# Spellbound
Untangling English Spelling

Robbins Burling

SHEFFIELD UK    BRISTOL CT

Published by Equinox Publishing Ltd

UK: Office 415, The Workstation, 15 Paternoster Row, Sheffield, South Yorkshire, S1 2BX

USA: ISD, 70 Enterprise Drive, Bristol, CT 06010

www.equinoxpub.com

First published 2016

**British Library Cataloguing-in-Publication Data**
A catalogue record for this book is available from the British Library.

ISBN-13 978-1-78179-130-1 (hardback)
          978-1-78179-131-8 (paperback)

**Library of Congress Cataloging-in-Publication Data**
Burling, Robbins.
Spellbound: untangling English spelling / Robbins Burling.
pages cm.
Includes bibliographical references and index.
ISBN 978-1-78179-130-1 (hb) — ISBN 978-1-78179-131-8 (pb) 1. Spellers. 2.
English language—Orthography and spelling—Handbooks, manuals, etc. I. Title.
PE1145.2.B87 2015

421'.52—dc23
                                          2014039976

Typeset by CA Typesetting Ltd., Sheffield
Printed and bound in Great Britain by Lightning Source UK Ltd., Milton Keynes, and Lightning Source Inc., La Vergne, TN

# Spellbound

# Contents

# Preface

There was once a time when English spelling reform was regarded as a respectable topic for serious debate. During the first half of the last century, notables such as George Bernard Shaw in England and Andrew Carnegie in the United States were active supporters of reform. Spelling societies on both sides of the Atlantic explored the kinds of changes that were needed, and debated ways to bring these about. In the mid-twentieth century, extensive experiments with a reformed spelling known as the "Initial Teaching Alphabet" (ITA) were conducted in Britain, the United States, and Australia. Thousands of children were taught to read with a radically revised spelling. Initial reports were enthusiastic, but then doubts arose, educational fads changed, and schools everywhere retreated to our traditional orthography.

More than fifty years have now passed since the experiments with ITA came to their unhappy end, and through all these decades spelling reform has been left to an eccentric, although enthusiastic, fringe. For everyone else who happened to think about it, spelling reform has been little more than a topic for ridicule. These have been lonely decades for those of us who are incompetent spellers, and who wish that our children and grandchildren could avoid the years of struggle that we had to endure in order to become literate.

Recently, books about spelling that are intended for a wide audience have once again begun to appear. Some have even been reviewed in the popular press. Three notable examples are David Wolman's *Righting the Mother Tongue* (2010), David Crystal's *Spell It Out* (2012), and Simon Horobin's *Does Spelling Matter?* (2013). These tell us a great deal about the nature and history of English spelling, and all three authors recognize the difficulties of our orthography. Nevertheless, Crystal and Horobin both come down firmly against reform, arguing that we have far too much invested in our present spelling for any change to be practical. Wolman, a confessed bad speller himself, is less one-sided, but even he seems to regard reform as hopeless. It is time for a book that presents the reformer's point of view.

Spelling is rarely regarded as an exciting topic, but it is an important one. As a wretched speller myself, I find our present spelling both infuriating and fascinating. I do not mean to infuriate anyone by supporting what many people dismiss as a lost cause. Rather, I hope that I can show the fascination of the problem.

\* \* \* \* \*

This book has been long in the writing and much longer in the thinking. Indeed, I have shouted my anguish about the horrible state of English spelling ever since I discovered my own disability while struggling through the second grade at the age of seven. I needed all the decades between then and my retirement before I earned the luxury of sufficient time to complete the project.

Even people who have no more than an average ability to spell seem to forget how much time and effort they needed to learn to read and to write "correctly." They often regard spelling-reform advocates as more amusing than persuasive, so I was surprised when so few of my friends and acquaintances laughed when I told them that I was writing a book about spelling. Many, indeed, offered their help. An old friend, Peter Fries, who had worked with Kenneth Goodman, tried, with truly impressive patience, to explain Goodman's position to me. Another old friend, this one from Norway, Bente Ailin Svendsen, and a new friend to whom Bente introduced me by e-mail, Arne Torp, were exceedingly helpful about clarifying the language situation in Norway. I have never met John Wells but no one will be able to read this book without recognizing my debt to him. He was good enough to set me straight on a number of matters via e-mail. I could not possibly have written this book had I not been able to build on his work. I was enlightened by attendance at meetings of the English Spelling Society, and in particular by conversations and correspondence with Masha Bell. Keith Bub, President of the Initial Teaching Alphabet Foundation, generously sent me a computer font for the ITA alphabet and granted me permission to use it in this book. My daughter, Adele Yunck, sent me the wonderful poem by Gerald Nolst Trenité called "The Chaos." Knowing her father's incompetence with such matters as punctuation and spelling, she also did a yeoman job of proofreading.

It is my good fortune to have two close friends who, even though they are good spellers themselves, did not laugh when I admitted, timidly at first, that I was tempted to use a piece of my retirement to write a book about spelling. Thomas Trautmann encouraged me from the start. As Tom has done with many of my earlier writings, he read every page that I wrote. He directed me firmly, and always sagely, to expand some parts but to drastically revise others. He even told me, in no uncertain terms, which parts should be thrown away. My partner, Sheila Procter, also read every page, some of them several times and at several stages. It has been a bit of good luck that Sheila is English. She has been subjected to endless questioning about how our accents differ, and how they are the same. She helped me, always, to remember that a single orthography needs to be as good for British, Australian, and all manner of other accents, as it is for North American. Sheila has an acute ear for our language, and she pushed me, always, to be clear and never to get lost in linguistic jargon. Her contribution is particularly impressive because she really does not believe in spelling reform. To both Tom and to Sheila: my warmest thanks.

# Part I

# 1   What Needs Fixing?

English orthography satisfies all the requirements of the canons of reputability under the law of conspicuous waste. It is archaic, cumbrous and ineffective; its acquisition consumes much time and effort; failure to acquire it is easy of detection. Therefore it is the first and readiest test of reputability in learning, and conformity to its ritual is indispensable to a blameless scholastic life.

Thorstein Veblen, *Theory of the Leisure Class* (1899)

I already knew that something was badly amiss when I was seven years old and hit the second grade. I had a serious, and I mean *serious*, disability. For a large proportion of the words that I wanted to write, I simply could not remember which letters my teacher wanted me to use. I wasn't much worse than most of my classmates at reading. Through the muddle of *flea*s and *see*s, *bear*s and *care*s, *fight*s and *write*s, and all those absurd *-ough*s of *though*, *rough*, and *cough*, I could usually make out what words were intended by the strings of letters in my reading books. But it was utterly impossible for me to reproduce them in the way that was approved by my teachers. I well remember a particularly grim morning, probably in the third grade, when I sat at my undersized desk and simply could not figure out how to spell "of." I knew that the letters I tried were wrong (already a big advance from the first grade) but I could not come up with a sequence that seemed right. The most sensible spelling I could think of was "*uv*." That did look a bit odd, but I could not imagine any way to fix it. I had, by then, been so often made to feel stupid because of my dysfunctional spelling that I was reluctant to humiliate myself by asking my teacher or a classmate for help. I was in a serious pickle, and just how I solved my problem I no longer remember. Perhaps the bell rang for recess. Whatever happened, my misery is painfully burned into my memory.

Sometime during my early school years we began to have spelling bees. Even in the 1930s, when I was in the third grade, the teachers in my school were usually careful not to humiliate children in front of their classmates. No one was held up for ridicule for making a mistake when adding 13 to 17 or for singing off-key. Better to give these children some extra help. But spelling bees were an exception to this humane tolerance of weakness. They were deliberately designed to humiliate those who didn't manage to spell in an acceptable way. We needed to be shamed into working harder, to have our moral fiber stiffened. When, however, I was the first to make a mistake and the first to sit down in a spelling bee, my reaction was not "I must try harder" but "Why is English such a stupid language?" That, I now know, was the most intelligent possible reaction to a spelling bee, but I was also perceptive enough to keep my mouth shut. My teachers blamed the victim.

My problem was clear: much too early and much too well, I had grasped the idea that letters are supposed to stand for sounds. I learned this unfortunate lesson before I had even toddled into kindergarten. I had a set of blocks with letters on their sides, and my mother explained that the letters stood for the sounds in words. She even told me which sounds some of the letters stood for. She meant well. She probably even believed what she told me, but I was fatally pointed in the wrong direction. Years passed before I overcame the naive expectation that if *s* could stand for the hissing noise in *bus* then nobody should object if I used the same *s* for the identical hissing noise in *cent*. Big mistake!

I did, gradually, learn to spell some words in a reasonably conventional manner, but I never caught up with my classmates. Mysteriously, they were able to remember those arbitrary jumbles of letters. Through all my tribulations, please understand, I was never illiterate. I was even quite capable of writing when the threat of correction and the presumption of laziness or stupidity were removed. When we were in the fifth grade, a good friend moved to a different town. He could not have been as bad a speller as I was, or at least I never remember him sitting down ahead of me in a spelling bee, but spelling cannot have been his strong point any more than it was mine. After he moved, he and I had a lively written correspondence and, since neither of us was fussy about such matters, our spelling did not matter at all. I don't remember ever catching him in a spelling mistake but it would never have occurred to me to look for one. Many years later, my mother admitted to me that she had sometimes read our letters when she found them loose in the living room. She did not approve of reading other people's mail, not even that of her eleven-year-old son or of his eleven-year-old friend, but she found them irresistible because our spelling was so hilarious.

Later on in grade school, a teacher once said, "Robbins, if you would only try harder, you could spell just as well as Mary does." She was wrong. I did try. It was, in fact, the only grade school subject that was enough of a challenge to require me to work at it. But it was futile. I am certain that some people are born with a strange ability to remember the way words are spelled, just as some other people can tell you, in a twinkling, the day of the week on which the 3rd of September will fall in 2072. I was not so blessed. Telling me that I could spell as well as Mary, if only I would try, had the same kind of cruelty, though admittedly not to the same degree, as telling

Mary, whose glasses were the thickest in the class, "If you would only try harder, you could see just as well as Robbins." I like to believe that I have used my precious cerebral synapses for something more important than remembering how to order my letters in the way the authoritarian teachers of my childhood thought best.

Perhaps I was in the eighth grade when a teacher said, "If you don't know how to spell it, Robbins, look it up in the dictionary." A more ridiculous bit of advice is hard to imagine. Most importantly, I didn't even know which words I didn't know how to spell, so I would have had to look up a whole clutch of words on every page that I wrote. By the eighth grade, I had managed to get *of* under reasonable control, but if I really didn't know how to spell a word, how was I supposed to find it in the dictionary? If ever there was a way to stifle someone's urge to write, it is by telling him to spend hours scratching around through the pages of a dictionary, searching for words that he doesn't know how to spell. Rather than tell me to use a dictionary, my teacher could have given me genuine help by admitting, "I'm sorry, Robbins, but I can't help being distracted by unconventional spelling. It would help me a lot if you would get someone who is a good speller to go through your papers before you hand them in, and have them give you the conventional spelling wherever your spelling differs from the dictionary. You can fix up those words and then I won't be distracted by trivia. I'll be able to concentrate on what you have to say." Sadly, no teacher was ever thoughtful enough, or mature enough, to deal with my spelling in that way. Instead, they just knocked off a few points from my grades, so that by the time I finished high school, they had convinced me that my verbal aptitude was on the frail side. I thought I had better stick to more technical topics and keep away from writing. Fortunately, my teachers in math and science were sufficiently mature to ignore my spelling. They could see past that detail, and see that I understood their lessons.

Years later I became a teacher myself. Occasionally, before an exam, a jittery student would wave a hand and ask, "Professor Burling, do you take off for bad spelling?" I loved the question. It invited me to pull myself up to my full professorial dignity and say in the most pompous tone that I could muster: "I have always felt that careful attention to the orthographic conventions of our language is a characteristic of a very limited imagination." The class needed just a few seconds to untangle my syntax, but their eyes would then widen in astonished delight. They would grin. I assured them that I was virtually blind to unconventional spelling, which I am, and that I almost never noticed a misspelled word in an examination, which was true. My colleagues told me that their students were awful spellers. As far as I have ever been aware, mine were not. Even if I had wanted to punish them for their spelling, I would not have been capable of doing so. I think I was a better exam reader than my finicky colleagues, because I was never distracted by such a trivial matter as spelling.

After I became a teacher, but before the days of computers and spell-checkers, faculty members used to communicate a good deal by circulating typed memos. I will always cherish the comment of a teasing colleague who told me how much he enjoyed getting a memo from me because he could always be confident that it was the genuine article rather than a forgery. No one else on the faculty was capable of spelling as badly as I did.

If you find few spelling "errors" in these pages, the credit must go entirely to my spellchecker. It does its job extraordinarily well, and I loathe it. I learned to be a proudly defiant bad speller, delighted to offend anyone who was so insecure that he (they were usually "hes" not "shes") had to prop up his confidence by flaunting his skill with the chaotic conventions of English spelling. My plan, as I began to write these pages, had been to turn off my spellchecker. I wanted you to see that I had not been fibbing when I wrote about my spelling disability, and I wanted you to realize that you can read with understanding even when a writer refuses to knuckle under to Webster or the *Oxford English Dictionary*. I thought that if my spelling bothered you so much that you didn't want to keep reading, you probably shouldn't be reading my book anyway. I felt sorry about your terrible hang-ups, and sorry that you waste the precious synapses of your precious brain on something as trivial as spelling. You would surely do better to use those synapses for more creative matters, but I knew no way to help you, except to show you that it is possible to spell unconventionally and still be understood.

I bumped into reality as soon as I asked two good friends to read some chapter drafts and to give me their suggestions for improvement. I told them that I had deliberately turned off my spellchecker and I asked them to ignore whatever "errors" in spelling might have crept in. This, I quickly discovered, they found utterly impossible. Every page of every chapter came back with my "errors" corrected. Memories of my teachers' red marks came flooding back. No more than my schoolteachers could these kind and helpful friends ignore my spelling. With great reluctance I turned my spellchecker back on, and if you find few "errors" in the remaining pages, you must blame that on that loathsome checker.

It is too late for me to profit much from a spelling reform. Indeed, no one who reads well enough to have any power or influence over educational policy will gain much from reform. Educated adults have a large vested interest in the spelling that they managed to learn. It is our children who would profit. It is our children who could make better use of the hours now wasted in learning to spell. Fewer of them would reach adulthood without gaining literacy. Children cannot influence educational policy, but for the sake of their children and grandchildren, adults ought to be willing to support reform.

The remainder of this book falls into two parts. The first part, through Chapter 6, is relatively general. I sketch the history of how English spelling managed to become so tangled, and I argue, I hope persuasively, that our present spelling contributes seriously to the high rates of illiteracy in the world's English-speaking nations. I consider the differences among spelling systems and the relation of spelling to the spoken language. How did English spelling descend into such a mess? What, if anything, might be done about it? What problems need to be dealt with when designing a better spelling system? I describe the alarming but little-noticed fact that, with every passing decade, new irregularities are added to our spelling. I say something about successful reforms in several other languages. Mostly, however, I focus on English and on the consistent failure of every attempt to bring more order to our spelling.

The second set of chapters, 7 through 12, is considerably more technical than the first set. I examine what a better spelling system might be like. I consider the problems in creating a spelling that is equally well suited for speakers of all accents and who come from everywhere in the world that English is spoken. For anyone who hopes to bring reforms to our spelling, it is the diversity of English accents that presents the most difficult challenges, but this is not the insuperable problem that it is sometimes imagined to be.

I do not propose a particular set of reforms. Dozens of reforms have already been proposed, and many are described in the Appendix. Any of these would be better than our present orthography, but most suffer from being better suited to the accent of the spelling's designer than to the accents of speakers from other parts of the world. What is needed now, I believe, is not another proposal, but a careful consideration of the criteria that a good proposal should meet, along with some realism about the steps that would be needed to bring about a serious reform.

American readers may notice that I use the word "accent" in a way that American linguists generally avoid. In popular American usage "accent" most often means "foreign accent"— the way an Italian or an Indonesian might pronounce English, or the way an American might pronounce Italian or Indonesian. However, I will be writing about the varied pronunciations used by native speakers of English, which American linguists usually call "dialects." I will use "accent" as British linguists use it, because it refers specifically to pronunciation, while "dialect" can refer to any part of language that varies—not only pronunciation but vocabulary and grammar as well. Spelling is supposed to reflect pronunciation, and therefore "accent" is the best word to describe the kind of language variability that makes spelling reform so difficult.

Except for the smug pleasure that some people feel when they make fun of the "bad" spelling of others, spelling is rarely regarded as either a gripping or an amusing topic. I am under no illusion that a reformed spelling has much chance of replacing our present mess in the near future. Nevertheless, I am fascinated by the question of what a better spelling system might look like, and what would be needed to get a better one accepted. My hope is to persuade others to join me in my fascination.

# 2 What Happened to English Spelling?

It is a pity that Chawcer, who had geneyus, was so unedicated. He's the wuss speller I know of.

Artemus Ward, *Artemus Ward in London* (1867)

## The Marriage of Anglo-Saxon with French

The known history of our language begins with inscriptions written in what we now call "Anglo-Saxon." The language arrived in Britain in the heads and on the lips of fifth-century migrants from the European continent. Inscriptions written in ancient runic characters give us the first hints of the way they spoke, but for several centuries literacy remained a rare skill. In Britain, as elsewhere in Europe during the second half of the first millennium, priests and monks did most of the reading and writing. On the Continent, the vernacular languages of Romance-speaking Europe were drifting away from their ancestral Latin, but Latin must still have been much easier for speakers of early French, Italian or Spanish than it was for speakers of Germanic languages such as Anglo-Saxon. The relative ease of learning Latin probably slowed the development of vernacular writing in Romance-speaking areas, and Latin continued to be used both by the church and for secular writing. In Britain, the few people who were literate more often wrote in their own language. The monasteries became the most important centers for Anglo-Saxon writing, even while they continued to use Latin as well.

The few who did write during Anglo-Saxon times were far more casual about their spelling than writers are today. Scribes needed to stay close enough to convention to let their readers to recognize the words that their letters stood for, but the limits were broad and no one expected consistency. As the centuries passed, and as the spoken language gradually changed, scribes would quite naturally adjust their spelling to fit the changing ways of talking, but in the absence of any notion of correctness, spelling could vary from one monastery to another, from one writer to another, or even from one instance of a word to another. Often, writing reflected the local accent of the writer. Even in Anglo-Saxon times, literacy did slowly spread and, as it did, spelling grew a bit more uniform, but the idea that a word should have just one "correct" spelling had to wait for the time, several centuries later, when paper and printing allowed a radically increased use of the written word.

The conquest of England by the Norman French in 1066 brought the early hegemony of written Anglo-Saxon to an abrupt end. The new rulers spoke French, and a few of them could even write it. French became the language of the new regime, and in the monasteries, where most writing took place, the monks began to write in French where they would earlier have used Anglo-Saxon. Except for some continuing use of Latin, Norman French became the language of both the government and the church, and it was used for all serious writing. Relatively little written English survives from the first two centuries of Norman rule, and what did survive lost whatever uniformity had developed before the conquest. The bulk of the population, of course, continued to speak their familiar Anglo-Saxon dialects without ever writing or reading anything in any language. The few who did continue to write in Anglo-Saxon wrote in ways that reflected their local accents.

Inevitably, the French and Anglo-Saxon languages began to influence one another. The more ambitious locals, those who hoped to share the prestige, power, and riches of their conquerors, soon set about learning the conquerors' language. Like bilinguals anywhere, they would have freely used words from one language when speaking the other. They probably found it especially tempting to borrow words from the more prestigious French into the less prestigious Anglo-Saxon so that, as the generations passed, more and more French words entered Anglo-Saxon speech. The first step in borrowing from one language into another must have been the work of bilinguals, but French words then found their way to ever-wider circles of the population. French words flooded into spoken English, and then they flooded into written English as well.

In 1204, the Normans lost control of their continental possessions in Normandy. Their resulting isolation from continental French probably helped the developing English language gradually to reassert itself for both speaking and writing. By 1300 most residents of Britain, even those of French ancestry, were learning English as their first language. Even for the upper classes, French became an acquired language rather than a native one, and in the fourteenth century, after nearly three hundred years of French dominance, English began, once again, to be used as a medium for serious writing. In 1362, English was accepted as an official language in Parliament. By then, spoken English had absorbed massive numbers of French words and, even as English came to be written more often, French retained its high prestige. When French words were spoken in sentences that were otherwise English, they must have been well adapted to English pronunciation, but when they were committed to parchment, even in an otherwise

English context, it would have seemed natural, even elegant, to spell them in the French way. These French spellings brought serious complications to written English, but until printing began, scribes had broad license to adapt their spelling to the changing spoken language.

Through these centuries, of course, most of the population never wrote or read anything in any language. Whether writing was done in French or English mattered little to them, but by the time English regained its importance as a written language, French words had found their way into the colloquial speech of every illiterate farmer. The re-emerging written English, with its large French component, had changed so much from the language used before 1066 that we give it a new name: "Middle English." Since we know it only in its written form, "Middle English" is, of course, a name for the written language, not for the spoken one. Colloquial speech would certainly have had more continuity across the decades and centuries than writing, but the three centuries between the Norman Conquest and the acceptance of English in Parliament gave ample time for the spoken language of the most humble Englishman to be heavily influenced by French. As English overtook French as the colloquial spoken language, even among the elite and educated members of the population, it had nothing like a fixed or standard spelling, and the continuing prestige of French must have made it seem entirely reasonable to use French spellings for French words, even when most of the surrounding words were English. The seeds of our spelling problems had been sown.

## Paper and Printing

Paper had been manufactured in China as early as the second century CE, but 1200 years were needed for its manufacture and use to find their way across Central Asia and through the Middle East to Europe. At the end of the fourteenth century, however, the manufacture of paper finally reached all the way to England and it quickly became much more plentiful, and much less expensive, than parchment had ever been. More people could now have something to write on, and more people duly found reasons to write. Even without printing, paper made writing useful to a growing fraction of the population, and as paper spread, so did literacy.

About a century after paper arrived, it was followed by the printing press and by movable type. Europeans attribute the invention of movable type to Johannes Gutenberg, whose famous Bible was completed in Mainz by 1456, but printing, like paper, had come much earlier to eastern Asia. Even movable type had been used by the Koreans for two centuries before it reached Mainz. Nevertheless, Gutenberg gets the credit for its first successful use in Europe, and once printing with movable type had been shown to be possible, the art and technology quickly spread across the continent.

In 1476, William Caxton, an Englishman who had learned the new trade in Holland, returned to London, where he set up England's first print shop. Caxton and the many printers who followed him were hardly more consistent in their spelling than the earlier scribes had been. From our modern perspective, indeed, they were wildly inconsistent. We are so accustomed to the uniform spelling of modern English that we have difficulty putting ourselves in the position of a writer, reader, or printer during the century after Gutenberg. Since no standard spelling existed, printers, like writers who had been limited to pen and ink, felt free to vary their spelling, almost at whim. The same word might be spelled in more than one way on a single page, even in a single sentence. Printers liked to justify their lines to make the margin on the right as straight as the one on the left, so they sometimes chose a longer or shorter spelling simply to give each line its desired length. However bizarre this may seem to modern spellers, it would not have seemed odd to printers or readers of the early sixteenth century. They simply lacked any fixed rules about the spelling of each word.

The first printing of the King James Bible appeared in 1611, and Shakespeare's First Folio was completed in 1623. This was almost a century and a half after Caxton had brought printing to England, but both the First Folio and the King James Bible still flaunted all sorts of variant spellings. Even the idea that there ought to be just one "correct" way to spell each word was slow to take root. *Pity, pyty, pitie, pytie, pittie,* and *pyttye* can all be found in early printed English (Scragg 1974: 71). Variable spelling did nothing to slow the spread of printing, however, and printing vastly expanded the availability of reading material. Literacy became valuable to far more people than it could ever have been when writing was done by hand on something as scarce and expensive as parchment.

## French Influence

The arrival of printing in Britain coincided with a vogue for fancy French spellings. These failed to reflect the phonetic habits of English speakers, but even when surrounded on the page by English words, many of these French spellings settled firmly into written English. It would have looked vulgar to alter an elegant French word to make it reflect the sounds of spoken English. Re-spelled French words would have seemed as crude and uneducated as a sensible *laf* would look now to any reader of English who is already familiar with *laugh*. With unclear conventions for older English words, and with a massive injection of French conventions, the divorce between English pronunciation and English spelling had begun. Middle English spelling was off to a very bad start.

The effort to make English writing look more elegant came at the time when spelling, under the impact of printing, was becoming progressively more standardized. Some of the more florid re-spellings were abandoned before spelling became fixed, but with increasing standardization, irregular and non-etymological spellings of many words became frozen. These have contributed to the view that English spelling was never really intended to represent the sounds of the language. Any sequence of letters will do as long as we can all agree on the sequence that is needed for each word.

French spelling brought all sorts of anomalies to English writing. No *h* had been pronounced in spoken French since long before the Normans brought their language to England. This is why French speakers who learn English often have trouble with the English *h*: *"I 'ope 'e 'as 'ad an 'appy time 'ere"* is not simply a silly caricature. *H*'s really are difficult for French speakers. Nevertheless, *h* was, and still is, written at the start of many French words. This *h* reflects the ancient pronunciation of Latin, but it was no more pronounced in the French of 1066 than it is pronounced in Paris today. The useless *h* in *heir*, *honor*, *honest* and *hour* was dragged into written English, where it remains, as silent, and as useless, as ever. Having long disappeared from speech, it represents well over a millennium of conservative writing habits, first in French and later in English.

Not every silent initial French *h* remained silent in English, however. Spoken English, both before and after the impact of French, has had plenty of native words with a well-pronounced initial *h*: *her*, *his*, *high* and *hair*. This native *h* made it tempting for English speakers to pronounce the *h*'s that they found in written French, just as they pronounced them in English words. Unless you have an accent such as Cockney, you probably pronounce the *h* in *hostess* and *hotel*, even though no French speaker has pronounced it in the corresponding French words for well over a thousand years. At some point, ignorant English speakers began to pronounce *hostess* and *hotel* with the same *h* that they already used in *his* and *hers*. Such pronunciations are known as "spelling pronunciations," and they begin as simple mistakes. At first, they must have sounded as silly as *hour* or *honor* would sound to us if the *h* were pronounced. Silly or not, spelling pronunciations have a way of spreading, and by the time they have spread to the entire population they can no longer be counted as "mistakes." Now, we all pronounce the *h*s in *harmonious* and *hotel*, even though these found their way into the language as spelling pronunciations, either ignorant or pretentious (or, most likely, both).

So we now have words like *hour* and *honest* that we both spell and pronounce in the French way and that bring a small but annoying irregularity into English spelling. We have a second set of words, including *hotel* and *harmonious*, in which we have regularized the spelling by creating new and non-etymological spelling pronunciations. A third set of words, including *able* and *ability*, were borrowed from French, but had their spelling revised in English by losing the silent French *h* of *habile* and *habilité*. The revised spelling of *able* and *ability* effectively immunized these words from any danger of succumbing to a new pronunciation (Scragg 1974: 41).

British and American speakers, who sometimes like to believe that they speak the same language, are divided by *herb*. The British generally use a spelling pronunciation with a pronounced *h*, while Americans, by saying *erb*, remain closer to the French original. A few British speakers may scorn Americans for "dropping the *h*" from *herb*, but Americans would be equally justified in scorning the British for using a vulgar spelling pronunciation. We are left with spellings for many English words that fail to reflect either modern pronunciation or etymology in any reliable way.

*Mice*, *lice*, *cinder*, and *ice* are old English words. In Anglo-Saxon times, they could be sensibly spelled with an honest English *s*: *mys*, *lys*, *sinder*, and *is*. Unfortunately, the French often spell their *s* sound with the letter *c*, and it must have looked elegant to imitate French practice by using *c* in these words. That is why we now write *mice* and *lice* with a *c*, where the Anglo-Saxons had used *s*. The singular forms, *mouse* and *louse*, have clung to their original *s*, so ever since English writers began to tart up *mice* and *lice* with a pretentious French *c*, everyone who aspires to conventionality has had to use an *s* for a singular *mouse* or *louse* but switch to a *c* as soon as the *mice* or *lice* multiply. Every child who wants to avoid red marks on his papers has to remember which words are spelled with *c* and which with *s*. *Herb*, *able*, *mouse*, and *mice* form only the tip of the very confused iceberg of irregular spellings. They do as much to obscure as to reflect the etymology of English words.

## More Chaos

As French spellings invaded written English, their unpredictability began to undermine the phonetic principle, but the real disaster came later. By the sixteenth century, the printing press had spread across Europe. Books were becoming much more widely available, and printers in England tried to make words look more important by using extra letters that had no etymological justification. Honest old English words were sometimes given a vaguely classical look: *dette* was re-spelled as *debt*, *doute* as *doubt*, *samon* as *salmon*, *ceptre* as *scepter*, *receite* as *receipt*. Most of these words have held on to their older pronunciations even as their spellings brought grief to generations of young spellers.

Words that were re-spelled in ways that had nothing to do with any genuine etymology have sometimes acquired spelling pronunciations. These bring the sound and spelling into greater harmony, but they obscure the etymology. English once had a word that was written as *vitals* and that simply meant "food". Someone gussied up the spelling as *victuals* and then people tried to pronounce it that way too. The new pronunciation should offend anyone who prizes etymology, but the word is going out of fashion, probably because so many people lack confidence in either its pronunciation or its spelling. An older *catif* was re-spelled, and eventually re-pronounced, as *captive*; *cors* became *corpse*; *olifaunt* became *elephant*; *trone* became *throne*. In his dictionary of 1755, Samuel Johnson noted that some people pronounced the *l* of *fault* while others did not. This intrusive *l* must, by now, be universally pronounced, but it has not a shred of etymological justification. The *l* was added because someone once supposed that it would look fine even if it was not pronounced. We now pronounce it, as well as write it, but it tells a false etymological story. The older *cedule* was re-spelled as *schedule*—elegant perhaps, but surely more florid than necessary. This pretentious new spelling has now been blessed with two different spelling pronunciations: *shedjule* in Britain, *skedjewel* in America. The British pronunciation is closer to the original. The American pronunciation is etymologically absurd but, of course, most Americans regard the British pronunciation as the absurd one (Scragg 1974: 57–9). The *l* in *could* picked up its written *l* by contagious analogy from the *l* in *should* and *would*. Now all three words have anomalous spellings. The *l* of *should* and *would* is no longer pronounced. The *l* of *could* never was pronounced.

More irregular spellings found their way into English writing at the end of the sixteenth century when writers made a deliberate effort to give contrasting spellings to homophones—words such as *right* and *rite* that have different meanings but are pronounced identically. Since homophones rarely bring ambiguity to speech it is not at all clear why spelling them as homographs—words that are spelled identically—should bring ambiguity to writing. Plenty of homographs still grace English orthography without causing the slightest confusion. *Bear* can mean an animal or *bear* a burden. *Saw* can be a tool or the past of *see*. *Sap* can come from a tree, or refer to a fool. *Sound* can be something you can hear, or it can mean "in good condition." These, and many other pairs of words, are used easily with the same spelling. They occur in contrasting contexts, and the context tells us which meaning is the right one. Their identical spelling gives us no more problem than their identical pronunciation. Nevertheless, we now distinguish many other homophones in writing by using different spellings: *week/weak, rain/reign, feat/feet, roam/Rome, lone/loan*. Anyone who imagines that we need contrasting spellings for homophones ought to be puzzled by our casual willingness to pronounce them identically. Distinguishing homophones by their spelling may bring some eccentric joy to folks who have been lucky with their spelling genes, but the different spellings bring nothing but grief to children and poor spellers.

Ever since the invasion of French words into our language, English speakers have been enthusiastic borrowers. We welcome words from other languages and feel that they have greatly enriched both our speech and our writing. We adapt their pronunciation to our English habits, but we are more willing than are the speakers of many languages to retain foreign spellings even when they are surrounded by native English words. As borrowed words with their foreign spellings accumulate, any remaining expectation that spelling should reflect pronunciation is further undermined.

The impact of French, the use of elaborate spellings to make words look more important, the attempt to have spelling reflect etymology, the retention of foreign spelling in borrowed words, and even the effort to distinguish homophones by different spellings have all contributed to a divorce, or at least an estrangement, between English spelling and English pronunciation. We have learned not to expect pronunciation to be a reliable guide to spelling. Nor can we expect spelling to be a reliable guide to pronunciation.

## Modern Decay

Well-meaning friends who know about my spelling disability have tried to encourage me by suggesting that the imaginative spelling used in text messages might be enough to shake up tradition and allow significant improvements in our spelling. I am skeptical. Texting arose in a very special environment, where the length of the message is severely limited and punching in words on a tiny keyboard is a delicate exercise. However nimble your thumbs, you will never type out a message on the cramped keypad of a cell phone as quickly as you can write it on paper, let alone type it on a standard keyboard. The keypad of a cell phone cries out for abbreviations, and abbreviations have duly blossomed: "how r u 2day. have a gr8 1." The sheer fun of such abbreviations turned them into a game. Who could invent the most ingenious shortcuts? Who could pack them in most densely? Who could use them most outrageously? Who could interpret them most skillfully?

Absurdly, but probably inevitably, these spellings provoked outrage: David Crystal quotes the *Daily Mail*, a London newspaper, in which a terrified journalist wrote that texters are "vandals who are doing to our language what Genghis Khan did to his neighbours eight hundred years ago. They are destroying it: pillaging our punctuation; savaging our sentences; raping our vocabulary. And they must be stopped."[1] This was over the top, for sure, but it probably expressed a widespread attitude among those ancients who had passed their thirtieth birthday. The attitude was certainly common enough to prevent texting from having any but the most marginal influence on traditional spelling.

Texting was never likely to have any appreciable influence on mainstream spelling, but our writing conventions are by no means immune to change. Alarmingly, in fact, we add new irregularities with every passing decade. We have become so accustomed to abbreviations that we hardly notice that they have burdened us with a new set of spelling conventions. UN, EU, USA, CIA, FBI, TV, NBC, CBS, BBC, IBM, DVD, DDT are only a few tips of a very large iceberg. In a sense, to be sure, their spelling is beautifully regular. If we see these words spelled we can usually pronounce them, and if we know how they are pronounced we can usually spell them. This is more than can be said for many of our more conventional words, but these new ones bring a new, although secondary, spelling system to our written language, one that is largely limited to twenty-six possible syllables.

Even with abbreviations like these, however, we cannot always be confident about pronunciation. If an abbreviation includes a vowel, we sometimes pronounce it as if it is an ordinary word. CERN, which stands for *Conseil Européen pour la Recherche Nucléaire*, is pronounced as a single syllable, rather than as a sequence of the four names for the four letters. But does "CERN" rhyme with *turn* or with *cairn*? NASA, NATO, UNESCO, and ASEAN are also pronounced as ordinary words, although written with capital letters. We can only know the pronunciation of the second letter of NASA and NATO by hearing them spoken. The first half of HIV/AIDS is pronounced as a sequence of letters; the second half like an ordinary word (aich-eye-vee/aids). All of these seem to be "words," but if they are spoken aloud, the speakers need to know which are pronounced by the conventions of normal spelling and which are pronounced as a series of letters. A new elementary particle is spelled "ð" and pronounced as "do-mezon." Is it old-fashioned of me to be uncomfortable about a word that I do not know how to pronounce? Is it a *doe-mezon*, or *doo-mezon*?

It gets worse: names like *PayPal* and *YouTube* squeeze out the normal space between words, turning these names into single words that have capital letters where capital letters never used to be found. *eBay* and *iPod* start defiantly with lower-case letters, but sprout capitals in the middle. *Xstrata* is a "globally diversified mining group" with a previously forbidden consonant cluster. If you want an "archive for electronic reprints of scientific

---

1.  *Daily Mail*, 28 September 2007. Cited in Crystal (2008), p. 9.

papers" you might try *arXive*, but watch out! That "X" in the middle of *arXive* is not the twenty-fourth letter of the English alphabet, but the Greek letter chi, and will you please pronounce it as the Greek letter should be pronounced! A British firm is cutely named *Eighti9*, and a weight-loss drug has been baptized, unpronounceably, as *Qnexa*. The completely unpronounceable *lincCRNAS* is the name of a molecule similar to messenger-RNA. *ZERO1* is a place where "Principles of artistic creativity will be applied to real world innovation challenges." The very name would seem to be a good example of an "innovation challenge." And please remember to capitalize all the letters in "*ZERO1*."[2] With a bit of imagination, many of these words can be pronounced, though not by the rules we learned in school.

How many such words can our written language sustain? These words enter the language one by one. By itself, each word is easy to learn, and a "word" like CERN gives us a welcome escape from any need to cope with a name as long as *Conseil Européen pour la Recherche Nucléaire*. We have excellent reasons for using these abbreviations. Still, month by month and year by year, words like these bring an ever-longer list of irregularities to our written language. New readers do not have the luxury of learning these words gradually. They are simply piled on top of all the earlier irregularities of English orthography, and they make reading and spelling even more difficult for our children than it was for us. They join the rest of our chaotic spelling to condemn too many people to illiteracy. They are a far greater threat to our language than the playful abbreviations of text messaging.

## Writing and Speech

This tangled history has left English with a much less satisfactory spelling system than most languages of Europe. A German or an Italian who knows how to pronounce a word but who has never seen it written has a good fighting chance of guessing its usual spelling—of getting it "right." Even a French speaker who encounters a new word in print can usually arrive at its correct pronunciation. An English speaker needs lots more luck. In the days before spellcheckers, Germans and Italians didn't need to scrabble through a dictionary as often as Americans or Britons. Germans and Italians are much less likely to suffer the embarrassment of a shameful error.

French spelling, to be sure, is messier than German or Italian. Indeed, French vies with English for the dubious honor of being the worst-spelled language of Europe. Whatever the beauties of "la belle langue," no French

---

2. These examples are culled from *The Economist*: 12 January 2012, p.83; 25 February 2012, p.79; 3 March 2012, p.8.

speaker should point with pride to conventional French spelling. In particular, no one should be sanguine about a language that finds so many ways to spell words that have identical pronunciations. French speakers ought to be outraged by the absurdity of the four different spellings that are required for four forms of the "regular" verb that means 'to speak': *parler* (infinite), *parlé* 'spoken' (past participle), *parlai* 'I spoke' (first person singular, past definite), and *parlez* 'you (all) speak' (second person plural, present). All four are pronounced identically.

All the many verbs of the first conjugation go through the same changes, and this is considered to be the most "regular" of the conjugations. These spellings reflect pronunciations that, many centuries ago, were different, but that long ago became identical. French children, like students of French as a foreign language, must struggle with these spellings even though they reflect nothing at all in modern spoken French.

In spite of these orthographic absurdities, French spelling does have one great advantage over English. Readers of French who know the system can usually make an excellent guess about how to pronounce a previously unknown word, even when encountering it in print for the first time. In French, for example, the letter *c* is almost always pronounced like an *s* when it is followed by *e*, *i*, or *y*, but like a *k* when followed by *a*, *o*, or *u*. English has borrowed so many French words, and embraced so many of its spellings, that this French habit has invaded English. That is why *c* is pronounced in one way in *cent*, *city*, and *cymbal*, but in a different way in *cabin*, *cousin*, and *cure*. This is a needlessly messy rule. French has a great many rules that are at least as messy as this one, but once learned, the rules hold up very well. The challenge for a French speaker is not that of figuring out how to pronounce a word when it is seen in print for the first time. That is usually straightforward. Rather, because French offers several ways to spell many of its speech sounds, the challenge is to remember how to spell a word that is well known from speech. Learning when to write *parler*, *parlai*, *parlé*, and *parlez* is a serious problem for every French child.

Unlike French, English spelling throws up almost as many challenges for a reader as for a writer. One reason that English speakers keep their dictionaries handy is to find out how to pronounce an unfamiliar word. Seeing a new word in print is not likely to be enough. How would you pronounce a word spelled *blove* if you should see it in print? Should it rhyme with *move*, or *love*, or *cove*, or should it be pronounced in still another way? When in doubt, reach for your dictionary. People whose languages are spelled rationally rarely have this problem. Even the French do not often need the kind of help that English readers do in order to learn the pronunciation of a new written word. English even has pairs of words that are spelled identically but pronounced differently: *tear* with one pronunciation means 'water from the eye,' but with another pronunciation it means something you can do to cloth; *lead* has one pronunciation to mean 'guide' but a different one to mean 'a kind of metal.' One pronunciation of *wind* means 'moving air,' while another means 'turn, twist.' *Minute* can mean 'very small' or 60 seconds. How is a poor foreigner to know that *goes* and *does* do not rhyme?

Spanish, Dutch, and German all have more orderly spelling than either French or English. The spelling of Italian and Finnish is even better. If you have learned the spelling conventions for one of these languages, and if you know how to pronounce a word, you can generally spell it correctly, or at least you can make a very good guess. Reciprocally, if you know how to spell it, you can generally pronounce it correctly. None of these languages burdens children with the problems that French and English children must cope with. Within the past few decades, the Norwegians, Germans, Dutch, and Spanish have all introduced modest spelling reforms that have made good spelling systems even better. What, then, has gone wrong with English? Why do readers and writers of English need to struggle with such a mess? Why do we cling to a system that forces English-speaking children to take so much longer than other children to learn to read and write? Why do we use a system that leaves so many of our children illiterate? Why, indeed, do we put up with it?

# 3 Reading, Spelling, and Illiteracy

"Do you spell it with a 'V' or a 'W'?" inquired the judge. "That depends upon the taste and fancy of the speller, my Lord," replied Sam.
                                        Charles Dickens, *Pickwick Papers* (1837)

## Reading and Illiteracy

Periodically, Americans work themselves into hysterics about the dreadful state of their country's primary education. Books are written, statistics on illiteracy trotted out, national commissions formed, programs pushed, slogans invented: "No child left behind," "Back to basics," "Head start." Fatigue then sets in and the hysteria subsides until it is discovered, yet again, that millions of adult Americans cannot read the warning labels on a can of drain-cleaner or the instructions on a bottle of aspirin. We then look for something or someone to blame: segregated neighborhoods and segregated schools that short-change minorities; illiterate parents who cannot help their children; schools of education that promote faddish but hopeless teaching methods; too much phonics; too little phonics; and always, of course, not enough money: "Just give us an adequate budget, and we will solve every problem!" But no amount of money is ever enough, and the problems refuse to go away.

Quite apart from the hysterics, however, we really do find a good deal of plausible evidence that children in English-speaking countries take substantially longer to learn to read than children do elsewhere (Seymour *et al.* 2003; Thorsdad 1991; Oney and Goldman 1984; Landerl *et al.* 1997). These studies strongly suggest that our spelling, which is much less orderly than that of most European languages, seriously interferes with the ability of English-speaking children to learn to read. The most convincing demonstration of the English delay is the ambitious study by Philip Seymour and his colleagues. This team compared the early reading abilities of children in no fewer than fourteen European countries where thirteen different languages are spoken and taught. They found that English-speaking children in Scotland took approximately two and a half years to reach what they call a "foundation level" of reading. Children who were learning highly regular systems of spelling, such as those used for Finnish or Italian, achieved the foundation level within their first year of school. French-, Portuguese-, and Danish-speaking children, whose spelling is less regular than Finnish or Italian, but not as chaotic as English, were in between. They learned more quickly than English-speaking children but not as quickly as the Finns or Italians.

There are complications. Children in Scotland start reading instruction when they are as young as five, while in other countries reading instruction may begin as late as seven. We should not expect younger children to learn as quickly as older ones, but we would hardly expect the younger ones to take two and a half times as long. We might also question whether it is possible to establish a "foundation level" of literacy that can be accurately compared across thirteen languages. Questions have also been raised about the variability of syllabic complexity in different languages. The Germanic languages, including English, have complex consonant clusters, such as those in *splits* and *strength*, so their syllables are more complex than those of Romance languages. Perhaps complex syllables make reading more difficult, and perhaps they hold back English-speaking children. The similarly complex syllables of German do not appear to hold back German-speaking children, however, so perhaps syllable structure does not matter that much (Landerl *et al.* 1997).

In spite of such complications, the evidence that we have points in a single direction: English orthography seems, consistently and seriously, to retard the acquisition of literacy. I know of no observational evidence that points in the opposite direction. Until we have counter-evidence, we need to presume that English spelling must bear a good deal of the blame for the extra difficulties that English-speaking children have with reading. In the face of the evidence, I find it disturbing that those who raise alarms about the reading crisis in English-speaking countries rarely point to our irregular orthography as a major contributor to the problem. We take our traditional orthography for granted, and we expect our children to adapt to it. Only eccentrics suggest that we might adapt the orthography to the people instead of struggling to adapt the people to the orthography.

## Reading Instruction

Reading is the central and essential component of primary education. If children do not learn to read, all else will fail, but both educators and self-appointed crusaders in North America and in Britain have argued endlessly about how reading can best be taught. It is often the more traditionally minded worriers who want phonics to come first. They may insist that children cannot be expected to read much of anything until they learn the twenty-six letters of the alphabet and the sounds that these letters most often stand for. These people advocate what has been variously called "systematic phonetics," "intensive phonetics," "decoding," "code-emphasis," or, more simply, "phonics-first."

Lined up against the phonics enthusiasts are those who, perhaps more imaginative or, at least, more willing to experiment, would rather emphasize meaning and content than dwell on the dreary details of sounds and letters. Seeing, all too clearly, the chaos of our traditional spelling system, they do not want to burden six-year-olds with intricate spelling rules. Instead of artificially isolating sounds and letters, they urge the teaching of whole words. It is words, phrases, and sentences, after all, that carry the meaning, and it is words, phrases and sentences that need to be understood. So a second group of experts push what has been variously called the "whole-word" method, "meaning-emphasis," "sight-reading," "look and say," or even the "whole-language" method. The jargon that I find least misleading for the opposing positions are "code-emphasis" and "meaning-emphasis." These terms are a bit less contentious than most of the others, and they are less likely to seem mutually exclusive. They acknowledge the plain fact that both code and meaning need to be dealt with by every learner and by everyone who wants to help a learner with reading. These terms can help to focus the arguments over when and how the different components of reading should be emphasized, and they avoid the trap of imagining that one method is all that is needed.

In the United States, a third explanation is sometimes offered for our educational failures: the alarming nature of our stratified and segregated society. Parents from poor and excluded groups are more likely than other parents to be illiterate or only weakly literate, so they cannot give their children the kind of help that our middle-class schools expect from parents.

## Code-Emphasis

A steady stream of books and articles, some hysterical, others turgidly analytical, have offered their remedies for the awful state of American education and, in particular, for our high rates of illiteracy. An uncompromising best-seller of an earlier generation was written by an enthusiast named Rudolf Flesch. His book, *Why Johnny Can't Read—And What You Can Do About It*, was first published way back in 1955, but it is still well worth a read. It was a slashing, no-holds-barred attack on any method for teaching reading that failed to emphasize phonics. With no hint of compromise, Flesch advocated phonics and then more phonics. Teach children how the letters sound, he insisted, and they will be able to read. He accused American schools of education of ignoring phonics and pushing outrageous teaching methods that he referred to as "look and say." These methods, he believed, had catastrophically delayed the acquisition of reading skills. Giving up on the schools, Flesch tried to persuade parents to take over where teachers and, especially, the teachers of teachers had failed. He hoped that parents would start their children in the right direction by teaching them phonics and, in that way, immunize them against the confusions of "look and say." His book represents the absolute extreme of the code-emphasis method of reading instruction.

Flesch's book supplied parents with no fewer than 72 pages of word lists, most of them with exactly 72 words, all nicely parading in four columns of 18 words each. The first of these pages has 68 three-letter words, each with *a* in the middle, and a single consonant on each side: *mat, ham, fan, hag, nap*, and so on. The four remaining words are two examples each of *pass* and *mass*. (British readers note: Flesch, like most Americans, would have pronounced the vowels of *pass* and *mass* just as he pronounced the vowels of *pan* and *man*.) If children could be persuaded to sit still long enough to learn to recognize the 72 words on the first page, they should have gained a good idea of the most common pronunciations, both of *a* and of the seventeen consonants that are used in the examples.

Later pages introduce increasingly complex features of English spelling: the four short vowels of *pet, sit, hot*, and *but*; simple, and then increasingly complex, consonant blends (clusters), and additional ways to pronounce the vowel letters. On the 23rd page of examples, two-syllable words are rather tentatively introduced, and three-syllable words arrive on the 39th. Page 72, the last, has such impressive words as *innocence, butterfly, selfishly, January*, and *invitation*. All these words are spelled in reasonably regular ways. Words with less-regular spelling are left for later, but children who can recognize the words on Flesch's many pages ought to have gained a solid basis for sounding out a useful proportion of English words when they are first encountered in reading. Once children have learned to read these words, Flesch argued, they will have learned the most important relationships between English sounds and English letters, and they should be ready to take on connected prose. Children of kindergarten age or even younger, he believed, can learn the sounds that the letters stand for, and in that way recognize the written forms of many words that they already know from speech. With judicious parental help, they should arrive at first grade well immunized against the damage that can be inflicted by confused teaching methods. Here, in Flesch's program, we find the logical extreme of phonics-first methodology.

When browsing through Flesch's book, it is easy to miss the fact that a good many very common words never appear on the lists. Only a dozen two-letter words are included. These include such essential words as *be, me, we, he, or, at, so*, and *no* and some that may be less essential, such as *ox, ax, pa*, and *ma*. Flesch is teaching children to recognize letters and pairs of letters, rather than words, so if the word can be inferred in a written context, the absence of such common words as *of, if, on*, and *to* may not matter. The suspicion does arise, however, that Flesch avoided words that are spelled in irregular ways. *Too* is found in his lists, for example, but *to* and *two* are not. Still, it may be entirely reasonable to teach the regularly spelled words first, and expect the meanings of words with less-regular spelling to be recognizable with help from the context in which they are used.

Can children be persuaded to slog through 72 pages, most of them containing nothing but 72 disconnected words? Altogether, the pages have more than 5,000 words, but since many are repeated two or more times, they have far fewer than 5,000 *different* words. Some children seem to have been able to manage all these pages. At any rate, some parents reported impressive success, even with children who had struggled and failed with other methods. Other children, I am afraid, would rebel in boredom long before reaching the seventy-second page. Whether because of childhood boredom, or simply because of the conservatism of schoolteachers and professors of education, Flesch's book failed to usher in the revolution in reading instruction that its author had hoped for.

Neither discouraged nor repentant, in 1981, a quarter-century after *Why Johnny Can't Read*, Flesch gave birth to a second book, this one called *Why Johnny Still Can't Read: A New Look at the Scandal of Our Schools.* Here he insisted that educational research, in the decades since his first book appeared, had overwhelmingly supported his argument in favor of phonics. Still, he failed to persuade the educational establishment to forget all methods except phonics. Many educational experts, to say nothing of practicing teachers, advocate a healthy phonic component in reading instruction. Few have been as one-sided as Flesch.

## Meaning-Emphasis

On the other side of the educational divide, no one in recent decades has been more influential than Kenneth Goodman, a long-time Professor of Education at the University of Arizona. "Whole language" is Goodman's term for his favored method, and he leaves little place for the direct teaching of phonics. Goodman repeatedly ridicules the eagerness to break the whole language up into small pieces, and especially the urge to tear words into letters, or into the sounds that the letters stand for. He wants children to have the whole language, not its shattered bits. He writes:

> Effective reading . . . is not accurate word recognition; it is getting to meaning. And efficient reading is using just enough of the available cues, given what a reader brings to the reading, to make sense of the text. (Goodman 1996: 8)

I have never found a place where Goodman explains how a reader can "make sense of the text" without at least some degree of "accurate word recognition." He writes as if these are alternatives, but of course they are not. Surely word recognition is a necessary step on the way to meaning.

Goodman writes, "People learn both [reading and listening] in the same way" (ibid.:15). He can only make such an assertion by ignoring the obvious fact that children learn to read only after they have been chattering for several years. By the time they begin to read, they are highly skilled at extracting the meaning from the spoken words and sentences that they hear from others, and they know how to put their own words together into phrases and sentences. The trick of reading is to figure out how the visible written language relates to the audible spoken language that they already know. Because written language is absolutely dependent on spoken language, learning to read and write is utterly different from learning to understand and speak one's first language. It is simply silly to imagine that reading and listening are learned in the same way.

Anyone who doubts the crucial role of the spoken language in learning to read should think about the struggle that profoundly deaf children have with reading. Since they lack a spoken language as a base on which to build, deaf children need to learn both the meaning and the written form of words at the same time. Some congenitally deaf children succeed. Many never do. For all of them, it is a struggle. Indeed, it is reported that "only about 25 percent of the profoundly deaf would be classified as functionally literate (where literacy is defined as fourth-grade reading ability). About 50 percent of the deaf with hearing loss greater than 85 decibels have virtually no reading comprehension" (Rayner and Pollatsek 1989: 208–11).

I can remember only two lessons from my first five years of school that I found genuinely interesting, so I may not be typical. Once, we went outside and drew chalk circles on the sidewalk to represent the sun, earth, moon, and inner planets, all drawn in proportion to their size and distance from one another. We learned how small and insignificant the earth is in that context, and we learned that Pluto would have to be drawn far off in a distant town. That was fun! My other happy memory was the time, certainly no later than second grade, when our teacher stood in front of her sitting pupils and explained that letters stand for speech sounds. That was interesting, a most welcome change from most of school, which I regarded as a serious restriction on my freedom, hardly an opportunity to gain either useful or fascinating knowledge. Whether or not my interest in letters and their sounds was shared by my classmates I have no way of knowing, but even if Goodman finds phonics dull and dislikes tearing words into small pieces, children should profit from learning how letters, and combinations of letters, sound. Some of them will even find it interesting!

Far from minimizing the importance of sounding-out, I would suppose that the single most important step on the way to reading comes when children learn to sound out written words that they already know from speech, but have never before encountered in print. For a language that is spelled as badly as English, sounding-out is by no means a trivial skill, but it is an essential skill for every new reader. Learning to sound out English words needs time and practice, but as their skill improves, it allows new readers to understand a vastly wider written vocabulary than can be learned by brute memory. Even adults continue to sound out words when encountering an unfamiliar proper name or technical term. Sounding-out is impossible without an understanding of the way the marks on paper are related to the sounds of the spoken language. That relationship is what we call "phonics," and it means that phonics is essential for reading. Some children seem to be able to learn the necessary phonic skills by practice and experience—by generalizing from examples. Other children find this very difficult, and they need help.

I cannot have been the only new reader who found phonics interesting, and we ought to be able to speed up everyone's learning with a bit of explicit instruction about the relation between sounds and letters. Very few children will ever learn to recognize, let alone spell, thousands of written words unless they can relate them to the spoken words that they already know. A few deaf children manage this difficult feat, but it is a terrible struggle for them. When hearing children can learn to sound out words that they have heard, but never before seen, they can escape primers with controlled vocabulary. They can then improve their skill in the most natural way possible—by reading.

For decades, advocates of phonics have competed with those who call their methods "look and see" or "whole language." The innocent lay person might be forgiven for wondering why these should be in such fierce competition. Surely new readers need to learn that letters represent sounds. At the same time, I can agree with Goodman that reading English is not merely a matter of phonics. In order to achieve any reasonable fluency, learners will need to recognize whole words without having to take each one laboriously apart into its individual letters and sounds. An early attention to phonics ought to get children off to a good start, but no one should imagine that nothing else is needed.

## Blame the Society

Code-emphasis and meaning-emphasis do not exhaust the debate. A third perspective on reading failure is found in Jonathan Kozol's book, *Illiterate America*. This book was published in 1985, but its arguments must still be taken seriously. Unlike Flesch or Goodman, Kozol was not much concerned with pedagogy, but he was deeply concerned about the social conditions that he believed fostered illiteracy. Kozol was as angry as Flesch about the miserable results of American reading instruction but, instead of focusing on teaching methods, he wrote about the ethnic, class, and racial divisions of American society. It was these divisions that Kozol blamed for denying effective education to an enormous, and growing, number of American children. He was alarmed by the number of American parents, disproportionately immigrant, poor, or black, who were illiterate themselves and who were unable to give their children the kind of help that American schools expect from parents. In 1955, Flesch had hoped that parents could step into the breach where the schools were failing. Thirty years later, Kozol argued that millions of illiterate American parents simply lacked the skills or knowledge that would allow them to step into any breach at all.

Kozol painted a dismal picture of illiterate America. Our society assumes literacy, but Kozol claimed that as many as a third of American adults are illiterate, or at least "functionally" illiterate, whatever that vague term may mean. Tax forms, census forms, bills, direction signs and street names, warning labels on boxes and bottles, to say nothing of newspapers, magazines, books, and messages carried home to parents from school, are all a mystery to someone who cannot read. Worst of all, illiteracy is passed on from one generation to the next, and this at a time when fewer and fewer jobs are open to the illiterate millions. Illiteracy begets poverty and poverty begets criminality. Our prisons hold far more than their share of illiterates.

Kozol abandoned any hope that the schools would ever be able to teach reading to children from impoverished and illiterate homes. He wanted, instead, to mobilize communities to spread literacy to the millions of adults who, he believed, were hungering for it. In 1985, he had a rather touching hope that once the great American public was alerted to the dreadful problems of illiteracy, then a groundswell of alarm and compassion would persuade literate lay people to step into the breach and tutor the folks whom the schools had never reached. He foresaw reading rooms in the poorer parts of our cities where an army of thoughtful neighbors or concerned students would help another army of the people who so badly wanted to read. These are beautiful thoughts from an angry man who spent much of his energy in an effort to bring literacy to those who had missed out. One can only wish that he had been more successful.

## Cooler Heads

In the effort to describe the great range of prescriptions for improving literacy, I have deliberately chosen writers who have taken extreme positions, but in doing so, I have been unfair to the great majority of teachers, and teachers of teachers. Flesch, Goodman, and Kozol all wrote with an eloquence and passion that comes from a confidence about possessing the Truth, and they demonstrate the diversity of viewpoints that have marked the debates. All have appealed to wide readerships, but most of the reading establishment is less polarized than the writings of these three authors would suggest. Already, in 1966, Jeanne Chall, a long-time professor of education at Harvard, published the first edition of her masterful survey of the state of reading instruction in both the United States and the United Kingdom (*Learning to Read: The Great Debate*, 1996). Chall reviewed the massive research, and reported on her seemingly endless visits to class-rooms and equally endless interviews with teachers and administrators. She came down in favor of an early emphasis on the "code" (i.e. phonics), and supported her position by an appeal to huge amounts of research. At the same time, she fully recognized that we read in order to extract the meaning from the print (the rather banal point that Goodman keeps insisting on, as if it is a radical view), but she saw an early emphasis on the code as a helpful, even necessary, means of reaching the meaning. She denied the claim that too much emphasis on the code would undermine attention to meaning and her calm and careful work reassures me that, far from undermining meaning, an early code-emphasis consistently speeds up the ability to read with both understanding and pleasure.

Since Chall wrote her book, hundreds of other books and thousands of research papers have appeared, all based upon even more hundreds and thousands of research hours. In a fat collection of his papers, Keith Stanovich (2000) not only reports the results of his own research, but reviews the research of hundreds of other scholars. He confirms my initial bias (and Chall's conclusions) that some grounding in phonics speeds up the learning process. Like Chall, Stanovich never forgets that extracting the meaning is the goal of reading, but he is confident that the over-whelming conclusion from masses of careful research is that children need a solid grounding in phonics if they are to reach the meaning with any ease. Marilyn Adams (1994) insists that some children come to school with no knowledge of the alphabet. They may not even realize that letters can represent speech sounds. The parents of these children are often poor and from minority backgrounds; they may be barely literate themselves. Such parents can hardly give their children a rich experience with reading, and it is such children who are most at risk of failure. They leave school tragi-cally ill-equipped for life in the twenty-first century. The consensus of all these authors, based on a mass of research, is that while the goal of reading is certainly that of extracting meaning from texts, children are more likely to reach that goal if they are given some help with phonics.

Textbooks have been written that attempt to bridge the gap between those who strongly emphasize phonics and the code, and those who do not want to tear words into pieces. One example is a tome of nearly 500 heavy but well-referenced pages by another School of Education professor named Michael Pressley. His book, *Reading Instruction That Works*, was first published in 1988 (3rd edition 2006). Presumably intended for prospective schoolteachers, its message is revealed in its subtitle: *The Case for Balanced Teaching*. At great length and with great care, Pressley argues that children need both phonic skills and word-recognition skills, hence the "balance." I feel certain that Pressley is absolutely correct. I remain mystified that anyone has ever doubted it or that the case ever needed to be made.

## Spelling

Having struggled with English spelling since the first grade, I find myself baffled by the absence, in the writings of Flesch, Goodman or Kozol, or even in the writings of better balanced and less hysterical authors, such as Chall, Pressley, Stanovich or Adams, of any suggestion that the chaos of English spelling might be one important contributor to our debacle of illiteracy. Flesch writes eloquently about the need for phonics and he castigates the schools for ignoring it, but he takes conventional English spelling as a given. Goodman finds no problem with our present spelling system, and he even imagines that reading and spelling should be easy for children if teachers would only adopt his whole-language philosophy. Kozol points his accusing finger at racism and social class, but he never suggests that our spelling might also contribute to our high rates of illiteracy. Adams writes at great length about the problems of teaching phonics in the face of the irregularities of English spelling, but the possibility that we might try to fix the spelling, instead of the children, seems to be beyond her imagination. Stanovich refers to an enormous amount of reading research but, like Adams, he takes our present spelling for granted. Why do none of these passionate people ever suggest that our broken spelling has something to do with the problem?

People who write books about reading are themselves highly literate. They read easily and often. Perhaps they have forgotten how many years they needed to learn to read, let alone to spell "correctly." Perhaps they are among the lucky ones to whom spelling came easily, and perhaps they imagine that all of us should find it as easy as they did. Having survived elementary school, they see no abnormality in the several years that English-speaking children need to gain literacy. They may not realize how easily and quickly Finnish and Italian children learn to read. Good spellers also seem unable to grasp the fact that some elementary schoolchildren are, like me, either incapable of mastering English spelling, or too cussedly independent to knuckle under to its absurdities. Too many English-speaking children simply give up and never learn to read or write.

Anyone who has managed to avoid the theoretical arguments of the reading experts is likely to take for granted the idea that the way to start children on the road to literacy is to show them how our letters are pronounced. Sadly, the relation between English sounds and English spelling is rarely simple. All too often, the relation is too complex to be easily discovered. Every vowel letter can represent more than a single spoken vowel; for example, "*o*" can stand for any one of the six different speech sounds in *odd, honey, cost, go, do, woman*. We have spoken vowels that we can spell in more than a dozen different ways: *goat, mauve, beau, yeoman, sew, go, soap, doe, rope, oh, yolk, brooch, soul, glow, owe*. I have never outgrown my astonishment that so many of my friends can remember which spelling is required for which word. Wouldn't even good spellers learn more quickly and easily if they did not need to squander their limited memory on something as ridiculous as a dozen ways to spell the vowel sound of *goat*?

English consonant sounds are spelled less chaotically than our vowel sounds, but even they can sometimes be spelled in several ways: *find/phone/ laugh*; *cake/kite/back/quilt*; *shove/sure/assure/chef/nation*; *measure/vision/ beige*. Complications like these make English phonics far more difficult than the phonics of most other alphabetic languages. With such a complicated spelling system, we should not be surprised that children need so much time and effort to learn to read English, or that so many children simply give up. It must be the complexities of our sound-to-letter correspondences that tempt people like Goodman to minimize the importance of phonics and reach, instead, for the whole word.

In spite of the chaos, English does have islands of phonic consistency. The combination *ch* generally represents the sound of *chin, choose, chew, chop, much*, and *each*, so spotting a *ch* will usually help a child who tries to sound out an unknown word. True, new readers will eventually have to learn that *Chicago* and *Christmas* and a scattering of other words have misleading *ch*'s, where they ought to have a more sensible *sh* or *k*. Still, as a first try, the pronunciation that starts the syllables of *choo-choo* is an excellent guess for any early reader who encounters a written or printed *ch*.

Many other consonant letters have reasonably consistent pronunciations: *b, d, f, h, j, k, l, m, n, p, r, t*, and *v* are all quite reliable. Even some vowel letters can usually be interpreted correctly: *oy* and *oi* nearly always represent the spoken vowel of *boy* and *choice*. We should not need two ways to spell the sound, but that is a more serious problem for a writer than for a reader. Except for a few exotic words such as *matinee*, *ee* sounds as it does in *meet* and *see*. It is *not* the case, however, that every word whose vowel is pronounced like the vowel of *see* is spelled with two *e*'s. We also need to cope with *be, flea, ceiling, field, visa, Pete, phoenix*, and *people*. The sound/ letter correspondences of our consonants are far from perfect, but they can still be a great help to a struggling new reader. Children who learn enough sound/letter correspondences can start to puzzle out unfamiliar written words that they already know in speech. They will get less help from the vowel letters than from the consonants, but even the consonants should be enough to get them started with connected prose. Even Goodman ought to grant that much to the advocates of phonics.

But sounding out the consonants is simply not enough for anyone who wants to read English, and if you want to write English, you cannot fudge the vowels. Children who learn how the *a* of *hat* is pronounced may be confused by *hate*. To be sure, we have a rule for that. The final *e* in *hate* may, itself, be silent but it changes the pronunciation of the earlier vowel. That is an awkward rule, but children can usually understand it. Before *a*, *o*, or *u*, the letter *c* generally sounds like *k* (*cat*, *cop*, *cup*) but before *e*, *i*, or *y* it is more likely to sound like *s* (*cent*, *city*, *cycle*). Is every mature English reader aware of this rule? Would children be helped or confused by being told about it?

Other rules abound. Here, for example, is a rule for which I have a certain fondness, perhaps because I felt so triumphant when I finally untangled it. I extracted this rule from a book by Richard Venezky, a book that has many such gems. (Venezky uses angle brackets, < >, to enclose examples that have conventional American spelling. Slants, / /, enclose symbols that stand for "phonemes," the distinctive speech sounds of the spoken language.)

> Before final <ll> and medial or final clusters composed of a pronounced <l> plus another consonant, <a> corresponds not to /æ/, but to /ɔ/, as in *almanac*, *alternation*, *call*, *chalk*, *mall*, *psalm* [sic!], and *walk*. This shift does not occur before medial <ll>, however. Compare, for example, *call–calliper*, *fall–fallacy*, and *mall–mallard*. Before a silent <l> plus another consonant, <a> usually corresponds to /a/ (*almond*, *balm*, *calm*, etc.). (Venezky 1999: 179)

If you spend enough time puzzling through this paragraph, you will find that it describes this bit of English spelling with admirable precision, even if not with admirable lucidity (although I do not know how *psalm* slipped into this list of words). It is possible that a rule, such as this one, can bring enlightenment or joy to some people, but I have some serious doubts that it could ever coax a ten-year-old (or even me) toward better spelling, let alone reading. I could not remember this rule any more successfully than I can remember which words get by with < l > and which require < ll >. I don't even want to *try* to remember it! If a professor of linguistics (me!) can find no help or solace from this rule, we might hesitate to burden youthful readers with it. We could, and Venezky does, write more rules than anyone could possibly use or want and, alas, English also has irregularities that cannot be covered by any rule at all. What rule can tell a struggling new writer that *table* and *label* want their two final letters in different orders? How, except by brute memory, can anyone know that *literal*, referring to an accurate quotation, is conventionally written with just one *t*, in spite of the "rule" that a short vowel is supposed to be followed by a doubled consonant? Fonics can phail. Every writer who is condemned to traditional English spelling must, sooner or later, resort to brute memory. Context and guessing can help a reader. They offer less help to a writer.

My own impossible spelling almost never interferes with my ability to read. Even now, I am rarely aware of whether I am dealing with a British or an American publication unless I encounter a "whilst" (British) or a "gotten" (American). Recently I was surprised to learn that people on one side of the Atlantic are supposed to write *realise* while those on the other side prefer *realize.* I still do not know which side writes in which way, and I do not care. Why, I always wonder, do such trivia seem so important to so many people?

It is spurisrnig to ralezie taht wehn slkield raderes are swohn wrdos in wcihh the ltretes, oehtr tahn the iiatnil and fainl, are bdaly srcemabld, tehy can slitl raed tehm wihtuot hgue dicuffilty. It helps if the words are anchored at the beginning and end with their usual letters but, in between, the letters can be juggled quite freely without making the words totally unrecognizable. This seems to tell us that we don't process letters in sequential order, but take in whole words as units. If we swallow words whole rather than process them letter by letter, should we, as Goodman suggests, avoid tearing the words into pieces, and teach children to read whole words? I think not.

Children who are just starting to read cannot be expected to read words in the same way as fluent adults read. Only by encountering words repeatedly does a reader become skilled enough to process them as single chunks. To teach children to read by recognizing whole words restricts them to the limited number of words that they have memorized, and to the few whose meaning can be guessed from their context. This means hopelessly dull reading materials. It cannot be denied that the irregularities of English spelling make sounding-out a rather chancy endeavor, but even chancy sounding-out is better than trying to memorize the thousands of written words that are needed if a story or a book is to bring joy to an early reader. To be sure, too much sounding-out can slow down new readers to the point that they lose track of the context and miss the meaning. Too little sounding-out, however, will mean that so many words are misunderstood that the passage loses coherence. The sad truth is that neither sounding-out nor learning whole words is an entirely satisfactory way of learning to read English. The irregularities of English spelling put barriers in the way of every method that has ever been tried. Only a radically revised spelling system could make learning to read English less difficult.

# 4 Reforms for Other Languages

"She knows that it's not my fault if I don't know how many Z's there are in LOSER."

Lauren Child, *Clarice Bean Spells Trouble* (2005)

## Printing and Conservatism

With every passing generation spoken languages change. New words are coined, new pronunciations are mouthed, new grammatical forms emerge. The written language can adjust quickly to changing vocabulary and a bit more slowly to changing grammar. Until printing came along, writers even had a good deal of freedom to spell as they liked, so spelling, too, could adapt, even if slowly and irregularly, to changing pronunciation. As printing spread across Europe in the centuries after Gutenberg, however, it brought a gradually increasing uniformity to the written languages. Printing encouraged standardization, so readers became familiar with more uniform spellings. It became increasingly difficult to adjust spelling to the changing spoken language until, finally, even the most modest change could be fiercely resisted by conservative readers.

In spite of such conservatism, many languages have undergone reforms, some cautious, a few revolutionary. Deliberately planned changes have brought the spelling of several European languages into closer harmony with speech, but the motives of the reformers have not always been benign. Political antagonisms have sometimes been more important than linguistic good sense in encouraging reforms. The reforms that have been successful should give us hope, but the outrage that has so often met reform proposals should also make us cautious.

## German

Like English, German has many diverse accents and, also like English, it is spoken in several different nations. Rather surprisingly, the German reforms have been less encumbered by political antagonisms than many reforms and attempted reforms in other languages. German, however, has never been spelled as chaotically as either French or English are now spelled, so reforms have been less disruptive for German speakers than they would be for speakers of French or English. That has not saved the Germans from fierce disputes.[1]

Until 1871, when Bismarck imposed political unity over what we now think of as Germany, spelling varied from one region to another. As late as the third quarter of the nineteenth century, the schools of Hanover, Leipzig, Stuttgart and Berlin all followed their own separate orthographic guidelines. The regional differences were not so great as to interfere seriously with understanding, but political unity seemed to call for a unified spelling.

German speakers have been more willing than English speakers to deal with spelling reform in a formal way. In 1876, just five years after political unity, a gathering that became known as the "First Orthographic Conference" was held in Berlin. After much debate and much disagreement a few changes were proposed, but when Bismarck heard about them, he furiously vetoed the proposals. This early effort at reform came to an abrupt end.

Nevertheless, educational authorities in Switzerland, Austria, and the various German states drew up guidelines for spelling in their schools, and by imitating one another's guidelines, they managed to bring about a good deal of unity. Then, in 1880, on the basis of these scattered but reasonably consistent reforms, Konrad Duden published his *Complete Orthographical Dictionary of the German Language*. This became the de facto, and sometimes the de jure, authority on German spelling. In spite of Bismarck's opposition, the individual German states, as well as Austria and Switzerland, had sufficient autonomy to make their own decisions. By the turn of the century considerable unity had been achieved. At another Berlin conference, this one in 1901, other modest changes were proposed, and these were also widely accepted in the German-speaking areas. These changes, together with general acceptance of the authority of the Duden dictionary, brought effective unity to the orthography, even though many inconsistent spellings remained.

In English-speaking countries, efforts toward spelling reform have almost always been the work of eager individuals or unofficial interest groups, but official governmental bodies, most often education departments, have played a central role in German reforms. Even during the cold war, when the Iron Curtain divided the German Democratic Republic in the east from the Federal Republic of Germany in the west, representatives from the two Germanys, together with those from Austria and Switzerland, gathered at international meetings and tried to reach agreement on ways to unify and improve an orthography that, compared to English,

---

1.   On the German reforms, see Sally Johnson's excellent book, *Spelling Trouble?* (2005).

was already very good. Even Luxembourg, Italy, and Hungary, all of which have German-speaking minorities, sent representatives to these meetings.

Only in the 1990s, however, after German reunification, was agreement finally reached on a number of reforms. The most important concerned the spelling of loan words and proper names, and various aspects of punctuation. The bulk of the vocabulary was left alone. These proposed reforms seemed sufficiently modest and non-controversial that the educational authorities of the various states and nations prepared to implement them in their textbooks. Publishers prepared new editions that incorporated the changes.

Then, however, as has often happened after years when spelling reform has been deliberated in a relatively quiet and unpublicized way, the wider public suddenly became aware of the impending changes. Outrage erupted. In October 1996 *Der Spiegel*, a national news magazine, screamed on its title page "Save the German Language." Well-known German writers, notably Günter Grass, who later received the Nobel Prize for Literature, objected vociferously to the planned reforms. The conservative newspaper *Frankfurter Allgemeine Zeitung* had already accepted and introduced many of the proposals, but, when the issue became public and emotional, the newspaper flounced back to the older standard. The issue found its way to the Constitutional Court, which eventually ruled against the objectors, and the ruckus gradually subsided. Many of the reforms have, by now, been accepted, not only in the German states, but in Switzerland and Austria as well. The German language is still spoken, and the predictions of linguistic disaster seem not to have been fulfilled. Readers are surely growing accustomed to the new standard, and they will certainly be ready to defend it with passion whenever further reforms are proposed.

## The Former Yugoslavia[2]

After the Iron Curtain fell and Yugoslavia began to fracture into its parts, the linguistic battles that erupted make the arguments in Germany look like a sedate debate. The German reforms were driven by a desire to reduce regional variation, but the Yugoslav reforms were driven, instead, by political rivalry. As Serbia, Croatia, Bosnia, and Montenegro became separate nations, their leaders promoted orthographic differences rather than unity. The disputes over language reflected the fierce political rivalries in a nation that was coming unglued.

After the Second World War, "Serbo-Croatian" had been promoted as the national language of Tito's unified Yugoslavia. Slovenia in the north-

2.   On Yugoslavia, see the excellent account by Robert D. Greenberg, *Language and Identity in the Balkans: Serbo-Croat and Its Disintegration* (2004).

west and Macedonia in the southeast were recognized as having distinct languages that were appropriate for local use, but everything spoken between the Slovenian and Macedonian extremes was considered to be "Serbo-Croatian," and this was the single official language of the unified nation. It was the language of government and the language of the army, and, except for the Slovenians and Macedonians, it was the name given to the daily speech of all Yugoslavs. This wide linguistic unity was felt to be needed in order to support a unified resistance to threats from the Soviet Union. Linguistic differences were played down, hidden under the common label of "Serbo-Croatian." Yet this label could not hide the fact that it was the Roman Catholics who called themselves "Croatians" and who wrote with the Roman alphabet, while the Orthodox Christians wrote with the Cyrillic alphabet and called themselves "Serbian." In daily speech, of course, people used their own local accents. Those who called themselves "Serbians" spoke in the same way as neighbors who called themselves "Croatians," while Serbians from one part of the country spoke quite differently than Serbians from another part.

The scrambled ethnic and religious divisions of what was once Yugoslavia have never corresponded closely to the political divisions, but, except for some of its border areas, Serbia in the east is relatively homogeneous. Most people in Serbia consider themselves to be Serbs. In the west, Croatia is predominantly Roman Catholic, but it has a substantial minority of Orthodox Christians who identify themselves as Serbs. Smaller minorities have other ethnic identifications.

Lying between Serbia and Croatia is Bosnia, an ethnic hodgepodge. Many Serbs and Croats live in Bosnia, but so do others who identify themselves as "Muslims." The spoken language of the Muslims is not much different from that of their Croatian and Serbian neighbors, but as adherents of a different religion, they are regarded as belonging to a third ethnicity. They are the Bosniaks.

When Croats, Serbs and Bosniaks live side by side, they speak with virtually identical accents. Those who live further apart speak somewhat differently from one another, of course, and even though Serbian, Croatian, Bosnian, and Montenegrin are all mutually intelligible, particular words and particular grammatical forms have been seized upon as symbols that are supposed to show that they speak different languages. Fierce battles have raged over how to write the "languages" of the four newly independent nations. Every political conflict was mirrored by a linguistic conflict. To assert political differences it has been felt necessary to assert linguistic differences. The linguistic battles over written standards have been particularly fierce, but even the forms to be used when speaking are contested. The choices of how to write and how to talk have become hopelessly entangled with political loyalty.

In 1991, with Tito dead and the Soviet threat removed, united Yugoslavia began to shatter into its component parts. Instead of being a symbol of unity, as Serbo-Croatian had once been, language became the major symbol by which leaders tried to distinguish their own group from all the others. Dictionaries, grammars and handbooks that offered instruction on ways to make their writing, and even their speech, "more correct" poured from the presses. "More correct" usually meant displaying more differences from the "languages" of the other groups.

The language battles of the former Yugoslavia have been focused more on vocabulary and grammar than on spelling, but they illustrate the way that language can be used either to unite or to divide. Every pair of languages and every pair of accents are alike in some ways but different in others. Languages do not, of themselves, bring either unity or division but politicians can seize on linguistic differences as a way to denigrate their opponents. Language can be a symbol that unites people. It can also be used as a symbol to inflame mutual antagonisms.

We have excellent reasons for working toward a better way to spell English. Passionate nationalism is not one of them.

## Norwegian

In the course of the last century and a half, it may be Norwegian that has undergone the most radical orthographic reforms of any European language. Like the disputes in the former Yugoslavia, the Norwegian language disputes have been entangled with politics and nationalism, but Norway has long been a thoroughly democratic nation, so the issues have always been debated peacefully, even if endlessly. The Norwegian experiments began in the nineteenth century, and they have been as passionately disputed as any in Europe. They offer an illuminating example of the kinds of struggle that can entangle a people who are, in most other ways, thoroughly sensible and rational.[3]

We speak of Norwegian, Danish, and Swedish as different "languages" but the spoken languages are hardly more different from each other than the various accents of English are. Scandinavians do not learn each other's "languages" any more than British and American speakers learn each other's "accents." When Scandinavians meet, they understand each other's "languages" as easily as British and American speakers understand

---

3.   Einar Haugen's *Language Conflict and Language Planning* (1966) gives an excellent history of the Norwegian spelling reforms. I am greatly indebted to Bente Ailin Svendsen and to Arne Torp, both of the University of Oslo, for reading an early draft of this section and offering many insightful comments and suggestions.

each other's "dialects." We think of the Scandinavian "languages" as more different from each other than British and American "accents" only because the Norwegians, Danes, and Swedes each use differing spelling conventions.

For several centuries, Scandinavia had two major political centers, one in Stockholm, the other in Copenhagen. Each had its royal family and its own civil government. Each center developed its own, somewhat different, conventions of writing and spelling. For much of this time, the areas that now form Norway and Denmark were politically united. Their king and their political center were in Copenhagen, and the region that is now Norway was a sparsely populated northern realm, settled largely by farmers and fishermen. The accents of Norway and Denmark, or at least most of them, were then, as they are now, mutually intelligible, and a single system of writing, sometimes called "Dansk-Norsk," served both parts of the realm. Denmark, however, was on the losing side of the Napoleonic wars, while Sweden had been clever enough, or lucky enough, to have sided with the victors. When peace finally came, as one part of the settlement the area that is now Norway was detached from Denmark and placed under the jurisdiction of the Swedish crown. As a result of the transfer, the Norwegians managed to maneuver themselves into more autonomy from the Swedish state than they ever had when attached to Denmark. Norway acquired its own parliament, and the Norwegians gained an increasing sense of themselves as a people who were different from both the Danes and the Swedes. An important symbol of their uniqueness was an increasing insistence that the Norwegian language was different from both Danish and Swedish. If Sweden and Denmark had different "languages," then Norway needed its own "language" too. If the Swedes and the Danes showed their differences by the way they wrote, then the Norwegians needed a third way to write that was different from either of the others.

The result was not just one, but two, quite different, reforms. The more radical reform was primarily the invention of a single man, Ivar Aasen, who in the mid-nineteenth century developed an orthography that was based largely on the rural accents of western Norway. Some Norwegians regarded these rural accents as less "corrupted" by Danish influence than the language of the capital city, then called Christiania. From this point of view, rural Norway was the place to find the "real" Norwegian language. Other Norwegians, however, felt that the accent of backward farmers was not at all suitable for their needs. The residents of Christiania were more likely to prefer their familiar way of writing, even though it was identical to Danish. Of course, the enthusiasts for reform accused people in the capital of writing in a "foreign" language. Those in the capital reciprocated by disdaining writing that was based on the speech of farmers.

However much it was scorned, the new writing system did, gradually, gain support, though mostly not in the urban areas. It became known as

"Landsmål." Like the English word "country," the Norwegian word *land* can mean either "nation" or "countryside"; depending on their preferences, Norwegians might regard Landsmål either as proudly representing the nation or as something belonging to the rural countryside—romantic, no doubt, but hardly suitable for serious writing. Whatever the opposing viewpoints, Landsmål did clearly demonstrate that it was entirely possible for Norwegian to be written in more ways than one. Landsmål acquired its passionate advocates.

Dansk-Norsk, the written form of the language that had been used when Norway and Denmark were united, was hardly ideal, even for the form of Norwegian that was spoken in the capital. A second set of reforms, less radical than that of Landsmål, and less disturbing to the urban residents of Christiania, began by tinkering with the spelling of Dansk-Norsk in order to bring it closer to the spoken forms used by educated urban Norwegians. The first changes were relatively modest, but they pulled the written language a bit closer to the spoken language of urban Norway. Today, this is known as Bokmål, "Book Language." Even the cautious early changes evoked passionate opposition and heated parliamentary debate. The more rural and more radically changed writing system came to be called Nynorsk, "New Norwegian." Endless attempts have been made to find a compromise between Nynorsk and the more conservative Bokmål, and in that way to create a single writing system, but full unity has eluded all efforts.

The political struggles between the adherents of the two "languages" have often been fierce, and the struggles to reform Bokmål have been fierce as well. Nevertheless, many Norwegians did believe that the spelling of Bokmål could be made more Norwegian and less Danish, and they also argued that a revised spelling would make it easier for children to learn to read, particularly children from less-privileged homes. Even for Bokmål, many reforms came to be accepted, though never without initial resistance. The government could not control how either publishers or private writers chose to spell, but it could control the spelling of school texts. In reaction to one reform, Oslo mothers gathered to cross out the disliked new forms in new textbooks. They wrote their preferred, more conservative, spellings into the books. In spite of such opposition, Bokmål did grow away from its Danish roots, though never far enough to satisfy the fervent supporters of Nynorsk.

Today, Norwegians travel about their country easily. They move for education or for work, and all Norwegians become familiar with Norway's diverse spoken accents. They have no more difficulty understanding each other than American and British speakers do, but still Norway has been unable to escape its linguistic divide. In democratic Norway, the two "languages" must be given equal status. Every government document must be printed both ways. Every schoolbook must be printed in both "languages." Every child must learn to read both. Students, anywhere in Norway, have the right to write their examinations in the "language" of their choice. Television announcers must be chosen to represent both "languages." But there are far more than just two forms of spoken Norwegian, and from an early age all Norwegians grow accustomed to hearing many spoken varieties of their language, not just two.

The long struggle to reform Norwegian orthography is an example of the deep attachment that readers often have to whatever they find familiar. The writing that we are familiar with seems so clearly correct that we resist any change. If the fewer than five million Norwegians in a small and homogeneous nation find it so difficult to agree on a single way to write, what hope can there be for the scattered nations and the more than three hundred million people who call their language English?

Norwegians sometimes justify having two "languages" on the grounds that simply by having two competing written forms, everyone is liberated to speak, and even to write, as they choose. When only a single way to write is acceptable, its authority can be oppressive. Any deviation risks censure. With two competing standards, it becomes easier to deviate from both. When no single form is universally accepted as "correct," all are freer to follow their own preferences. Perhaps the two written forms even foster the health of the many spoken accents. Certainly the accents of Norway are rich and varied, and Norwegians face little pressure to adjust to a well-defined spoken norm. Even the written standards are probably less constrained in Norway than in Britain and America. For all the fierce struggles, two competing standards may be less oppressive than a single monolith. Or so some Norwegians like to believe.

## Hangŭl of Korea: A Cautionary Tale[4]

The Norwegian reforms that brought Nynorsk and Bokmål into existence were intended not only to bring the written language closer to the spoken language, but also to demonstrate, even to flaunt, the linguistic differences between Norwegian and Danish. In this, they resembled the Yugoslavian reforms, which were also intended to assert the differences among the languages. The German reforms, instead, were intended to bring unity and to allow speakers of German, wherever they lived, to use the same written

---

4. An excellent description of the Hangŭl writing system can be found in Geoffrey Sampson, *Writing Systems: A Linguistic Introduction* (1985). On its history, see also Kim Chŏng-Su and Ross King, *The History and Future of Hangeul: Korea's Indigenous Script* (2005).

conventions. None of these reforms, however, required the kind of radical changes that are needed if English is to become easier to spell. For a truly dramatic example of orthographic reform, we need to turn to Korea. Not since runes went out of fashion has any European language undergone the kind of radical reform that has come to Korea. The reforms in Korea were intended neither to unite the Koreans nor to divide them but, quite simply, to make it easier for them to learn to read and write. In this respect, the reforms are closer to the goals of most English reformers than to the more nationalistic goals of the advocates of Nynorsk, let alone the enthusiastic chauvinists of the former Yugoslavia. Sadly, no less than five centuries were needed for the writing system known as "Hangŭl" to be fully accepted. It is not an encouraging precedent.

Of all the writing systems in use today, it may be Hangŭl that comes closest to a perfect representation of its spoken language. Hangŭl is the darling of linguists, and it should delight everyone who longs for a better way to spell. The history of Hangŭl, nevertheless, has been a rocky one, and the half-millennium that passed between its invention and its final acceptance should worry anyone who hopes for a quick fix for English. Hangŭl shows the promise of orthographic reform but it also shows the serious problems that stand in its way.

Like Vietnam and Japan, Korea lies on the periphery of China, and China has always had a powerful influence on its smaller neighbors. The Korean spoken language has a totally different origin than Chinese, and its core vocabulary remains utterly different from Chinese. Nevertheless, the Koreans, like the Vietnamese and the Japanese, borrowed an enormous number of Chinese words into their language, just as the English borrowed an enormous number of words from French and Latin. The Koreans even adopted Chinese characters for writing their language, although the characters must always have been much more difficult for Korean speakers than for the Chinese. Many characters hint at the Chinese pronunciation of the words they represent, even if they do so imperfectly and irregularly. They have no relation at all to the pronunciation of native Korean words. The differences between the Korean and Chinese spoken languages mean that the Chinese characters have always imposed an extra burden on Korean readers and writers. Even more than in China, the ability to read and write was limited to scholars who had the privilege of a long and arduous education.

From 1418 to 1450, the king of Korea was a man named Sejong. During his reign, Sejong convened a group of scholars and charged them with the design of a new writing system for Korean. This was intended to reflect the spoken language of Korea in a way that was impossible with Chinese characters. The work may have been done primarily, or entirely, by the scholars whom King Sejong had appointed, but Korean tradition holds that the king himself had a major part in the design of the new way of writing. Whoever was actually responsible, the result was the extraordinary Hangŭl orthography.

Hangŭl is described in some detail in the Appendix to this chapter, but the most important general point is that its symbols are constructed so that they represent the sounds of the language at three levels of complexity. The basic and simplest level of Hangŭl has just five symbols for five consonants: ㅁ *m*, ㄴ *n*, ㄱ *g*, ㅇ *ng*, and ㅅ *s*. It is not likely that anyone who is unfamiliar with these symbols would suspect that they are stylized pictures of the vocal organs, but they are. The little box 'ㅁ' that represents an *m* is a picture of a mouth. Western readers might expect a mouth to be round, rather than rectangular, but its squared-up shape would be easily recognized by any Korean familiar with Chinese characters, because the character for "mouth" is a square. The Korean ㄴ represents a sound that is similar to English *n*. It is a stylized picture of the tongue with its tip curled upward to articulate against the roof of the mouth, as it does when pronouncing *n*. ㄱ represents a speech sound that is similar to the *g* of *go*. This, too, is a picture. Here, the tongue is humped up at the back to articulate against the soft palate, as when pronouncing a *k* or a hard *g*. The circle is a picture of the throat in cross-section, and it is used for the sounds that are made furthest back in the throat. The symbol for *s* is ㅅ. It is a picture of a tooth, the place where *s* hisses.

Strokes are added to these five basic symbols to form the other consonants. For example, ㄷ represents the sound of *d*. It is formed from the symbol for *n* by the addition of a top horizontal line. Both *n* and *d* are articulated by pointing the tongue tip upward against the roof of the mouth. The symbols for other consonants are formed by adding other strokes to the basic symbols. Hangŭl has about thirty symbols of this kind, and they are the closest that it comes to the letters of western alphabets.

In addition to the consonant symbols, which tend to be rather blocklike, Hangŭl has another set of symbols for the vowels. These are more elongated than the consonants. All the symbols, and the ways in which they are related to each other, are described in the Appendix to this chapter.

These letter-like symbols are not simply strung together one after another as are the letters of European alphabets. Instead, they are clustered together to form complex symbols that represent entire syllables. These form the third symbolic level of Hangŭl. Syllables have no special role in western writing systems but in Chinese each character represents exactly one syllable. The scholars who designed Hangŭl were well acquainted with the syllabic nature of Chinese writing, so they would have found it natural to create symbols for Korean syllables too. The Hangŭl syllable symbols, however, have an utterly different internal structure from Chinese characters. Each Korean syllable is represented by a cluster (rather than a sequence) of the letter-like symbols. Western alphabets represent just one kind of phonological unit, roughly, the phoneme. Hangŭl represents three phonological levels: phonetic features, phonemes, and syllables. It was a brilliant invention. Readers who are interested will find a more detailed description of Hangŭl in the Appendix to this chapter.

For Korean speakers, Hangŭl writing is very easy to learn. A Korean is supposed to have once said of Hangŭl, "An intelligent man can learn it in a single morning. A stupid man needs a few days." More time than this is surely required for easy fluency, but Korean children do not need spelling bees. When first learning to read, Koreans can be helped by understanding how the letter-like symbols are constructed from their parts and how these letter-like symbols are, in turn, grouped into syllables, but with increasing fluency, they have no more need than western readers to tear apart each word or syllable into its components. Fluent Korean readers surely learn to read the syllable signs, or even familiar sequences of syllable signs, as single chunks, just as western readers learn to read entire words as chunks.

The design of the Hangŭl script was completed in 1444, the same decade in which Gutenberg first showed Europeans that printing with movable type was possible. By the 1440s, the Koreans had been printing with movable type for more that two centuries, but they had used the older Chinese-based script. Once it was available, Hangŭl began to be used by writers of popular fiction, and it was especially popular among women, few of whom would ever have had the chance to learn the older writing system. No school was needed to teach Hangŭl. It could be passed from friend to friend. Could English speakers pass on the ability to read from friend to friend if our spelling were as easy to learn as Korean?

The new alphabet, however, was far too easy to suit the taste of the literate Korean elite. Fifteenth-century Koreans who knew how to read the older writing system had a vested interest in it. Their scholarly scorn for Hangŭl should be easy for us to understand because it was so similar to the attitude of many fluent readers of English today. Hangŭl must have looked at least as simplistic and childish to the fifteenth-century Korean literati as simplified spelling now looks to fluent readers of traditional written English. If everyone could learn to read, moreover, the hard-earned skill with the older writing system would no longer be so valuable. The Korean literati reacted just as many literate readers of English do today to proposals for simplification. The proposals looked childish and they threatened vested interests. The literati rejected them.

In 1504, a king who was less concerned with disseminating knowledge than King Sejong had been, prohibited the study or use of Hangŭl. For the next four centuries the new writing system waxed and waned in importance. It might be good enough for women and peasants who would never be capable of learning the more prestigious Chinese-based writing system, but better people deserved something better. Hangŭl, however, could be so easily learned and passed on that it was not simply forgotten. No school or trained teacher was needed to learn Hangŭl, only a helpful friend. In spite of the prestige of the older writing system, Hangŭl refused to disappear.

Korea became a Japanese colony in 1910, and only in 1945, at the conclusion of the Pacific War, did it regain its independence. During the colonial period, Japanese became the official language of Korea, but Hangŭl was, for a time, taught in the schools. Mixed forms developed in which the grammatical words and affixes were written in Hangŭl while most lexical roots—nouns, verbs, adjectives—were written with Chinese characters. Japanese colonialism probably helped Hangŭl by turning it into a symbol of national pride, and this may be the reason why, in 1938, the colonial government banned its use in Korean schools. Immediately after the Second World War, however, when Korea finally emerged from colonial rule, Hangŭl came into wide general use. North Korea, more autocratic and nationalistic than the south, banned all use of Chinese characters. In the south, characters have continued to be sprinkled through texts but, even there, the trend has increasingly been toward using more Hangŭl and fewer characters. No longer is Hangŭl dismissed as mere childish scribble, suitable only for women and peasants. Even as we admire Hangŭl, however, its five hundred years in gestation should worry us. If a spelling system as splendid as Hangŭl needed so much time to become fully acceptable, how much time will be needed for a better spelling of English to become respectable?

## Reforms Elsewhere

Reforms have been attempted in many other places, sometimes successfully, often not. The most radical orthographic reform of the twentieth century was certainly the Turkish switch from the Arabic to the Roman alphabet. During the Ottoman Empire, the Arabic alphabet was used for Turkish, just as it continues to be used in many of the world's predominantly Muslim nations—in Urdu-speaking Pakistan and in Persian-speaking Iran, as well as in the countries where the dominant language is Arabic. After the First World War, most of the non-Turkish-speaking parts of the Ottoman Empire were torn away. What was left was predominantly Turkish in speech. Kemal Ataturk, the leader of the new Turkey, imposed the change from the Arabic to the Roman alphabet, and the new alphabet came to symbolize the newly modernizing nation. Such a radical change could never have been carried out without a powerful and autocratic leader who could impose his will. This is not a model that offers much hope to people living in democratic nations.

The Maoist regime in China, no slouch on the authoritarian side, imposed two reforms, neither as radical as the reform in Turkey. The more important reform simplified a large number of characters. This did not radically alter the way Chinese is written, but did reduce the complexity of many characters. The simplified characters are now used everywhere in mainland China, while the traditional characters continue to be used in Taiwan, and even in Hong Kong. Anyone who wants to read Chinese from both the mainland and elsewhere must now learn two forms of a large number of characters.

The second, and more radical, Maoist innovation was the romanization known as "Pinyin." Several other romanizations of Chinese had already been developed, both for scholarly purposes and for representing Chinese personal and place names when they were embedded in a written European language. Pinyin, however, was the first romanization to have official backing. It has been used to introduce schoolchildren to the variety of spoken Chinese that is variously known as Putonghua, Mandarin, or Standard Chinese. Pinyin has also been used to show the pronunciation of difficult characters and to represent Chinese words in foreign-language contexts, but it has never been used to replace the characters.

For many hundreds of years, Vietnam was ruled as a province of China. As in Korea, Chinese characters were modified and supplemented in ways that allowed them to be used for writing the Vietnamese language, but the Chinese-based characters were as difficult for speakers of Vietnamese as they were for Koreans. When Catholic missionaries from Portugal reached Vietnam in the early sixteenth century, they adapted the Roman alphabet to Vietnamese, and used it in their teaching and evangelism. A century later, a French Jesuit priest named Alexandre de Rhodes regularized and systematized the romanization, and it is Rhodes who is generally credited as the originator of the modern Vietnamese orthography now known as "Quoc-ngu." Rhodes wrote a dictionary and he established a tradition among Vietnamese Christians of using Quoc-ngu, but the older Chinese-based writing also remained in use for three more centuries. In 1910, however, the French colonial administration adopted Quoc-ngu for official purposes, and by the time of Vietnamese independence after World War II, it had become the universal writing system of the country. It is well adapted to the language and it has contributed to the high rate of literacy among the Vietnamese people.

The reforms of Vietnamese and Korean, and even those of German and Norwegian, were successful in the sense that they eliminated some irregularities and made the writing systems easier to learn, but reforms have failed at least as often as they have succeeded. The French recently had a chance to drop many of the circumflexes from *î* and *û*. These little hats are a distant echo of an *s* which long ago was pronounced and spelled in these words, but centuries have passed since it went silent. All that remains is the useless circumflex, as in *forêt*. It tells readers nothing whatever about the pronunciation of modern French, and its only effect is to force every French child, and every foreigner who aspires to write French, to remember which words need a circumflex and which do not. Even such a trivial simplification as dropping this long-dead accent was met by outrage. The circumflexes remain safely in place.

## Failure and Success

The examples of successful reforms and the examples of reforms that failed both hold serious lessons for those of us who would like to see English reformed. First, they show us how varied the motives that drive reformers can be, and they warn us that some of the reasons for reform should be firmly rejected. We should fiercely resist the political motives that have led some reformers to assert their differences by using different spellings. It is more difficult to design a spelling system that is equally suitable for all the diverse accents of English than to design a spelling for a single homogeneous accent, but that cannot be avoided if we are to keep our language unified. I would want nothing to do with any English reform that did not maintain the worldwide unity of written English.

The reforms that have succeeded, as well as those that have failed, also show us that we must always expect resistance. From the condemnation of Hangŭl by Korean scholars five hundred years ago to the outrage of Günter Grass when he felt threatened by some modest reforms for German, skilled readers have always found it easier to continue with what is familiar than to make the effort to learn something better. Skilled readers can be cruelly indifferent to the struggles of their own children. When threatened by such a timid reform as a dropped circumflex, even outspoken political radicals can become timid social conservatives, and the reforms needed for English are not for the timid.

We must expect that change will take a long time. We can hope that it might come more quickly than the half-millennium that the Koreans needed before they would fully accept Hangŭl, but reform is not a task for a decade. We can also note with satisfaction that reform is not, after all, impossible. The Germans and the Koreans have managed to reform. What, then, stops the speakers of English?

# Appendix to Chapter Four
# The Hangŭl Writing System

I look with awe on the Hangŭl writing of Korea. No other writing system that is in wide use today is more perfectly adapted to the spoken language, and no other writing system is so easy to learn. Only a few minutes are needed to appreciate its beauty.

*Consonants* The five consonant symbols in the first row in Figure 4.1 were described earlier: ㅁ is a stylized picture of the mouth; ㄴ pictures the tongue with its tip pointed up toward the roof of the mouth; ㄱ is also a picture of the tongue, but here it is hunched up at the back; ㅅ is a tooth; ㅇ is a cross-section of the throat. These are the five basic consonant symbols and they represent, respectively, *m, n, s, g,* and *ng/h.*

|  | bilabial | apical | sibilant | velar | laryngeal |
|---|---|---|---|---|---|
| Lax continuants | m ㅁ | n ㄴ | s ㅅ | g ㄱ | ng/ɦ ㅇ |
| (nasals and s) |  |  |  |  |  |
| Lax stops | b ㅂ | d ㄷ | ɟ ㅈ |  |  |
| (voiced stops) |  |  |  |  |  |
| Tense aspirated stops | pʰ ㅍ | tʰ ㅌ | cʰ ㅊ | kʰ ㅋ | h ㅎ |
| (voiceless, aspirated stops) |  |  |  |  |  |
| Tense continuant |  |  | ss ㅆ |  |  |
| (aspirated continuant) |  |  |  |  |  |
| Tense unaspirated stops | p ㅃ | t ㄸ | c ㅉ | k ㄲ |  |
| (voiceless, unaspirated stops) |  |  |  |  |  |
| Liquid |  | l ㄹ |  |  |  |

**Figure 4.1** The Hangŭl consonants (from Sampson 1985)

The remaining consonant symbols are sorted into columns according to the place in the mouth where they are articulated: the bilabial sounds in the first column are made with the two lips; apicals are made with the tip (the "apex") of the tongue articulating against the roof of the mouth; sibilants hiss near the teeth; velars are made by articulating the back of the tongue against the soft palate (the "velum"); laryngeals are articulated way at the back of the throat, closest to the larynx. The rows in Figure 4.1 show the manner in which the consonants are produced. For Korean, these are traditionally described rather differently than they are described for western languages, and the terms in parentheses in the leftmost column may be more familiar to western readers. The Roman letters that are next to each Korean symbol give a good approximation to their pronunciation. The only consonants that are likely to be unfamiliar are *j* and *ɦ*. These are explained below.

The symbols in the first row in Figure 4.1 are stylized pictures of the vocal organs. All the symbols in the lower rows are modifications of these topmost symbols. Phonetically, the rows are distinguished from one another by the manner in which their consonants are articulated. For European languages, we usually distinguish the spoken consonants by such features as voicing (*b* is voiced, *p* is not), and nasalization (*m* is nasal, *b* and *p* are not). For Korean, it is customary, instead, to distinguish consonants as "tense vs. lax" and "stop vs. continuant." Tense sounds are made with more muscular effort than lax sounds. Continuants allow a continuous flow of air, while the stops briefly cut off the flow. Readers unfamiliar with linguistic terminology may find it easier simply to use the Roman letters that are beside each Korean symbol. These show the approximate pronunciation of each Korean symbol.

At the end of a syllable, the slightly squashed circle stands for the speech sound that linguists usually symbolize as *ŋ*, and that we spell in everyday English as "*ng*." In Korean, as in English, this sound is found only at the end of a syllable. The squashed circle is also used at the beginning of a syllable, but there it stands for a voiced *h*. This is similar to an English *h* except that the vocal cords vibrate. The phonetic symbol for this speech sound is *ɦ*. Like both *ng* and English *h*, the Korean *ɦ* is made at the back of the throat. The circle, then, stands for either *ɦ* or *ŋ*, depending on whether it is first or last in the syllable. Our English habits make it seem odd to use the same written symbol for two such different speech sounds, but since they occur at different places in the syllable, *ɦ* at the beginning, *ŋ* at the end, they cannot be confused, and the circle does well for both. ㅈ is a lax or voiced stop that is made at approximately the location of ㅅ(*s*); *j* is the linguist's phonetic symbol that represents the sound of the Korean ㅈ.

Except for the top row of "letter-like" symbols shown in Figure 4.1, all the symbols are constructed from smaller symbols that stand for features of the phonemes. In the second row, ㄷ and ㅈ differ from the symbols in the top row only by the addition of a horizontal top line. The symbol for *g*, also in the second row, is ㄱ, but it too has a horizontal top line. This top line, then, is a symbol that means "lax stop." The bilabial *b*, ㅂ, is also a lax stop, but its top line is pushed down, keeping it distinct from *m*,ㅁ, from which it is derived.

The symbols in the third row represent tense aspirated sounds. ("Aspirated" simply means "accompanied by a puff of air," like *p*, *t*, or *k* at the start of an English word.) Except for ㅍ, the aspirated consonants are all made by adding a horizontal line to the symbols for the lax consonants, so the added line of these symbols indicates tense aspiration.

The symbols for the tense continuant and for the tense *un*aspirated stops are made by doubling the symbol for the corresponding lax sounds. Doubling can be understood as the symbol for tense consonants that are *not* aspirated.

Down at the bottom of the table, the last consonant is ㄹ, the symbol for the sound of *l*. This is modified from ㄷ, which is the symbol for *d*. Since *l* and *d* are both articulated with the front part of the tongue tip touching the roof of the mouth, it is appropriate for their symbols to be similar. In these ways, the consonant symbols of Hangŭl show both the manner of their articulation and the place in the mouth where they are articulated.

*Vowels*. The vowels of Korean are shown in Figure 4.2. These are more linear than the blocklike consonants. The symbols for the high front unrounded *i* (similar to the English vowel in *heap* or *keen*) and the high back unrounded *ɯ* are, respectively, vertical and horizontal lines. These are the basic vowel symbols upon which all the other vowel symbols are built. (If you want to try to pronounce the sound of *ɯ*, you must spread your lips into the position you would use for "ee," as in *keep*, but try to say the vowel of "boot" without moving your lips. We have nothing like this vowel in English, so English speakers sometimes find it difficult to articulate. This vowel can be described as "high, back, and spread," meaning that the tongue is high in the mouth and pulled back, while the lips are "spread" wide, the opposite of "rounded."

|  | front | | back | |
|  | unrounded | rounded | unrounded | rounded |
|---|---|---|---|---|
| high | i ㅣ | | ɯ ㅡ | u ㅜ |
| mid | e ㅔ | ø ㅚ | ɤ ㅓ | o ㅗ |
| low | æ ㅐ | | a ㅏ | |

Figure 4.2 Hangŭl vowels (from Sampson 1985)

The symbols for the other four back vowels are built on either the vertical *i* or the horizontal *ɯ*, but each one has an added small tick on one side or the other. Three of these back vowels can, in turn, be joined to the vertical symbol for *i*. When joined, the three resulting symbols stand for the front vowels with the same features (unrounded or rounded; mid or low) as the corresponding back vowels. For example, the low unrounded *back* vowel is ㅏ. The corresponding low unrounded *front* vowel is ㅐ. The symbol for the front vowel differs from the symbol for the corresponding back vowel only by the addition of the second vertical line. This extra line can be taken to mean "front."

*Syllables.* Syllables are salient features of all spoken languages, but they are ignored in western alphabetic writing. It would have been possible for King Sejong and his scholars to ignore the syllables of Korean and to string the symbols of Figures 4.1 and 4.2 in a line in the same way that we string together the consonant and vowel letters of the Roman alphabet. However, the Korean inventors of Hangŭl were familiar with Chinese writing, where each character stands for exactly one syllable, so the scholars collected their "letters" into blocks, with each block standing for exactly one syllable. In this way they mimicked Chinese characters, even while giving the Korean symbols an internal organization that is utterly different from anything Chinese. If the vowel of the syllable is represented by a predominantly vertical symbol (a symbol standing for a front vowel), the vowel is placed at the right, while the consonants are then written on the left. The initial consonant is at the top, the final consonant at the bottom. If the vowel of the syllable is written by a predominantly horizontal symbol (standing for a back vowel), it is placed halfway down, with the initial consonant above the vowel, and the final consonant below. The characters for the syllables are then strung together in a line to represent words and sentences. The way in which syllable signs are constructed from the smaller "letter-like" symbols is shown in Figure 4.3.

| constituents | | | | syllable | pronunciation | meaning |
|---|---|---|---|---|---|---|
| | ㅏ | | | 아 | /a/ | (a suffix) |
| ㄷ | ㅏ | | | 다 | /da/ | all |
| | ㅏ | ㄹ | | 알 | /al/ | egg |
| ㄷ | ㅏ | ㄹ | | 달 | /dal/ | moon; sweet |
| ㄷ | ㅏ | ㄹ | ㄱ | 닭 | /dalg/ | hen |

**Figure 4.3** Formation of Hangŭl syllables (from Taylor 1980)

Like the letters of the Roman alphabet, the Korean symbols can be used to represent the words of any language. With the help of Figures 4.1 and 4.2, the reader should be able to confirm that the English word "ungentlemanliness" lurks in the sequence of Korean symbols found in Figure 4.4.

언젠틀먼리네스

**Figure 4.4** "Ungentlemanliness" in Hangŭl (from Taylor 1980)

The letters of western alphabets symbolize one kind of spoken phonetic segment. The letters may do their job well, as they do in Finnish, or with irritating irregularity, as in English, but, ideally, each letter should represent one phoneme. Korean writing symbolizes not just one kind of spoken segment, but three: first, the features of the sound system, in particular the place and manner by which the speech sounds are articulated; second, the sequential consonants and vowels, the phonemes; and third, the syllables. The syllabic aspect of the writing system must have been important to the designers of Hangŭl, because it gave the writing an obvious, although superficial, similarity to Chinese characters. In both Chinese and Korean, blocklike symbols of considerable internal complexity stand for syllables, but the internal structure of the Hangŭl syllable signs is utterly unlike the internal structure of Chinese characters. Korean syllable signs are far more logically constructed than Chinese characters. We can only look with awe at this brilliant intellectual achievement of the fifteenth-century Koreans.

# 5  Failed Reforms for English

"It is a damn poor mind that can think of only one way to spell a word."
Attributed to Andrew Jackson, US President (1829–37)

## Reformers and Their Opponents

Serious and reasonable proposals for English spelling reform began within a century of the introduction of printing. One of the earliest was by a man named John Hart, who in 1569 published a book called *An Orthographie*. Hart was a skilled phonetician and he made concrete proposals for a spelling that would be easier for English speakers to learn than the system then in use. At the time when Hart wrote, *u* and *v* were different forms of the same letter, no more different from one another than modern *a* and *a*. They were distinguished not by their pronunciations, but by their position in the word. Similarly, ſ, the so-called "tall *s*," had a different shape from our *s*, but these, too, were alternative forms of the same letter. Hart began his book with these sentences:

> Orthographie is a Greeke woorde ſignifying true writing, which is when it is framed with reaſon to make vs certayne wyth what letters euery member of our ſpeach ought to bee written. By which definition wee ought to vſe an order in writing, which nothing cared for vnto this day, our predeceſſors and we haue ben (as it were) drouned in a maner of negligence, to bee contented with ſuch maner of writing as they and we now, haue found from age to age. Without any regard vnto the feuerall parts of the voice, which the writing ought to repreſent. (Hart 1969 [1569])

Like modern reformers, Hart advocated a spelling that stayed close to the phonetics of the language. In the orthography then in use, he saw the vices of "diminution" (too few letters), "superfluite" (use of superfluous letters), "mysplacing" (usurpation of one letter by another) and "disordering" (failure of the order of the spelling to correspond to the order in which the letters are pronounced) (Venezky 1999: 214). Hart advocated the separation of *v* from *u*, and of *j* from *i*, seventy years before this was generally accepted.

Also like reformers today, Hart faced strong opposition. Richard Mulcaster was a teacher and distinguished schoolmaster. In his book, *The First Part of the Elementarie*, published in 1582, Mulcaster argued against reforms such as those that Hart had proposed, and he appealed to the importance of tradition. "Tradition," at the time when Hart and Mulcaster were writing, was less oppressively uniform than it is now, but it was still strong enough to make any threat of radical reform disconcerting to readers who had grown familiar with the spelling that was then conventional. The opposing arguments of Hart and Mulcaster anticipated the arguments, both for reform and against it, that have been made repeatedly in the four centuries that have passed since their time. Reformers have always advocated a spelling that reflects pronunciation more closely. Traditionalists always cite the dangers of any break with the past. Since the late sixteenth century, when Hart and Mulcaster wrote, every dispute has been won by the traditionalists. The comforting security of familiar spelling, along with the greater ease of doing nothing, has always trumped the uncertain benefits of change.

In the century that followed Hart and Mulcaster, a long series of reformers suggested changes of many kinds. They worried about double letters and silent *e*. Some wanted to re-spell "soft *g*" as "*j*." They all wanted to have written English reflect the spoken language more closely, but they focused on different problems. They were good at pointing out inconsistencies in the writing used in their time, but they showed little consistency themselves, either in the problems that they worried about or the solutions that they offered. Some even worried about such peripheral matters as the names of the letters or the order of the letters in the alphabet. Some worried about homographs. Printers groped for consistency in the spelling of particular words, but they failed to be consistent about using the same letters for the same speech sounds in different words.

While the reforms proposed by Hart and by his contemporaries and successors achieved little, spelling did gradually change. In particular, the seventeenth century saw a clear trend toward greater consistency in the spelling of particular words. The highly variable spelling that was used in the early days of printing cannot have disturbed poor spellers, but it was certainly an annoyance for printers who groped for some sort of consistent standard. They developed style sheets for their own use and they even tried to follow them. As they imitated one another's practices, variant forms were gradually shucked off, so they did, slowly, converge on a uniform standard. Uniform spelling came more slowly to private writing than to printing, but even private writers could not resist the example of the increasingly consistent spelling of print. Oddly, consistent spelling was sometimes cited as offering help to writers, even to writers who were poor spellers. If a word could be spelled in only one way, all the writer needed to do was to learn a single spelling, and stick to it.

Always, there were people who saw etymology as more important than phonetic consistency. In about 1711, Jonathan Swift addressed a letter to "the Most Honourable Robert Earl of Oxford and Mortimer, Lord High-Treasurer of Great Britain":

Another Cause . . . which hath contributed not a little to the maiming of our Language, is a foolish Opinion advanced of late Years, that we ought to spell exactly as we speak; which beside the obvious Inconvenience of utterly destroying our Etymology, would be a thing we should never see an End of. Not only the several Towns and Counties of England, have a different Way of pronouncing; but even here in *London* they clip their Words after one Manner about the Court, another in the City, and a third in the Suburbs; and in a few Years, it is probable, will all differ from themselves, as Fancy or Fashion shall dirrect: All which reduced to Writing, would entirely confound Orthography. (quoted by G. H. Vallins 1954:120)

This passage displays a misconception that can still be heard from those who are skeptical about reform. Accent variability is, admittedly, a difficult problem, and one major theme of Part II of this book is to suggest ways to reconcile variable speech with uniform spelling. Nevertheless, however much variability our spoken accents display, all have much in common. Even their differences are generally sufficiently systematic to allow a uniform spelling. If the differences among accents were not reasonably systematic, after all, we would not be able to understand each other's speech. Speakers of different accents should certainly continue to pronounce their words in the same varied ways that they have always done, even when reading the same letters from the same page. Swift badly exaggerated the problem of accent variability.

By 1700 the standardization of spelling was essentially complete. Since that time, changes have been few, and proposals for reform have more often been greeted by amusement and scorn than by serious thought. Samuel Johnson's *Dictionary of the English Language* first appeared in 1755. His spelling did not deviate in any significant way from the spelling that printers were already using, but his dictionary was so influential that it helped to freeze the spelling more firmly. Johnson himself seemed to regret the need to follow tradition. In the preface to his dictionary, he wrote, "I have often been obliged to sacrifice uniformity to custom; thus I write, in compliance with a numberless majority, *convey* and *inveigh*, *deceit* and *receipt*, *fancy* and *phantom*" (Johnson 1755). If Johnson regretted such unfortunate spellings, he still felt obliged to follow the conventions that were already familiar. His dictionary entered literate British homes and its spelling came to be accepted as the standard for private writing as well as for printing.

Simply by choosing one form from among the possible alternatives, Johnson helped to crystallize spelling practice. Printers and, somewhat later, private writers knew that they would not be criticized if they followed Johnson's spellings. As writers and printers groped toward spellings that would offend the fewest possible number of readers, they gradually winnowed out the variants. No one asserted authority, but the writing public came to imagine that a word could have only one "correct" spelling. Even at the end of the sixteenth century, writers were already urging the young to conform to spelling that was regarded as "correct," and by the eighteenth century, when Johnson's dictionary appeared, spelling had become a mark of education, good breeding, and social acceptability. Anyone who was concerned about his own reputation needed to follow convention. The tyranny of the dictionary was complete. Mirth at the expense of the poor speller has a long history in the English-speaking world.

Authoritarian traditions have a way of evoking a reaction, however, and a few people have always had enough imagination to propose repairing the spelling instead of the speller. One famous advocate of reformed spelling was Benjamin Franklin. He proposed a reformed alphabet and urged others to change. In a letter written in 1768 to a young "Miss Stevenson," Franklin sent a message that any enthusiastic reformer would still cheer.

> Craven Street [London],
> 28 September 1768
>
> Dear Madam:
> The objection you make to rectifying our alphabet, that "it will be attended with inconveniences and difficulties," is a natural one; for it always occurs when any reformation is proposed, whether in religion, government, laws, and even down as low as roads and wheel-carriages. The true question, then, is not whether there will be any difficulties or inconveniences, but whether the difficulties may not be surmounted, and whether the conveniences will not, on the whole, be greater than the inconveniences. In this case, the difficulties are only in the beginning of the practice. When they are overcome the advantages are lasting. To either you or me, who spell well in the present mode, I imagine the difficulty of changing that mode for the new is not so great, but that we might perfectly get over it in a week's time.
>
> As to those, who do not spell well, if the two difficulties are compared— namely, that of teaching them true spelling in the present mode, and that of teaching them the new alphabet, and the new spelling according to it, I am confident that the latter would be by far the least. They naturally fall into the new method already, as much as the imperfection of their alphabet will admit of. Their present bad spelling is only bad because contrary to the present bad rules. The difficulty of learning to spell well in the old way is so great, that few attain it, thousands and thousands writing on to old age without ever being able to acquire it. It is, besides, a difficulty continually increasing, as the sound gradually varies more and more from the spelling, and to foreigners it makes the learning to pronounce our language as written in our books almost impossible. (Franklin and Vaughan 1779)

In no discernible way did Franklin's advocacy of a better spelling influence either publishers or the writing public.

Noah Webster's *An American Dictionary of the English Language* (1828) did for American English what Johnson's dictionary had done three-quarters of a century earlier for the English of the home country, but Webster had a considerably stronger reforming streak than Johnson had. He wanted a new American language for the new American nation, and at times he spoke quite radically in support of deep changes for American spelling. Webster supported himself by sales of his widely used schoolbooks, however, and he could not risk offending the people who bought them. In his schoolbooks, Webster was more conservative than in his other writings, and by the time he had finished his dictionary his enthusiasm for reform had weakened considerably.

Webster did spell a few words differently from Johnson, and he is largely responsible for the scattered differences that now distinguish American spelling from British. The most salient single example of transatlantic differences may be *o/ou* in words such as *color/colour* and *honor/honour*. Both spellings had been used on both sides of the Atlantic but Johnson helped *ou* to win out in England. Webster settled on *color* and *honor*, perhaps as much from a nationalist desire to be different as for any practical advantage. He chose *-er* rather than *-re* in such words as *theater*, and he got rid of the final *-k* in *musick* and *publick*. He changed *c* to *s* in a few words such as *defense*. He allowed Americans to drop the final *e* from *axe*, and he tried, but failed, to do the same for *medicine* and *famine*. He proposed other reasonable spellings, such as *hed*, *giv*, *bilt* and *lether*, but these never had a chance (R. A. Wells 1973: 61–2; Ives 1979: 37–9).

Webster's spelling caused outrage in some quarters, but many of his choices were adopted, and he is usually given the credit (or the blame) for whatever modest differences there are between British and American spelling now. In fact, most of Webster's spellings had already been in use before they found their way into his dictionary, some of them in Britain as well as in America. Webster's real contribution, like Johnson's, was to consolidate practice that was already in wide use.

As with Johnson's dictionary in Britain, American readers took Webster's dictionaries to be authoritative, but the changes that are attributed to him hardly touched the mess that is English spelling. The differences between British and American practice are enough to show proficient modern readers whether the book they are reading originated in the United States or in Britain. The differences are also enough to irritate readers who fuss about such trivia. In the end, Webster's dictionary did more to freeze American spelling than to revise it. In both Britain and the United States, the idea took firm hold that each word could have one, and only one, "correct" spelling. Any deviation from the standard came to imply either carelessness or incompetence or, more likely, both.

After Johnson's dictionary had stabilized orthography in Britain, the innovations credited to Webster were the most substantial that have come to English spelling. Fortunately, these were sufficiently modest to let British and American speakers read one another's writing with ease. We can still claim to write, as well as to speak, the same language.

## Nineteenth- and Twentieth-century Reform Movements

The final quarter of the nineteenth century brought a modest burst of interest in reform. It was a time when respectable people could openly support a more rational spelling. In the United States, the "Speling Reform Asoshiashun" was formed in 1876, with its headquarters in Boston. In April of the following year, its Buletin No. 1 used a revised spelling in its title and headings, although in this hopeful paragraph it clung to tradition, even for its name:

> Never before in the history of the language has there been so much promise
> of a reform in our orthography as at the present time. The late renewal of
> the agitation led to the International Convention, of August 14–17, 1876.
> That convention proved that there was an amount of interest in the subject
> greater than even its friends had supposed. The time had finally come for an
> international organization to take in hand and guide to a successful comple-
> tion, the reform so happily begun. This was so evident, that at the close of
> the four days' meeting there was not a dissenting voice in the Convention,
> when the SPELLING REFORM ASSOCIATION was organized.[1]

In spite of this initial enthusiasm, the Speling Reform Asoshiashun seems to have left few marks on history, but in 1906 it was followed by a new organization, this one called The Simplified Spelling Board. Andrew Carnegie was a founding member and a generous benefactor, giving annual bequests of $20,000, a sum worth far more then than now. Carnegie also supported reform societies in England, where the Simplified Spelling Society (now the English Spelling Society) was founded in 1908. The American SSB produced a list of improved spellings for several hundred words that seemed ripe for reform, and in August 1906 President Theodore Roosevelt showed his sympathy by issuing an executive order directing the Govern-ment Printing Office to adopt the SSB's recommendations.[2] Among many other changes, *addressed* was to become *addrest*, *mould* would be *mold*, and *fulfill* would be *fulfil*. The order aroused the ire of Congress, however, and after a lively session in which Roosevelt was accused of usurping the Senate's authority, it voted against the revised spellings. Roosevelt backed

1.   http://upload.wikimedia.org/wikipedia/commons/9/95/1877_SpellingReform_
Bulletin_Boston.png
2.   http://www.johnreilly.info/trlist.htm

down, saying that other issues were more important than spelling. Nevertheless, a number of simplified spellings that were included in the list have now become acceptable, such as *dike* for *dyke* and *hiccup* for *hiccough*.

Like Carnegie, George Bernard Shaw was a generous financial supporter of spelling reform, and for a few decades reformers had the resources to promote their cause with some vigor. In his will, Shaw provided funds for a competition to design a new alphabet. The winner was an alphabet that should have allowed rapid writing, like the Gregg and Pitman shorthands, but it looked nothing like our conventional Roman alphabet. It was given the name "Shavian" in honor of its benefactor, but it was never a serious contender for a practical spelling system. (See the Appendix to the book.) This period left us with a handful of revised spellings, but the overall results were meager. Books and periodicals continued to be published in traditional orthography. Poor spellers remained the butt of jokes.

The most surprising venture into spelling reform may have been that of the *Chicago Tribune*, an otherwise conservative newspaper. Col. Robert McCormick, the *Tribune*'s publisher during much of the first half of the twentieth century, was an enthusiastic reformer. Under his direction, the *Tribune* experimented with a number of reformed spellings, although the particular words that were reformed changed somewhat as the years passed. The *Trib* was fond of *thru, tho, altho,* and *thoro* and, at one time or another, tried *clew, hocky, iland, crum* and *yern*. A few of the changes that the paper supported, such as *catalog* for *catalogue* and *skilful* for *skillful*, have now become accepted, at least partially, in American usage, but changing a few words at a time cannot bring significant improvement if new irregularities are introduced even more quickly. When McCormick died in 1955, the *Tribune*'s experiments came to an end. Perhaps it counts as a minor triumph that its innovative spellings did not seem to damage the *Trib*'s circulation.[3]

Frank Laubach was an evangelical Christian missionary who, in the mid-twentieth century, gained fame for his program to bring literacy to every corner of the globe. He devised alphabets for languages that had never before been written, and his once-famous slogan, "each one teach one," suggested how he expected literacy to spread. Laubach was best known for his literacy programs, but he also took a brief foray into reformed spelling for English. Like so many other reformers, Laubach had a touching expectation that, once people saw how much his revisions improved our spelling, they would enthusiastically adopt his reforms. In the *Intro/duc'shun* to his short book, *English Spelling Made Easy for the World* (1959), Laubach announced cheerfully, "Yoo ar reading dhu spelling ov dhu fu/ture!" and,

---

3. On McCormick's experiments, see: http://www.barnsdle.demon.co.uk/spell/histsp.html

on page one, he wrote confidently, "Dhis iz dhu new way too lern Ing'glish, too read it and too speak it" (iii, 1). A slash (/) was the unconventional symbol which Laubach used to indicate that the preceding vowel is long: *ha/t* "hate", *e/t* "eat", *fi/t* "fight", *bo/t* "boat", *fu/d* "feud".

> If dhu struggle for freedom and dhe struggle for survival turnz out to be a close raess, it cuud quite easily be/ true dhat we/ cuud looz our freedom or our lives—whichever we deside to give up, becauz we clung too dhu sinful spelling we inherited from our misguided but sainted ancestors. I do/n't no/w how yoo feel, but I for wun am not go/ing to sacrifiess us awl on the altar of spelling madness without raizing a howl. Dhis is my howl/.
> (Laubach 1959: Buuk II, Lesson I, p.19)

Laubach was less consistent than he might have been. He uses both "be" and "be/" in the same sentence. He explains that "hate" should be spelled "ha/t" but proceeds to spell "race" as "raess."

Laubach's proposals did not work out quite as he had hoped they would; in fact, he recognized only half the disaster of English spelling. His main concern was always reading and, in his proposals for a better spelling, he seemed unconcerned about the problems of the writer. He did not allow the same spelling to be used for two different speech sounds, so his spellings could not be ambiguous to a reader, but he freely allowed a single speech sound to be spelled in several different ways: *be*, *bee*, *eat*, *key*; *ride*, *chi/ld*, *high*, *my*, *I*, *ie* (eye). He allowed both *can* and *kick*, and *here* and *hear*, but he revised *ckemist* and *stomuck* because he needed *ch* for words like *church*. Laubach's spelling is a clear advance on our present spelling. It would make learning to read easier, but he seemed to be completely unconcerned about how people would learn to write when a single speech sound could still be spelled in several different ways. He offered little help to the fellow with a spelling problem. His reformed spelling, like that of so many other reformers, was first ignored and then forgotten.

## Initial Teaching Alphabet

The 1960s saw a flurry of interest in something called the "Initial Teaching Alphabet" or ITA. From the vantage point of a half-century later, the ITA looks like the final gasp of a century when serious people were willing to be serious about alternative spellings. The ITA was the invention of James Pitman, the grandson of Isaac Pitman, who had invented another alternative spelling, the shorthand that bears his name. The younger Pitman's ITA was an alternative alphabet for English that was intended to help children when they were first learning to read. ITA was easy to learn and it allowed children who were starting elementary school to begin both to read and to write much more quickly than could ever be possible with traditional English spelling. ITA was never promoted for general use, but only as a transitional alphabet that would get children started with reading and writing. After a year or two, they would need to move on to traditional orthography. It may be that Pitman would have liked to see ITA spread from helping early readers to serving as a new way for everyone to write English, but he was always careful to limit his public discussion to early reading.

The Initial Teaching Alphabet consists of 44 symbols. Of these, 24 are standard lower-case letters of the English alphabet, and 13 are constructed from two familiar letters joined as ligatures. The remaining 7 are letter-like symbols that have been modified from ordinary letters of our alphabet. Each of these 44 letters stands for one of the distinctive sounds (phonemes) of English. For a child to learn the 44 letters of ITA might seem to be a greater challenge than to learn the 26 letters of our traditional alphabet, but since the upper-case letters of ITA are simply enlarged versions of the lower-case letters, children escape the need to learn two different forms for the same letter. Eventually, of course, when making the transition to traditional spelling, children would have to learn the standard upper-case letters as well. The 44 letters of the ITA are shown in Table 5.1, with an example of their use below.[4]

**Table 5.1** Initial Teaching Alphabet

| Consonants | | | | | | | | | | |
|---|---|---|---|---|---|---|---|---|---|---|
| b | c | d | f | g | h | j | k | l | m | n |
| bib | cake | dad | fife | gag | hat | judge | kick | lull | mime | noon |
| ŋ | p | r | s | ʃ | t | v | w | y | z | ʒ |
| sing | pipe | roar | sauce | is | tot | valve | will | yes | zoo | vision |

| Joined consonants | | | | | Short vowels | | | | | |
|---|---|---|---|---|---|---|---|---|---|---|
| ʧh | ʃh | ʨh | ʥh | wh | a | e | i | o | u | ω |
| church | shush | thin | then | whale | at | egg | in | odd | up | book |

| Long vowels | | | | | | | | | | |
|---|---|---|---|---|---|---|---|---|---|---|
| ɑ | æ | au | ɛɛ | œ | ω | ue | ie | ɔi | ou | ɼ |
| father | ape | all | eat | oak | ooze | use | ice | oil | owl | earn |

U græt streŋth uv ita is ʈhat it lωks ɛɛnuf liek tradiʃhunul speliŋ tω ulau an intrested litret reedr uv iŋliʃh speliŋ tω reed it wiʈhaut muʧh difikultɛɛ, ɛɛvun if sumwhut slœlɛɛ. tω injɛɛnyus letrs, for egzampl, bœʈh lωk u bit liek u seɛkwens

4.   My use of the ITA font was made possible through the courtesy and with the approval of the Initial Teaching Alphabet Foundation, Inc. I give the foundation my warm thanks for its help.

uv tꞷ œs, but ᵺæ ar jͻind tꞷgeᵺr in dꞮfrent wæs. ᵺu vͻul uv *fꞷd* has u smaul lꞷp whiel ᵺu vͻul uv *bꞷk* laks u lꞷp. tꞷ enꞓwun hꞷ nœs trudiʃhunul speliꞑ, bœᵺ letrs lꞷk ꞓnuf liek u sekwens uv tꞷ o's, tꞷ mæk ᵺem ꞓsꞓ tꞷ rꞓd.

One ingenious letter is ꙅ, a backward *z*. This is used where traditional orthography uses the letter *s* to stand for the buzzing *z* sound. When ꙅ is used in such words as *haꙅ* or *biꙅy*, it looks enough like *s* to be readable by anyone who knows traditional spelling. At the same time, it looks enough like *z* to help a reader accept it as representing the *z*'s buzzing sound.

For a new reader, each letter stands consistently for just one speech sound, and the consistent spelling should help children to sound out the words easily and correctly. ITA spelling is utterly regular. Each symbol always stands for the same phoneme. This makes sounding-out much easier with ITA than it is with traditional spelling, so reading becomes possible and useful more quickly. Children who have learned the 44 letters of ITA should be able to read or to write all the thousands of words that they already use and understand when talking, although a new writer has no way to know whether to write the buzzing sound of *has* with ꙅ as in *iꙅ*, or with *z* as in *zoo*. Teachers of classes where ITA was tried reported that the children quickly grasped the idea that letters stand for the sounds that they already knew well from talking and listening.

ITA was first introduced experimentally in England in the early 1960s, and it aroused enough interest to stimulate experiments in the United States and Australia as well. Initial reports were enthusiastic. More than 100,000 children in Great Britain were estimated to be using ITA in the fall of 1965. In the United States ITA was reported to be in use to some degree in all 50 states and in at least 10% of all school districts, although not, of course, in every classroom of all these districts (Dewey 1971: 67). Children were reported to be able to read and write ITA much more quickly than they could read and write with traditional spelling. They could sound out words easily so their reading material did not need to be limited to a controlled vocabulary. Children were also able to spell any word in ITA that they could use in their own speech. Whatever they could say, they could also write. Children who learned ITA were reported to be lively writers of notes to one another. By the end of first grade they had become fluent readers and writers.[5]

For all its virtues, ITA faced steep hurdles. Few books had been printed

---

5. For a gushingly enthusiastic report on ITA see Riemer (1969). For a later and more balanced, though still very favorable, assessment, see Downing (1979). A book by James Pitman, the inventor of ITA, is, as would be expected, highly favorable, but it offers a thoughtful assessment nonetheless (Pitman and St John 1969). A weighty official review of the state of language arts in Great Britain, known informally as the "Bullock Report," gave good marks to ITA (Bullock 1975).

in ITA, so eager young readers had less to practice with than their contemporaries who learned traditional orthography. Brightly illustrated books to excite children about the joys of reading must have been rare. ITA learners could exchange notes with their classmates and teachers, but that must have been difficult with parents or cousins. Some parents must have felt excluded from their children's education, unable to help them. Nor did they have as much support as other children have from the writing that surrounds us on billboards and traffic signs, in magazines or soup cans. In spite of this lack of support, comparative studies of children who started with ITA and others who learned traditional spelling from the start consistently showed a decisive advantage for ITA.

After a year or two with ITA, the children needed to make the transition to traditional spelling. Many seemed to have made the move easily, and even after the switch children who had started with ITA maintained, for a time, their lead over those taught with traditional spelling. It was claimed that by learning to read so quickly and easily, they had acquired a confidence in their own ability and an understanding of the nature of reading. They could bring this with them when the time came to move to traditional orthography.

Perhaps, however, ITA merely postponed, rather than avoided, the problems of traditional orthography. Sooner or later, the transition had to be faced. Some who had started with ITA later blamed it for having undermined their ability to spell in the accepted traditional way. This author, who needed no help from ITA to fail at spelling, wonders if those who blame their bad spelling on ITA might not have been bad spellers even without their encounter with the new alphabet.

For whatever combination of reasons, after some years of experimentation the enthusiasm for ITA withered and then died. It is not clear how much of its decline was due to real problems with the transition to traditional spelling, and how much was simply the result of changing fashion in reading methodology. Whatever the reasons, ITA passed from favor. Of course, it was never promoted as a reformed spelling for adult readers, but if it had become widely used for introducing reading, its mere existence as a successful alternative to traditional spelling might have softened the opposition to a reformed spelling for other purposes. Experience with ITA might even have created a generation that knew two different spellings. Such people might have been less stubbornly opposed to changes than most skilled readers are today. Instead, enthusiasm for spelling reform became limited to a few eccentrics.

## The Myth of "Correctness"

English dictionaries usually describe at least three characteristics of each word in their collection. First, simply by printing the word, they show how it is conventionally spelled. Second, since our spelling is too chaotic to give an accurate guide to pronunciation, they generally use some sort of phonetic spelling to show how the word is pronounced. And, third, they give the meanings that the word can convey. For the writers of dictionaries, the definitions are, by far, the most difficult part. At least since Johnson, dictionary writers have collected examples of passages in which each word appears, often dozens of examples, sometimes hundreds. From these examples they work out the range of meanings that each word can express, and they summarize their findings in their definitions. This is an empirical and descriptive enterprise. The definitions given by any good, modern dictionary such as the *Oxford English Dictionary*, or *Webster's Third New International*, rest on a great deal of empirical research into how the words of the language are actually used—how speakers actually pronounce them, how writers actually spell them, and on the range of meanings that they can convey.

This is not, however, the way that many readers understand their dictionaries. Many dictionary users want to be told how the words are *supposed* to be pronounced and spelled and what they are *supposed* to mean. Instead of regarding dictionaries as a description of actual usage, readers often treat them as sets of instructions about how to speak and spell *correctly*. English speakers generally take for granted that there are correct and incorrect ways to talk and write, but they are often uncertain about what, exactly, *is* "correct." They turn to their dictionaries for help.

These contradictory views—of a dictionary that describes and a dictionary that prescribes—burst into public awareness in 1961 with the publication of *Webster's Third New International Dictionary*. This large and authoritative dictionary had the temerity to describe how Americans used words that had often been tabooed. It even included the horrid word *ain't*, on the entirely reasonable grounds that many people use the word, and everyone understands it. By the descriptive goals of the dictionary writers, that was all that was needed to ensure its inclusion in an unabridged dictionary. Many reviewers, however, felt that such a nasty word as *ain't* had no place at all in a dictionary, and they had a field day. The *Chicago Tribune* carried the headline "Saying Ain't Ain't Wrong: See Webster." The *Toronto Globe and Mail* was alarmed: "Where language is without rules and discipline, there is little understanding, much misunderstanding . . . A Dictionary's embrace of the word 'ain't' will comfort the ignorant, confer approval upon the mediocre, and subtly imply that proper English is the tool only of the snob." *Life* magazine said, "Webster's, joining the say-as-you-go school of permissive English, has now all but abandoned any effort to distinguish between good and bad usage—between the King's English, say, and the fishwife's" (R. A. Wells 1973: 74–9).

What these, and many other, readers took for granted is that an important part of a dictionary's job is to legislate "correct" usage. Simply to *report* usage was interpreted as conferring approval. Honest reporting was imagined to encourage the corruption and decline of our once-beautiful language. The outrage was an expression of a powerful myth: the notion that there is just one "correct" way to talk or to write. To speak or write in any other way is simply "wrong." In real life, as opposed to the mythology, people speak in many ways, and with varied goals that call for varied styles. But the myth of a single "correct" way of speaking is a powerful one.

High among the tests of correctness is spelling. Most English speakers presume that each word can have just one "correct" spelling. Any deviation from what is "correct" is a sign of ignorance, carelessness, or stupidity. If a dictionary merely reports the way people actually speak or write, how can we be confident that they have said it correctly? The dictionary might be reporting people's errors! The problem, of course, is that dictionary writers have no way to decide how words *ought* to be spelled. All they can do is report how writers and publishers have actually spelled them. Writers and publishers, in turn, cannot risk deviating from what dictionaries report, so they use dictionaries to find out how words *ought* to be spelled. The reasoning is entirely circular, but the circle seems impossible to break. The myth of "correct" spelling is so powerful that it keeps us chained to what already exists. Is there no way to break free?

## Reform

Dozens of proposals have been made for reforming English spelling. It is a game that anyone can play, and many have joined the fun. Several proposed reforms are summarized in the Appendix to this book. Most of them are beautifully designed for the inventor's own speech. Few, however, make any attempt to cope with the variability of our language. Unfortunately, a spelling that works splendidly in Philadelphia may not be well suited for Liverpool or Dublin, so the most difficult challenge for anyone who longs for something better is to devise a system that can be used equally well by all English speakers, wherever they live, and whatever their accents. No one who hopes to design a better spelling system can avoid careful attention to the diversity of our language.

In spite of the many proposals on offer, English writers have always avoided serious reform, and the reforms for other languages have regularly resulted in bitter conflict. Some, however, have been successful, and have brought written languages closer to daily speech. As these new spellings have become familiar, speakers have gradually accepted them. Not since Noah Webster's changes has English spelling had any real reform, however, and even Webster's changes were few and superficial. Fortunately, the reforms that Webster persuaded Americans to adopt are sufficiently trivial to let us easily read the writing of our cousins from across the water and from below the equator. At the same time, the diversity of spoken English accents does bring serious challenges to any attempt to design, let alone bring about, a reformed spelling. This diversity is one factor that, up to now, has undermined every attempt at reform. It will be addressed in detail in the chapters of Part II.

## Why Don't We Just Fix It?

Reform of English spelling has more often been ignored, scorned, and ridiculed than taken seriously. Why? The reasons are many—some nonsensical, some with a degree of merit—but whether foolish or reasonable, if the scorn is ever to be overcome, the reasons for it must be understood. I will offer six arguments that have been used by people who oppose reform. I will start with the silliest, and progress toward the arguments that would-be reformers need to take seriously.

**1. If the spelling were changed, we would need to change our pronunciation to fit the new spelling.** In its issue of January–February 2009, the *American Scientist*, hardly a fly-by-night periodical, included a Letter to the Editor that was reminiscent of Jonathan Swift. It said, in part: ". . . But English spelling? If it were phonetic, which dialect or accent would rule? Aside from geographical differences (regional, national), there will be temporal differences (historical evolution) . . . Could we order up a world-wide reform of English, including a provision that our children pronounce words exactly the same as we (the reformers) decide?"

The mind boggles at the misunderstanding displayed in this letter. The whole point of a revised spelling is to adapt it to pronunciation. The goal is certainly *not* to adapt pronunciation to the spelling. The misunderstanding is due to a failure to recognize something that ought to be obvious but apparently is not: a dozen people from a dozen parts of the world are fully capable of reading off the same page while speaking with a dozen different accents. This is true of our present spelling, and it would be just as true of any plausible reformed spelling. Because accents really do differ, any revised spelling would need to be a compromise among them, but everyone will continue to speak as they always have. No one will have to change their speech in any way.

There are, to be sure, complications and these will be dealt with in detail in Part II, but the principle is absolute: no one should be under the slightest pressure to change their spoken accent in any way whatever, in order to conform to any aspect of a reformed spelling.

It is spelling that needs to change to fit pronunciation. Pronunciation should never have to change to fit spelling.

**2. Homographs and homophones.** A very different justification for our irregular spellings is the idea that words with different meanings should be spelled differently even if they sound alike: *bare/bear*; *sight/site*; *write/right/rite/wright*, and hundreds of other sets of words are now distinguished by their spelling but not by their pronunciation. These are "homophones" because they sound alike, but they are spelled differently from one another so they are not "homographs." It is sometimes imagined that if we were to spell homophones in the same way (as homographs), we would bring impossible ambiguity to our writing. If *right*, *write*, *rite*, and *wright* were all spelled alike, how would we know, on encountering one of them in writing, which word it is supposed to stand for?

This question has two answers. One is that we already have a vast number of pairs of words with different meanings that are not only pronounced alike but also spelled alike: *box* ("fisticuffs" or a "container"), *trip* ("a voyage" or "a stumble"), *bank* ("a place for money" or "a river's edge"), *fine* ("ground-up small," "good" or "a penalty paid in money"), and, for good measure, what about *own*, *sap*, *sound*, *seal*, *die*, *pound*, *wake*, *left*, *used*, *like*, *light*, and countless others? Why have we not long ago been drowned in all this chaotic ambiguity? In fact, none of these homographs gives a reader any more trouble than the corresponding homophones give a listener. If we so easily assign the correct meaning to a homophone when we hear one, why should we have any trouble assigning the correct meaning of a homograph when we see one? We can safely bring writing into correspondence with speech by spelling homophones as homographs.

The second answer to the question of how we can distinguish homographs is more abstract. Homophones seem always to be used in very different contexts. In fact, if you collect sets of homophones you will find that they usually belong to different parts of speech. *Write* is a verb; *rite* is a noun; *right* is an adjective; and *wright* is rarely used in modern English except in a compound such as *wheelwright*. It is hard to find a context where two of these words could both be used. Other homophones are no different. *See* is a verb and *sea* is a noun; *to* is a preposition (*to school*) or it marks an infinitive (*to run*), while *two* is a number and *too* is an adverb. Different parts of speech are almost always used in such different contexts that listeners easily know which of them is being used.

Of course, there can be complications. *Box* is usually a noun when it means a container, but a verb when it describes a way to fight. Nevertheless, it is possible to ask someone to *Please box the cabbages*, where *box* has turned into a verb. This is not likely to mean *Please hit the cabbages with your fist*, however, so even here the context makes the meaning clear.

If homographs simply reflect the identity of homophones, they should bring no more ambiguity to paper than homophones bring to speech. *I will rite to you in the morning*; *That is the rite way to do it*; *Turn rite at the next corner*; *My ancestors were wheelrites.* These sentences are no more ambiguous when the *rite*s are spelled identically than when they are spelled as English convention now demands.

In the rare case where homophones do cause a problem, speakers quickly find a way to repair the spoken language. If you and I have accents in which *pin* and *pen* are pronounced in contrasting ways, I can ask you to *Please give me a pin* (or *pen*) and you will have no trouble knowing what I am asking for. In the southeastern United States, however, many people pronounce *pin* and *pen* identically. A physical *pin* and a physical *pen* are enough alike that *Do you have a pin?* could easily be misunderstood by an American from the South. Speakers of this accent have adroitly solved the problem. They refer to one type of *pin* as an *ink-pin*. *Pin*, when used alone, refers to the kind that pricks. Problem solved. Ambiguity avoided. Only when southern children move north, where they must deal with teachers who pronounce *pin* and *pen* differently, are they likely to run into trouble. I once heard a northern teacher correct a southern child by telling him not to say *pin* when he should say *pen*. The child, not being accustomed to hearing the difference between *pin* and *pen*, replied, perfectly reasonably, *That's what I said, "ink-pin."* For the teacher, who pronounced *pin* and *pen* differently, this was a needless redundancy. To the child it was a necessary means of avoiding confusion between two kinds of *pins*. Neither the teacher nor her pupil had any idea why the other seemed to be speaking so foolishly.

To be sure, we do have a few homographs that belong to the same part of speech. *Sun* and *son* are both nouns. *The sun/son came through the door* is, indeed, ambiguous. Why don't we trip over such sentences in speech? The answer is that the wider context almost always shows what we mean. Homophones such as *sun* and *son* do allow us to construct puns, and isn't it a shame that our present spelling system makes it difficult to commit puns to paper? Our conventional spelling destroys the fun. When we speak, we need to avoid ambiguity, so we find ways to prevent homophones from being ambiguous. If the spelling system is a faithful reflection of the spoken language, it will be no more ambiguous than speech. Homographs are no more likely to be ambiguous than homophones, and who would want a language without puns?

**3. Loss of etymological information.** Many of the irregularities of English spelling entered the language with foreign words. French words came into English with their French spelling, and other words continue to be spelled in ways that reflect their Greek, Latin, Spanish or Polish origins. At their best, such spellings tell us where the words came from. Most of us know that words that have *ph* where an *f* might have done just as well owe their *ph*s to Greek: *philosophy, telephone, phalanx. Laissez-faire* looks much more French than *lessay-fare. Weltanschauung* and *Wunderkind* are unmistakably German. But is etymology really a job for spelling? Do we really need to require every child to learn large numbers of exotic spellings in order to bring joy to enthusiasts for etymology?

The hints that our spelling gives about etymology are not as useful as is sometimes imagined. Indeed, considerable knowledge beyond the spelling is needed in order to guess the etymological origins of many of our words. Enough words have come to us from Latin, either directly or via French, that we may no longer even consider their spelling to be irregular. They are simply a part of the English stock of words. If we were to change *corona* to *korona, decimal* to *desimal*, or *judge* to *juj* would we really lose a reliable clue about the Latin origin of these words? How many readers find satisfaction in recognizing them as Latin now?

Because many words have been given a false classical gloss, it can be dangerous to accept apparent etymologies at face value. *Absolve, admonish, captive, corpse, describe, elephant, falcon, picture,* and *throne* all derive from good Middle English words that once were spelled *assoil, amonest, catif, cors, descryve, olifaunt, faucon, peynture,* and *trone.* Printers gussied up these words with a phony classical look, and then readers began to change their pronunciations to fit the spelling. Now, neither their spellings nor their pronunciations reveal their origins in any clear way (Scragg 1974: 54).

In fact, it is something of a myth that our present spelling is a good guide to a word's etymology. My aging Harcourt Brace dictionary from 1963 has 30 pages of words that start with *ca-*, but less than four pages of words that start with *ka-*. Most of the latter have a foreign origin. Some are proper names: *Kabul, Kaiser, Kalahari, Katmandu.* Those that are not proper names come from many languages: *kayak* (Eskimo), *kangaroo* (Australian), *kebab* (Arabic), *kapok* (Malay), *kaolin* (Chinese), *kabuki* (Japanese), and so on. *Ka-* tells us that the word is likely to have been borrowed from somewhere, but it doesn't tell us which language it was. We have a better chance of guessing the origin of a recent borrowing from its meaning than from its spelling. Words beginning with *ca-* are not only more numerous than those beginning with *ka-*, but most of them have belonged to English for a longer time than the *ka-* words. Nevertheless, the majority of the *ca-* words were also taken, ultimately, from other languages. Many come from French or, via French, from Italian, Latin, or Greek: *cabbage* and *cabin* are from French, *camp* from Italian via French. *Cabal* came to English via Latin, but ultimately from Hebrew. *Calf* (as a body part) and *call* are from Old Norse, *calm* from

Greek via Latin, *cam* (as in camshaft) from Dutch, *cambric* from Flemish, *candy* via Arabic from Sanskrit. We even have a few words, such as *care* and *calf* (as an animal) that have come to us directly from Old English. If you are fascinated by etymology, you would be well advised not to rely too heavily on the *ka/ca* difference in your search for a word's origin.

To be sure, we do have spellings that give us much more reliable hints about etymology than we get from *ca-* and *ka-*. Words that begin with *sc-*, such as *scissors*, *scene*, and *science* come from Latin. Words like *khaki* and *khan* that begin with *kh* generally have an eastern origin. *Khaki* comes from Hindi, *khan* from Turkish. When *ch* is pronounced like *sh*, as in *champagne*, *charades*, *machine*, and *Chicago*, you can be reasonably confident that its background is French. When *ch* is pronounced like *k*, as in *archive*, *chorus*, *school*, and *scheme*, the word probably goes back, sometimes via Latin, to Greek. All this may be fascinating, but only a small minority of our words provide such reliable hints about their origin.

A knowledge of etymology can surely be taught in better ways than by burdening children with irregular spellings. Etymological information might even have a better chance of being learned accurately if English did not have so many words that lead us astray.

**4. Loss of tradition.** Should we fear that a change in spelling would mean that our huge treasury of written English would suddenly become inaccessible? Would the threads that tie us to our past be broken? Would history be lost? This fear is not frivolous, but it is easily exaggerated. Everyone who can now read, of course, would retain their skill with traditional spelling. Older works that still have wide interest would certainly be republished in editions with the newer spelling. Future readers who have grown up with the new spelling might find the older spelling slow-going at first, but they should be able to learn it more easily than children learn it now. They would, after all, need only to recognize the words, not to reproduce their spellings.

After a spelling reform, scholars who want to bury themselves in ancient twentieth-century archives will need to learn to read the older spelling system, but that is the sort of thing that scholars love. Learning to read the old spelling would be no more difficult for a motivated scholar than learning to read is now for every child. They will have little need to write, let alone to spell, in the old-fashioned way, so they will escape the hardest part of gaining literacy now. Shakespeare and Chaucer would sound no different in a revised spelling than they sound in present-day spelling. Even now, we rarely see the spelling that Shakespeare and Chaucer used themselves. A revised spelling would not misrepresent their words.

**5. It looks childish.** There is no avoiding it. Any reformed spelling looks childish simply because it looks a bit like children's writing when they first catch on to the idea that letters represent the sounds of speech. If a new spelling were to come into general use, our associations with it would soon change. Nothing that is inherently childish contaminates a revised spelling except, perhaps, for a degree of naive childish simplicity, a trait that is hardly to be scorned. The spelling of German and Italian is much better than the spelling of English but nobody accuses either the Germans or the Italians of using a childish spelling. If a better spelling for English ever comes into general use it would soon lose its childish connotations, but a bit of time might be needed to overcome our initial reaction to it.

**6. Vested interest.** Finally, we come to the real reason that we cling to our garbled spelling. It has nothing to do with homographs, with the imagined need to learn a new pronunciation, or even with the loss of tradition or of etymological information. These are little more than excuses. The real reason that we cling to what we have is, quite simply, vested interest. Having learned to read our awkward spelling, and even having learned to reproduce it, literate adults have nothing at all to gain by a change. On the contrary, however wonderful the regularity of a reformed spelling might be, literate adults, including everyone with any sort of influence, prestige, or power in our society, has very little to gain and a good deal to lose from changing to a new spelling. Skillful readers do not read letter-by-letter. Rather, with a single, momentary, fixation of the eye (technically, a "saccade"), they take in an entire word, sometimes more. The best spelling system that we could design would, at first, make reading annoyingly slow. Readers would have to return to wholesale "sounding-out." This is possible but it would drag. With all due respect to the honorable B. Franklin, I believe that he badly underestimated the difficulty of making a change. Much practice would be needed before skill with a new spelling would equal our skill with the old. The skill would eventually come, but whatever the long-term gain, the immediate pain would be very real.

Enthusiastic reformers often underestimate the difficulties of using an unfamiliar orthography, even an easy one. Still, shouldn't we be willing to make the sacrifice for the sake of our children and grandchildren?

# 6　Is Reform Possible?

"I hold that a man has as much right to spell a word as it is pronounced as he has to pronounce it the way it ain't spelled."

Josh Billings, American humorist (1818–85)

## A Changing Language

Young people are always more open to innovation than their elders, and they take a special delight in linguistic innovations, partly no doubt, as a way to set themselves apart from the stodgy generation of their parents. In reaction to their children's innovations, older people may be inclined to bemoan the awful spoken language of their juniors. There is said to be a Babylonian clay tablet that laments the deplorable decline in the language of young Babylonians. It seems that ever since Babylon flourished, members of the older generation have imagined their language to be in danger of decay and collapse. What seems like deplorable decay to one generation, however, seems hip, exciting, and fun to the next. These attitudes help to keep spoken language in a continual ferment of change, and no attempt by parents or teachers to "correct" their children can stop the spoken language from drifting to new forms. Simply by living longer, it is the children who control the direction of change.

Parents, teachers, and editors can police youthful writing more effectively than they can ever police youthful speech. When the elders enforce traditional patterns of orthography and written style, the spoken language will inevitably grow away from the more conservative language that is inscribed on a clay tablet or printed in a book. For a century or two after printing began, individual writers could, within rather broad limits, choose their own spellings, so spelling, along with the words and grammar of print, could steadily adjust to the changing spoken language. If they wanted to be understood, writers had to put some limits on their idiosyncrasies, but as long as readers did not expect uniformity, both writers and the early printers were left with considerable freedom. The inevitable changes in the spoken language could be reflected in changes in the written language as well. When spelling became standardized, it also became so frozen that the slightest deviation from convention became a "mistake." Spoken English continues to change, but spelling seems to be helplessly fixed in one place.

Optimists are encouraged by small innovations. For half a century I have been told that the "thru" on traffic signs is a hopeful example of spelling reform. But one changed word among the thousands that are still spelled badly cannot nudge orthography far enough to offer much help. For every *thru* on a highway sign, a hundred other new words are added to our written language, each complete with woeful spelling. Even *thru* offers no real improvement. Would anyone seriously advocate re-spelling *to*, *blew*, *you*, and *hoot* as *tu*, *blu*, *yu*, and *hut*? We would do better to reserve *u* for *but*, *fun*, and *sum* than to let it be used in such an unfamiliar place as *thru*. Far from being a step forward, *thru* is just another word with another irregular spelling. It saves a bit of space on a traffic sign, but it represents no advance whatever toward a better spelling for the English language. Nor is text messaging, however ingenious and however much fun it may be, likely to have any but the most marginal influence on mainstream spelling. If piecemeal steps are to bring us any relief, the final system would need to be so clearly in mind that the many small changes would lead in a consistent direction. Random innovations will only add to the irregularities.

Printers want a single standard that will protect them from criticism. Private writing does not really need to conform closely to the printing standard, but as the idea took hold that there could be only one single "correct" way to spell a word, the printing standard became the standard for private writing as well. "Good" spelling became confused with good breeding, a good education, and a good mind. The bad speller faced scorn, ridicule, and failure in school. Admittedly, "good" spelling does allow people of otherwise limited talent to flaunt their skill to their unfortunate contemporaries whose talents lie elsewhere, but "good" spelling is really nothing but conventional spelling. When dictionaries report usage, and when usage clings timidly to the "authority" of the dictionaries, we have a closed circle from which escape seems impossible. Inexorably, what *is* comes to be interpreted as what is *right*. The hope that small and imaginative changes by private writers might bring reasonable spelling reform seems forlorn. Small and imaginative changes are more likely to add to the chaos than to bring order. Is there no way to break this circle of conformity?

## Two Patterns of Reform

The examples that were reviewed in the earlier chapters suggest that successful spelling reforms have followed one of two broad patterns. Reforms in European languages have generally been accomplished in a series of relatively small steps. Norwegian Bokmål is now substantially different from its Danish ancestor, but the changes came in well-spaced and modest increments. The same is true of the German reforms and, for all the emotional fireworks, even the reforms of the former Yugoslavia have hardly been revolutionary.

The more radical reforms of Korean and Vietnamese followed a different pattern. They required long periods when the new and the old writing systems existed side by side. Five hundred years were needed for Hangŭl to become generally accepted in Korea. Quoc-Ngu, the romanized script of Vietnam, had to wait three centuries after its invention before it came into general use in the twentieth century. Only in Turkey has a truly radical reform been achieved without a long period when the old and new ways of writing coexisted, but romanized Turkish was imposed by a powerful and autocratic leader during a convulsive period of revolution. History offers us no precedent that can give us hope that a radical reform for English could be accomplished within such a short time. English is spoken in democratic nations where conservative readers vote. Reform enthusiasts should not dream. People who can vote will not accept a sudden and radical change.

If we would rather not wait several centuries, as the Koreans did, we might opt, instead, for a series of incremental steps. Unfortunately, even modest increments face serious hurdles. Think of the fate of Teddy Roosevelt's aborted reform of 1906. It affected only a few hundred words, but since English has many thousands of words that need fixing, Roosevelt's reforms did no more than chip at the margins of what is needed. Even so, the topic was laughed out of court by the outraged members of the Senate. Roosevelt backed down.

More systematic reforms that would change no more than a few hundred words would be possible in principle, but probably not in practice. If *ie* were to become the universal spelling for the vowel of *tie* and *pie*, it should not be too difficult for readers to adjust to *chield, diemond, miel, sie, sien, fiet*, and *hie*. If reforms of this kind were introduced at long-enough intervals, readers should be able to adjust to one change before being burdened with another. Unfortunately, even such a simple change as this could not be introduced without some fiddling. Something would have to be done about *sieve, friend, field* and *view*, so that readers would not try to pronounce them with the vowel they were learning to use for *tie* and *pie*. Still, a series of reforms ought not to be too disrupting as long as each of them was reasonably modest.

Sadly, such reforms have little chance. In addition to the outrage that each change would evoke, each would require new schoolbooks and revised dictionaries. Publishers and printers might be delighted at the prospect of boosted dictionary and textbook sales, but purchasers would certainly rebel. Who wants a dictionary that, from the day it is printed, is doomed to early obsolescence? Readers would scream for the revisions to come to a rapid halt. I can hear the shouts of protest: "*Leave it alone!*" A long series of changes that bring a step-by-step repair will never fly.

## Resistance

Spelling reformers must deal with a paradox: an orthography that is reasonably good encourages readers to feel that spelling should be an accurate reflection of pronunciation. They may then be willing to accept modest changes that make a good spelling even better. When spelling is as bad as ours, however, we can almost forget that it does, after all, reflect pronunciation in some degree, even if it makes a bad job of it. Skilled readers of English may think of strings of letters as representing words more than they think of single letters as representing sounds. Children may even be taught by the "whole word" method that minimizes instruction in phonics. If phonics seems less important to readers of English than it does to readers of Italian or Finnish, then the English readers will have less sympathy for reforms than Italians or Finns do. The revolutionary nature of the reforms we need for English makes readers resistant to any change at all.

Parliamentary committees in Norway, and meetings of representatives from the German-speaking nations, have taken the responsibility for proposing and implementing changes in their orthographies. We have no history of planning such changes in the English-speaking world. It is difficult even to imagine a mechanism by which an international committee could be organized. But beyond the institutional difficulties, we can be certain that any prospect of reform, however modest, would meet at least as much outrage as met the Norwegian and German proposals. Since the reforms needed for English are far more extensive than those carried out for Norwegian or German, they would be more disruptive. A long series of reforms would be needed if each partial reform were to be kept modest. If the French could not rid themselves of a few useless circumflexes, what hope do we have of spelling *bed*, *bread*, *guess*, *many*, and *leopard* with the same vowel letter? It is no easier to imagine the average English reader submitting meekly to a long series of modest reforms than to imagine him surrendering to a radical reform that would take care of everything at once.

Even the most enthusiastic supporter of reform ought to be able to understand just how much each literate adult speaker of English has invested in our traditional spelling. It is all very well to insist that a revised spelling would be easy to learn, but anyone who has already invested the years that are needed to become a skillful reader has no reason at all to prefer a change. Goodwill toward the next generation is not likely to trump reading skills that took so long to master. This is not a place where goodwill stands much chance against vested interest. At least since Benjamin Franklin's time, spelling reform enthusiasts have imagined that learning to read a new spelling would be an easy task. In fact, skilled readers of traditional spelling would have to revert to "sounding-out," a relatively laborious process that adults use only when encountering an unfamiliar word. If a revised spelling were carefully designed, sounding out the words ought not to be difficult, but it would, at first, be frustratingly slow. Why would adults voluntarily submit themselves to such a painful exercise? The history of all the many spelling reforms that have been undertaken in the last century shows how much outrage is evoked by even modest change. And modest change is not what English needs.

I can imagine only one escape from this deep resistance to change: a long period when two orthographies are used in parallel. A decent new orthography that was used, at first, only for special purposes, would give readers, including children, a chance to grow accustomed to it. We could hope that its wider use might gradually spread. We could even fantasize that it might eventually spread widely enough to replace our present mess. I am, in other words, proposing a "Korean solution." I hope that something less than five hundred years would be long enough for a new orthography to be accepted for all purposes, but we should not imagine that it could happen quickly. To push for rapid adoption would do nothing but alienate skilled readers.

The stories of reform, and of opposition to reform, from Norway, Germany and Korea have recurring themes. Fluent readers everywhere have a powerful vested interest in the orthography that they worked so hard to learn. At first, reading even the best reformed spelling for English is certain to be slow and frustrating, but readers resist not only because of their skill with the established orthography. They have also built up a serious emotional investment in it. They cling to its familiar forms. Everywhere, the same arguments are repeated: "The reformed writing will cut us off from our heritage"; "It is ugly"; "It is childish"; "It lacks the beauty of traditional spelling"; "And anyway, it isn't needed because our present spelling works just fine." Reformers may have little sympathy for these excuses, but we had better understand them.

Random reforms are unlikely to lead in a sufficiently consistent direction to arrive at a satisfactory system. This means that a clear idea of the ultimate goal is essential. Just how we can reach an agreement on the final goal is not at all clear, but the chapters in Part II of this book are meant to be a contribution toward defining that goal.

## Reforms for Special Purposes

Enthusiasts for spelling reform may forget that English speakers have already become familiar with two kinds of serious and successful alternatives to conventional spelling. The most radical of these were Gregg and Pitman shorthand, Gregg primarily in the United States, Pitman in Britain.

A generation or two ago, stenographers still recorded speech with a shorthand that had no resemblance to traditional writing except for the direction of flow. Gregg and Pitman shorthand were written from left to right and from the top to the bottom of the page, but their characters were designed for speed, not for familiarity. Their symbols did not represent the letters of conventional spelling but, rather, the pronunciation of the words. Both shorthands used a phonetic orthography that completely avoided the irrational spelling of traditional English. A skilled stenographer could record speech as rapidly as people talked. Shorthand was once an essential skill for a good secretary, but it has been made obsolete by recording machines and computers.

A second, and very different, kind of reformed spelling can be found at the bottom of every page of any good dictionary of the English language. Here, you can expect to find a key to the set of symbols that show readers how each word in the dictionary is pronounced. The symbols vary a good deal from one dictionary to another, and they generally reflect the accents of the country in which the dictionary was published. Each set of symbols really amounts to a reformed spelling, although, in practice, they have rarely been used for anything longer than a single word. Several of these dictionary keys are shown in a table in the Appendix (pages 160-4).

The Initial Teaching Alphabet, described in the previous chapter, represents a third kind of reformed spelling. The symbols of ITA are closer than either shorthand or dictionary symbols to the spelling that reformers might advocate, but ITA was never promoted for general use. Since ITA has been abandoned, it can hardly be described as "successful," but it carries an important lesson: even the deeply skeptical must acknowledge that a reformed spelling is entirely possible. Children did learn to read ITA. Shorthands were, and dictionary keys still are, eminently successful "reformed spellings."

Nevertheless, a reform of English orthography for general use is simply not now in the cards. Nor does a long series of more modest changes have any serious chance of success. The only strategy that remains is to devise a spelling that can be used for special but limited purposes. Even restricted use would show that a reformed spelling is a realistic possibility, but it would not, perhaps for generations, replace our traditional orthography. A more rational spelling, one that could be used for a number of special purposes but that would not be an immediate threat to our traditional orthography, could still give everyone a chance to become accustomed to an alternative. Some of its uses would require general agreement about the spelling toward which we are aiming, and it would not bring the instant cure that is the dream of many passionate advocates of reform. The passionate must continue to dream.

## Extending Reform

We should abandon all hopeful fantasies of a sudden and radical switch to a new orthography. It would be a major advance just to agree on a single spelling that we could work toward. The criteria for choosing among the many possible reforms are considered in some detail in the next chapter, but let us suppose, for the moment, that we could achieve widespread agreement on an orthography that would be suitable for a general spelling reform. Let us also accept the clear fact that neither English-language publishers nor the huge mass of English-speaking readers will quickly be persuaded to adopt a better orthography for general purposes. It is not impossible, nevertheless, to hope that a better orthography could be used for limited purposes. If people grew accustomed to a better spelling in limited domains, they might even be willing, gradually, to expand its uses. To what purposes might such an orthography be put?

**1. Keys to pronunciation**. English readers already use revised spellings to learn how to pronounce unfamiliar words when they are first encountered in print. If you want to know how *granophyre* (a kind of stone) is pronounced, you can, if you have the same dictionary as I do, see that its pronunciation is shown by *gran'əfīr*. You can then search at the bottom of the page, where you will see how all the letters, including *a*, *'ə*, and *ī*, should be pronounced. You should then be able to pronounce the word as convention demands. News magazines sometimes need to show their readers how to pronounce a proper name, so they also use phoneticized spelling to help their readers get it right.

Such spellings are very helpful, and we all use them happily. No one worries that they might corrupt our sacred orthographic heritage. But however useful they are, they do suffer badly from a lack of standardization. The transcriptions used by magazines can be completely ad hoc. A dictionary needs to be internally consistent and the thousands of words that need to have their pronunciations shown must be spelled carefully and accurately, but every dictionary has its own system. The lack of standardization means that it is a rare dictionary user who bothers to memorize all the symbols. When we need to know what a symbol means, we search through the examples at the bottom of the page, and then promptly forget it.

If dictionary-makers and periodical publishers could ever be persuaded to agree on a single system, readers might become sufficiently familiar with its letters to avoid having to search at the bottom of the page every time they need help with pronunciation. As people became accustomed to the spellings that were used in their guides to pronunciation, they might even begin to look less "funny" than revised spellings look now. As the spellings became familiar, they would also face less resistance for other uses: to name new products, new businesses, new slang, even people's nicknames. Such a spelling might gradually spread.

Learners of English as a foreign language cannot now escape traditional spelling, but they will always need to be shown how English words should be pronounced. This is not something easily learned from traditional spelling. If teachers and the publishers of textbooks of English as a foreign language could show pronunciations with the same symbols that dictionaries use, the constituency that becomes familiar with a revised spelling would grow.

To be sure, this fantasy faces two very high hurdles. The first is to find a way to agree on a single orthography. It needs to be one that could be used by speakers of all English accents, and that could be used by dictionaries whatever the accent of their intended readers. The orthography would need to be "accent-neutral," one that could be used by all speakers of English, whatever their accent. The second and more difficult hurdle would be to persuade the dictionary-makers of the world to use the same symbols as keys to pronunciation. Will someone please volunteer to persuade them to unite behind a single set of orthographic conventions?

**2. A revised spelling for early readers**. The abandoned experiment with the Initial Teaching Alphabet has discredited any use of a revised spelling as a way to introduce children to reading. Parents were not always enthusiastic about ITA and, in truth, the alphabet was hardly the ideal way to write English. Some parents disliked its "funny" letters, and children who were quick to learn must have soon become frustrated on discovering that almost everything they might want to read was written in a different way than their first reading books. ITA could not even be typed on a standard typewriter, and it still cannot be typed on a standard computer keyboard. As long as there was nothing much to read in ITA there was not much motivation to learn it, and as long as very few people wanted to learn it, there was little reason to write or to print using its letters. The experiment came to a rapid but inconclusive end.

I would like to see more experiments with an orthography that looks less artificial to adults than ITA. Programs already exist that accept a text that is written with traditional spelling as input and immediately disgorge a translation in a revised spelling.[1] These programs make it possible to produce more, and more diverse, reading material than could ever have been produced when ITA was first tried. The programs that I have tried are by no means perfect. Their worst failing is with homographs that are

---

1.    At the time of writing, spelling translation programs are available at:
      http://www.wyrdplay.org/spelling-converter.html
      http://nuenglish.org/1-en-ProfessionalLinks.htm
      http://truespell.com

not also homophones, such as *live* ('dwell' or 'alive'), *tear* ('rip', 'water of the eye'), and *wind* ('moving air', 'wrap around'). They cannot choose the correct word, so they cannot chose the correct spelling.

Homographs such as these hardly bother us when reading. If you should read "*The wind is strong, so you better wind up the string,*" you might not even notice that the two *wind*s are pronounced in different ways. Any revised spelling needs to spell these words differently, but a simple conversion program has no way to know which of the two words is intended. Even that problem should be largely solvable if a reformed spelling becomes a serious possibility. Clever programmers have already taught computers to do a passable job of tagging words by their part of speech. It should be possible to link a program that assigns the parts of speech to a translation program. Together, they could use the context to select the correct word, and then spell it as it sounds. Very little final editing would then be needed. A good conversion program should be able to provide readers with all the reading material they could possibly want. Computer-savvy children would surely learn to select whatever they want to read, and have it translated instantly.

Homographs that are also homophones, of course, would be spelled alike in any new spelling system, just as they are in our traditional spelling, so they pose no problem for machine translation. A very large fraction of the documents that most people would want to read must already exist in electronic form, and these could be converted into a revised orthography with no more than minimal human intervention.

A reasonable orthography should quickly make children feel comfortable about reading, and give them confidence in their own abilities. In order to ease the transition from one spelling to another, any initial teaching orthography ought to cling as closely to traditional spelling as is compatible with accurate phonics. The demonstration that English can be written in more than one way should help to demystify spelling. If enough children (and enough parents) became confident about reading a revised spelling, the age at which children were obliged to shift might gently rise. Still, pushing a revised spelling for older children too quickly would only arouse opposition. For the foreseeable future, the goal of any teaching alphabet has to be to help children reach the point where they can easily switch to traditional spelling.

**3. Remedial instruction.** Millions of adults in the United States and in Britain are effectively illiterate. Illiteracy and poor reading ability seem to be less serious problems in places like Finland, where the spelling matches the spoken language very closely. An English spelling that more closely reflected speech might help both children and adults who have serious reading problems. It would be unwise to let a revised spelling become exclusively associated with remedial instruction, however. Even rapid readers would learn to read more quickly with a decent spelling.

**4. Defiant authors.** Spelling has acquired an importance that has nothing to do with its instrumental purpose, which is, quite simply, to show readers what word the author intends the reader to understand. Spelling has become a symbol of education and intelligence, a badge of the good, the true, and the beautiful. Poor spelling violates a kind of etiquette. It looks careless, sloppy.

The almost religious feeling about the importance of "good" spelling should be firmly resisted, and it might help if, now and then, a few brave souls would deliberately spell a word unconventionally. That would be a simple, although courageous, gesture of solidarity toward those of us who are crippled by our spelling. It might even gently coax readers toward more tolerance for diversity. Anyone who will not accept a bit of colorful variability in spelling is bereft of imagination. They are not the people to whom we should pander.

Alas, this may be too much to hope for. It may never be safe to defy even the silliest spelling convention. If, when reading drafts of these chapters, my own sympathetic friends found it impossible to refrain from correcting my "mistakes," how can I hope that others might become more tolerant?

## A "Korean" Solution

My fantasy is a "Korean" solution to our spelling problem: devise a good spelling system, persuade people to use it for limited purposes, and then hope it will gradually spread to wider use. It took half a millennium for Hangŭl to become fully accepted by most Koreans but we can hope that the transition to a better English spelling might go a bit more quickly. Unlike Koreans, we do not have to learn a new alphabet, only a better way to use our old one. If, when they first begin to read, enough children were to become familiar with a rational way to spell they might be more open to change than most speakers of English are now. Still, no one should imagine that spelling could change overnight. Decades, perhaps generations, will be needed before enough speakers of English grow sufficiently comfortable about a simpler spelling to be willing to use it for all purposes.

If what we want is a parallel orthography, we certainly want just one. Enthusiastic reformers have proposed scores of new spelling systems, none of which has ever gained any serious degree of acceptance. (See the Appendix, pages 151–64.) Most proposals are too narrowly based on a single accent to be generally acceptable. Some are obviously designed by Americans, others, just as obviously, by people from Great Britain. I will not propose yet another spelling system because I do not care to contribute to the Babel of competing proposals. What we need now is not another possible way to spell English, but some serious discussion of what a better spelling system should be like. We need a way to reach agreement on a single orthography that could be used immediately for special purposes and that has the potential for more general use. Only if we can agree on the orthography that we want can we hope to persuade anyone to use it for any serious purpose at all.

My purpose, in the remaining chapters of this book, is to contribute to a discussion of what we need, and of what a truly good spelling system should be like. These chapters are more technical than the earlier ones, but the technicalities cannot be avoided. Designing a spelling system that is better than the one we already have is child's play. Designing a spelling system that can be used equally well by speakers of all accents is a much greater challenge. But the first, and perhaps most difficult, challenge is to find a way to reach agreement on which of the many possible spellings we should unite behind.

# Part II

## Introduction

The six chapters that form the second part of this book are considerably more technical than the first six. They dig into the details of how we might construct a spelling system that would ease the task of learning to read English, but that would not favor one accent over all others. This requires a relatively detailed understanding of the sound system of English—not just of one accent, but of the way that speech sounds vary from one accent to another. We need to create a single spelling system that could be used by all English speakers, whatever their accent.

I will *not* propose a particular spelling system. We are already awash with dozens of proposed re-spellings (see the Appendix), and the last thing we need is still another proposal. Every one that I have seen would be a profound improvement on our present tangled orthography, but they all seem to be better designed for the accent of the designer than for the other accents of English. We need a spelling system that is "accent-neutral"—no better, but also no worse, for one accent than for any another. For this, we need to consider the nature and variability of all English speech sounds. As will become obvious, it is the vowels that give us the most trouble.

Before anything else, however, we need to consider just what criteria should guide us as we seek to construct the best possible spelling system.

# 7 The Criteria for a Better Spelling for English

"He respects Owl, because you can't help respecting anybody who can spell TUESDAY, even if he doesn't spell it right; but spelling isn't everything. There are days when spelling Tuesday simply doesn't count."

A. A. Milne, *The House at Pooh Corner* (1928)

## Spoken Language, Written Language, Dialect, and Accent

Language comes in two varieties, spoken and written. People who call themselves "linguists" and who study the nature and history of the world's thousands of languages, generally take it for granted that the spoken language is basic. Spoken language came first in human prehistory, after all, and, except for children who are severely deaf, it comes first for every growing child. The letters of our alphabet reflect the sounds of speech, even if they sometimes make a bad job of it. The order of words on a printed page differs little from their order in conversation. Children learn to read and write by discovering how the written marks on paper reflect the sounds and the spoken words that they have been learning since infancy. In all these ways, the written language depends on, and is derivative of, the spoken language.

In spite of this clear dependence, highly literate people often come to think of the written language as, in some ways, more important than the spoken language. The sounds that flow from our mouths are ephemeral, fading as quickly as they are produced. Written language endures. Spoken accents vary endlessly and chaotically, while written languages are relatively uniform and stable. It is the written language that is described in our dictionaries and, most often, in our grammar books. People make "mistakes" when they speak, or so it is often said. Writing is expected to conform to tighter standards. Writing carries our great literature.

So both spoken and written language are important, and anyone who is concerned with spelling must be concerned with both. In alphabetic languages, spelling is the point where spoken and written languages meet. The available evidence (to say nothing of common sense) strongly suggests that the more closely the spelling system reflects the spoken language, the easier it is for children to learn to read and write. The Finnish and Korean spelling systems reflect their spoken languages very closely, so children in English-speaking countries might well envy Finnish and Korean children for the ease with which they can learn to read their languages. The fit between the way we speak and the way we spell English is worse than the fit between the speech and writing of any other European language. Remember that the ability to read Hangŭl seems to have been passed from friend to friend for many centuries, with no help at all from any classroom. We have not only classrooms, but also a massive establishment of schools of education and squadrons of reading experts, yet still we have millions of adults who are effectively illiterate. I wish we could spell in a way that more accurately reflected the way we talk. I would like, even more, to spell in a way that could be passed from friend to friend without any classroom at all. Classrooms could then be used for more interesting activities. But I don't want anyone to have to change a single syllable of their spoken language. No new spelling system should require anyone to change either their pronunciation or the way they form their sentences. It is spelling toward which a reformer's efforts should be directed, not pronunciation and not any part of the spoken language. We need to be deeply concerned with the nature of the spoken language, not to change it, but only to be certain that it is accurately reflected in writing.

## Accent Diversity and Reform

Many decades ago, as a young man, I traveled to England with a knapsack (where I discovered that it was a "rucksack"). At a youth hostel, I had a conversation with a young English woman and, as Americans and Britishers often do, we compared our languages. At the end of the conversation she summed it up in her very English accent: "Well, it's awa language, i'nt it?" I giggled inwardly at her comment, but I was also startled by its arrogance. I have reported this conversation to many Americans, and they always burst out laughing. It never occurs to us to suppose that our beloved English language belongs any less to us than to our friends across the pond. More recently, I have told the same story to English people in England, and the first time I did so I was startled all over again. Unlike Americans, they didn't laugh. I had not realized that some people in England still seem to imagine that they have a greater claim on our common language than do the millions of people in other parts of the world who also count their language as "English." So: readers in England, beware! When I use the word "English," I usually mean the word to embrace not only the language of England, but also the language of the rest of the British Isles, North America, and parts of Southern Africa and the South Seas. I consider all these varieties to be equally worthy, and equally deserving, of the name "English." When I mean, specifically, the English of England, I will say so.

People in Boston speak differently from people in Atlanta. People in Manchester speak differently from those in Edinburgh. They vary in the words they use, and they vary in their patterns of grammar. They speak with many and diverse pronunciations. Constructing a spelling system that is perfect for a single homogeneous variety of a spoken language is child's play. The real challenge for English reform is to construct a single spelling system that is equally well suited to all the forms of a very diverse language. How do we cope with its diversity? If we want to bring English speech and spelling into better harmony, we need to know a great deal about how people in every corner of the English-speaking world pronounce their words.

Very good spellers may never have seen spelling as a problem. Even average spellers may forget their childhood struggles, but the desperate need for reform is obvious to those who are struggling toward literacy and to poor spellers of every age. Scores, probably hundreds, of reformed spellings for English have been proposed. Many of these are beautifully designed for the inventor's own accent, but make no nod to the rich diversity of English pronunciation. Unfortunately, what works splendidly for one accent may be less than ideal for another accent, so the real challenge for anyone who longs for a less-chaotic spelling is to devise a system that can be used equally well by all English speakers, wherever they live and whatever their accents. For this, we cannot avoid careful attention to the diversity of our language.

The successful spelling reforms of the last century have rarely avoided bitter conflicts, and they have as often been undertaken to increase, or even to exaggerate, the differences among languages, as to improve spelling or bring unity. Enthusiasts have sometimes had little interest in making learning and reading easier, but have wanted, instead, to assert differences from their neighbors. Virulent nationalism was the motivation for the "reforms" of the Serbs, Croats, Bosniacs, and Montenegrins. Even the peaceful Norwegians continue to work off their aggressions by quarreling over their spelling. Noah Webster's nineteenth-century reforms of American spelling were meant, in part, to establish a new written language for a newly independent nation, a language that would be different from that of the mother country.

The strength of English comes from its spread across so many continents, and as long as we all spell in nearly the same way, our writing cannot be used to symbolize just one particular nationality. I hope that we have long outgrown the kind of nationalism that fosters separate Croatian, Serbian, Bosnian, and Montenegrin "languages." I hope we have left behind even the relatively modest nationalism of Noah Webster. We should firmly reject any reformed spelling that threatens the unity of our language. We must be able to read each other's writing with ease.

Fortunately, the reforms that Noah Webster encouraged Americans to adopt were sufficiently trivial to let us easily understand writing from across the sea. We must not lose that ability. At the same time, the diversity of spoken English accents does pose some serious challenges for anyone who wants to reform our spelling. This diversity is one of the factors, though by no means the most important one, that has, up to now, undermined every attempt at reform. It needs to be dealt with in careful detail.

We should start by asking what we are aiming for in a revised system of spelling. What should guide us as we design a spelling system that avoids the barriers to literacy that our present spelling imposes? Any decent spelling for English should not only lower the handicap for bad spellers. It should speed up learning for everyone. At the same time, it must be flexible enough to represent all the great wealth of our language.

Unfortunately, the many desirable criteria for an improved spelling can conflict with one another. To meet one criterion perfectly could force us to compromise on others. The art of designing a better spelling system is to grope for a reasonable balance, but we cannot even look for a balance unless we know what we want.

## The Criteria

We need to ask just what criteria should guide us as we seek a better way to spell the language that we share. Those that follow should give us a reasonable place to begin.

**1. One sound—one symbol.** Ideally, each distinctive speech sound (phoneme) of English ought always to be symbolized by the same letter (grapheme) and, reciprocally, each letter ought always to stand for the same distinctive sound. This would mean, for example, that the letter *f*, in English, might be used for every instance of the speech sound that starts words such as *four*, *five*, and *photo* or that comes later in words such as *rafter*, *half*, and *laugh*. It also means that *f* would never be used to represent any other speech sound. This is the ideal. It is the goal toward which we should aim, although we know that in practice it is not always possible to reach this ideal. The complexities and diversities of English accents will sometimes force compromises, but the closer we can come to this ideal, the more satisfactory will be the orthography.

**2. Accent-neutrality.** A revised spelling should be "accent-neutral," no better and no worse for speakers of one accent than for speakers of another, no better for a New Yorker than for a Londoner, no better for a Scot than for an Australian. An accent-neutral spelling would require everyone to make some compromises so as to converge on a common spelling. Unlike the spellings of Norwegian, Swedish, and Danish, which symbolize their respective nations, a spelling that was accent-neutral would symbolize the linguistic unity of the English-speaking world. Although an accent-neutral spelling would have to be a compromise, it could still be much easier for everyone to learn than the chaotic spelling with which our children must struggle now.

Admittedly, the insistence upon accent-neutrality makes the task of designing a reformed spelling much more difficult than it would otherwise be. Creating a spelling that works splendidly for speakers of a single uniform accent is easy. Such alphabets have been designed repeatedly, and several are included in the Appendix to this book. Finding a decent compromise for two accents, let alone for dozens, is not easy at all.

**3. Resemblance to traditional spelling.** Any reformed spelling system ought to look as much as possible like the old one. This is only common sense. Switching to a new system should be no more painful than necessary. Shavian, the alphabet that won the contest for which George Bernard Shaw provided in his will, never had a chance because it was constructed with letters whose shapes were totally unfamiliar. Many of our letters, such as *b*, *d*, *m*, *n*, *l*, and *v*, can be used for the sounds that they usually stand for now. Familiar digraphs such as *ng*, *th*, and *sh* should do admirably to fill the gaps where our twenty-six single letters fall short. Traditional habits of punctuation and capitalization can be left alone. However much linguists may love them, we should probably avoid such "funny" phonetic characters as *ŋ* or *ə*. Even grave, acute, and circumflex accents would probably be a mistake. Too many readers would think they look too "foreign." Avoiding odd characters would also allow a new spelling to be typed on a conventional British or American keyboard.

**4. Pronunciation should not be affected by spelling reform.** In Chapter 5, I did my best to dispose of the silly idea that anyone's pronunciation would have to change in order to conform to the new spelling. The goal of spelling reform is to adapt spelling to the way we talk. It is *not* about adapting our talk to any sort of spelling. Every reader should be able to read from the same page while using his or her own accent, exactly as we do now.

**5. Over-distinguish, don't under-distinguish.** The first four points are easy to explain and, once stated, they ought to be obvious. I would not expect them to invite controversy. Now, however, we come to the most difficult part of designing a better spelling system: how do we compromise among different accents? In particular, how do we deal with the situation where speakers of some accents make a distinction between speech sounds even though they are pronounced identically by speakers of other accents? In the jargon of linguists, the question can be stated like this: when phonemes are in contrast in some accents, but merged into a single phoneme[1] in other accents, how should they be represented in writing? For English, all the serious problems of this kind are with vowels, not with consonants.

For example, many Americans pronounce *Mary*, *merry*, and *marry* identically, but some Americans, as well as most British speakers, pronounce each of these words differently. Those who pronounce them differently distinguish many other words by the same contrasting vowels. As a linguist might put it, some American speakers have just one phoneme that is used in all these three sets of words. Other Americans and most speakers from England have three contrasting phonemes, one for each of these three sets:

*Mary* vowel: vary, Sarah, dairy, fair, spare, etc.
*Merry* vowel: cherry, ferry, very, merit, etc.
*Marry* vowel: carry, arrow, narrow, Harold, etc.

In a satisfying bit of reciprocity, many Americans pronounce *pour*, *poor*, and *paw* differently, while most speakers in England pronounce them all identically. As with *Mary*, *merry*, and *marry*, speakers who distinguish *pour*, *poor*, and *paw* distinguish many other words with the same contrasting spoken vowels. Speakers in England who pronounce *pour*, *poor*, and *paw* identically generally use the same spoken vowel for all the other words as well:

*Pour* vowel: ore, wore, adore, before, etc.
*Poor* vowel: boor, sure, Moor, etc.
*Paw* vowel: awe, all, ball, ought, etc.

When some speakers use a single vowel for a set of words that others divide among three vowels, no spelling system can be ideal for everyone. To spell *Mary*, *merry*, and *marry* in the same way would seem absurd to most

---

1.  Anyone who feels shaky about the meaning of "phoneme" should realize that it simply means a distinctive speech sound of a language, a speech sound that is different enough from all the other speech sounds of the language to keep words distinct. The *th* of *thy* is different in pronunciation from the *th* of *thigh*. These two speech sounds are sufficiently different from each other to distinguish pairs of otherwise identical words, so they count as different phonemes. The initial phoneme of *thy* is also found in *this*, *them*, *bother* and *bathe*. The initial phoneme of *thigh* is found in *think*, *throw*, *thistle*, and *bath*. The vowel sounds of *pit*, *pet*, *pat*, *pot*, *put*, *pate*, *pout*, and *Pete* are sufficiently different to keep the words distinct, so the vowel sounds in each of these words count as distinct phonemes. *Do*, *shoe*, *boot*, *you*, and *flue* all have the same vowel phoneme in spite of their varied spellings. *Do*, *go*, and *pot* have different vowel phonemes, even though their vowels are spelled in the same way.

people in England, and also to a good many Americans who pronounce them differently. To spell *pour*, *poor*, and *paw* alike would seem equally absurd to most Americans. On the other hand, if we spell all six of these vowels differently we would give many people a spelling problem. Should Americans who pronounce *Mary*, *marry*, and *merry* as homophones need to spell them differently? Should speakers in England be forced to struggle with different spellings for the vowels of *pour*, *poor* and *paw*, even when pronouncing them all identically?

If we avoid using different spellings for different accents, as we certainly should, it seems better, on balance, to over-distinguish than to under-distinguish. It seems better to spell the vowels of these six sets in six different ways than to use the same spelling for words that some speakers pronounce differently. To distinguish all six of these sets of vowels in writing would require most people, in both Britain and America, to learn some spellings that seem arbitrary. Ideally, no one should need to use the same spelling for speech sounds that they distinguish, but everyone would have some words, such as *paw*, *poor*, and *pour* or *Mary*, *marry*, and *merry*, that they would need to spell differently, even though they pronounce them identically. That is, it is better to over-distinguish than to under-distinguish. Nobody, however, should need to cope with words such as *round*, *soul*, *you*, and *young* that in our present muddled system are spelled with the same vowel letters in spite of their differing spoken vowels. Nor would they be bothered by the outrageous range of choices that we all must make now, when choosing among the vowel letters of *maestro*, *aisle*, *bayou*, *eye*, *height*, *child*, *bite*, *diamond*, *tie*, *sign*, *guile*, *buy*, or *by*. Virtually every English speaker uses the same spoken vowel in all these words, and they should all be spelled with the same letters, too.

Determining exactly which words are pronounced with the same speech sounds and which are pronounced with different speech sounds in the many accents of English is the most difficult part of designing a better spelling system. Fortunately, the great majority of words are grouped into sets in much the same way in all English accents. It is these commonalities that allow us to consider English to be a single language, and it is these commonalities, also, that allow us to construct a far better spelling system for everyone than the system we have now. Everyone would have to learn a fair number of spellings that, like *Mary*, *merry*, and *marry* or *pour*, *poor*, and *paw*, reflect nothing in their own speech, but the number of these arbitrary spellings would be tiny by comparison with the number that we need to cope with now.

Of the fifteen criteria in this list, this is the one that is most difficult to explain and would be the most difficult to implement. It may also be the most important.

**6. Spell related words in different ways when this reflects their different pronunciations.** We have many pairs of related words that cling to the same spelling in spite of differences in pronunciation. Some of these have vowels that change in speech but not in writing: *heal/health, breathe/breath, wide/ width, meter/metrical, grade/gradual, divide/division, verbose/verbosity, profane/profanity, satire/satiric, sulfur/sulfuric.* Consonants, too, can change in speech but not in writing: *sign/signify, rigor/rigid, allege/allegation, evict/eviction, act/actual, quest/question.* The consistent spelling of these pairs is sometimes justified by suggesting that it reflects their semantic and historical relationships.

The fear of losing track of a relationship if the spelling changes is odd, because we have a great many other pairs of words that we easily recognize to be related even though their spellings differ: *clear/clarify, conceive/ conception, choice/choose, sober/sobriety, profound/profundity.* Consonants, too, sometimes change in writing in obedience to changing pronunciation, without ever threatening to obscure the relationships of the words: *divide/ division, describe/description, recede/recession, delicate/delicacy, safe/save, hoof/hooves, choice/choose, evolve/evolution, invade/invasion, submit/submission, galaxy/galactic,* and so on. We are left with rampant inconsistency. How is the poor learner to know whether related words need to be spelled differently so as to match their differing pronunciation, or spelled alike in order to suggest their relation to other words? Our present inconsistent spelling shows neither in any consistent or reliable way.

Perhaps some virtue could be found in spelling related words with the same letters even at the cost of ignoring pronunciation differences, but I have no idea just what that virtue might be. We have no trouble recognizing the relationship among words in speech even when we pronounce them differently. Why should we spell some words but not others in a way that obscures the differences in their pronunciation? Wouldn't foreign learners of English, as well as children, be less confused and less prone to mistakes if the spelling of *heal* and *health* reflected their different pronunciations, rather than their related meanings? If we spell *conceive* and *conception* with different vowel letters, why shouldn't we also spell *heal* and *health* with different vowel letters?

**7. Spell reduced vowels in the same way as the related full vowels.** English has many pairs of related words, one with a full vowel in a stressed syllable, the other with an unstressed and weak vowel that linguists call a "schwa" and write as "ə": *cóntrast/cəntrást; cónvert/cənvért; présənt/ prəsént.* Since dialects often differ in the vowels that are reduced, using the full vowel would have the advantage of allowing the same spelling to be used for both accents: American *cápəllary* and British *cəpíllary* converge on *capillary.* American *lábrətoree* and British *ləbórətree* would nearly converge on *laborotoree*. By spelling the reduced form of the vowel in the same way as the full form, the relationship between the words would be made clear.

Why do I want to spell related pairs like *heal* and *health* with different vowel letters, while I want other related pairs, such as *présent* and *presént* to have the same vowel letters? The answer lies in the extreme variability of the English schwa and the comparative stability of our other vowels, but a full discussion of reduced vowels must wait for Chapter 10, "The Unstressed Schwa." In addition to the schwas that have resulted from the reduction of full vowels, English has other schwas that have no obvious origin in any full vowel at all: *búttən, əbúv, sécənd*. We will need some way to spell these unchanging schwas, but that is also a topic for Chapter 10.

**8. Syllabic consonants.** Spoken words such as *kitten, button, little, bottle*, and *paddle* have little or no real vowel sound in their second syllable. The final *n* or *l* of these words forms a syllable that needs no help from any spoken vowel. Consonants like these are known as "syllabic consonants." Since the great majority of English syllables have clear vowel sounds that need to be represented in writing by equally clear vowel letters, readers might be puzzled if the second syllables of *cottn, satn, cattl*, and *brittl* had no vowel letter at all. If we had an obvious letter to use for a schwa it might be reasonable to use it here. It would represent the shortest of all possible spoken vowels—a vowel that has been shortened out of existence. Unfortunately, we have no such obvious vowel letter for this kind of syllable. *Kitun, butun, litul*, and *botul* might be hard for many readers to accept and, in any case, we might want *u* for something else, most likely for the vowel of *cut*, *up*, and *luck*. On the other hand, we might grow accustomed to *kitn, butn, litl*, and *botl*. And, just think how much ink that would save!

**9. Idiosyncratic pronunciations and traditional spelling.** English has many words that vary in pronunciation in idiosyncratic ways. Some people pronounce the *t* in *often*, others do not. Some pronounce the initial vowel of *economics* with the vowel of *fleece*, others with the vowel of *dress*. Some speakers rhyme *either* with *breather*, others pronounce it with the vowel of *flyer*. Americans can choose between two pronunciations for *vase, leisure*, and *aunt*. I have heard *poem* pronounced as *pome, powem*, and *poym*. And, of course, "I say *tomeyto* and you say *tomahto*." The only genuine virtue of our traditional spelling is that its messy relationship with pronunciation makes it relatively easy for everyone to use the same spelling for a word, even when it has two or even three different pronunciations. When we read aloud, we can read words such as *often, economics, poem*, and *tomato* in whatever way we have learned from our community. Our spelling does not coerce us into fitting our pronunciation to the sequence of letters that we find in writing.

These idiosyncratic irregularities give the spelling reformer a mass of messy problems—words with varied pronunciations that follow no general rule. What should we do about them? No one should feel any pressure to change pronunciation in order to fit the spelling, but even if a spelling is chosen by the flip of a coin it could influence future speakers. Think of the utterly ordinary word *been*. Most British speakers pronounce its vowel exactly as they pronounce the vowels of *green bean*. Most Americans pronounce *been* like the *bin* that used to hold coal, but a few pronounce it like the second syllable of *Big Ben*. In most accents these three vowels are clearly distinct from one another. Sets of words, such as *reed, rid,* and *red, teen, tin,* and *ten,* or *beat, bit,* and *bet,* demand three different spellings, but all three pronunciations of the vowel are in use for *been*. How should it be spelled?

We might encourage each writer to use the spelling that best fits his or her own pronunciation, but *been* is a very common word, and many readers would find it disconcerting to see it spelled in several different ways by different writers. We manage to understand speakers, whatever their pronunciation, but if our spelling is to be a compromise among accents, we should discourage idiosyncratic variability in spelling. We can stop a speaker who uses an odd pronunciation, and ask, "What was that you just said?" We cannot stop a writer who uses a quirky spelling in order to ask, "What was that you just wrote?" We really ought to agree on a single spelling for the word that we now spell "been," even while encouraging everyone to continue to pronounce it just as they always have.

For words such as *been*, for which there is no fully satisfactory solution, the least disruptive spelling would be the old and familiar one, as long as that corresponds to one of its current pronunciations. If *ee* continues to be used for the vowel sound of *fee, meet,* and *seen,* then it can continue as the normal spelling of *been* as well. That will be right for one group of speakers (most of them British), and it would at least look familiar to Americans, even if it suggested a strange pronunciation. It should not cause much trouble for anyone except for the (mostly American) children who will need to learn that the word is, from their point of view, spelled rather strangely. In the same way, by continuing to use the familiar single *e* in the otherwise reformed spelling of *ekonomiks*, we would favor those who pronounce the first syllable as *ek-* over those who pronounce it as *eek-*, but the written *e-* will be familiar to everyone who can already read.

Choosing a uniform spelling for words that differ idiosyncratically from one accent to another does have one serious drawback: it might encourage spelling pronunciations. Everyone ought to be able to continue speaking confidently as he or she has always spoken, but since any revised spelling would conform much more closely to pronunciation than our traditional spelling does, it might encourage readers to expect more similarity between pronunciation and spelling than they find now. This might tempt them to bring their speech into line with the marks on paper by using spelling pronunciations. That would be no disaster, and it might even help to keep the language unified, but I do not like to encourage spelling pronunciations.

Hundreds of decisions about idiosyncratic variability of this sort would be needed before we could have a settled orthography. Deciding just who should make these decisions and just how they should be made is even more difficult than the particular decisions about particular words. Nonetheless, it is important to remember that the ideal spelling for the vast majority of words would be completely clear.

**10. Patterned variation.** Americans generally pronounce *agile*, *fragile*, and *fertile* with a reduced vowel and no stress on the second syllable: *ágəl*, *frágəl*, *fértəl*. The same Americans, however, usually pronounce the final syllables of *éxile*, *ínfantile*, and *réconcile* with a full vowel. Most speakers in England pronounce all six of these *-iles* with the full vowel that we all use in *isle*, *I'll*, and *reconcile*. We could struggle to find a special spelling to mark the American difference, but in this case it is probably simpler to ignore the Americans and use a single spelling for the final syllable of all these words. That would reflect British pronunciation, but the irregularity is unlikely to bother mature American readers. It should not matter much even to an American writer. It would simply be one of many places where reduced vowels are spelled more fully than they are pronounced (see Chapter 10).

**11. Homophones and homographs.** In Chapter 5, I argued at length that homophones such as *right*, *rite*, *write*, and *wright* do not require different spellings. If the spoken context tells us which of these words a speaker intends, then the written context should surely tell us, just as clearly, what word the writer intends. The fact that homophones survive so easily in speech shows us that the two words occur in such different circumstances that a listener can easily grasp which word is intended. We should not, however, confuse such innocent homographs with words such as *bow*, *tear*, *lead*, *wound*, or *minute*, all of which can represent two unrelated words that differ in pronunciation. These pairs of words are simply unlucky enough to be spelled in the same way in spite of their different pronunciations. They are not homophones and they deserve different spellings. (See Chapter 5 for additional discussion.)

**12. Proper names.** Unlike most of our words, proper names belong to particular people or to particular places. Even if English speakers could be persuaded to use a reformed spelling for their daily reading and writing, some would bitterly resist any suggestion that their own names should be re-spelled. Their feelings should be respected. No one should be required to change the spelling of his or her own name. In the last century Norway has had extensive spelling reforms but nobody was required to re-spell their names. As a result, archaic spellings are still common among personal names. If that is a problem for anyone, it is the owners of the names who must cope with it. To foreigners, the Norwegian family name, *Wang*, looks oddly Chinese, but it is pronounced as if it were spelled *Vang*, so it sounds safely Norwegian. If someone wants to burden everyone else with the need to remember the peculiar spelling of his name, let him do so. We really ought to welcome an occasional archaically spelled name. It would be a refreshing assertion of personal idiosyncrasy.

Place names could be treated in much the same way. They are not as personal as people's names, but the people of Albuquerque or Terre Haute, Leicester or Worcester, ought not to have to change the spelling of their city's name simply to suit the whim of some enthusiast for reform. Let the inhabitants of each state, province, county, city, and village decide how to spell the name of their home.

How do we deal with foreign place names? We now follow French spelling for *Paris* but, unlike the Parisians, we pronounce the final *s*. Should we spell it to match French pronunciation or to match our traditional pronunciation and French spelling? What do we do about *Rome?* The Italians both spell and pronounce their capital as *Roma*. Should we follow their spelling or spell it as we pronounce it? When the Chinese government settled on a new romanization that they call "Pinyin" to replace older and more cumbersome romanizations, publishers in English-speaking countries quickly fell into line and adopted the new spellings. We now write, and even say, *Beijing* instead of *Peking*, and *Chongqing* instead of *Chungking*. There is certainly an advantage in using the same spelling whether writing in English or in the language of the place being named, but the choice is not always simple. The Chinese do not actually write with Pinyin. Chinese names, like all Chinese words, are normally written with Chinese characters. Pinyin is really a phonetic transcription that shows readers, both Chinese and foreign, how to pronounce the name. Pinyin does not show us how the Chinese write either their personal names or their place names. Still, if we know the rules, we can use the Pinyin spelling to figure out how to pronounce them.

It would be least disruptive simply to continue to spell foreign place names as we have spelled them in the past. In the long run, spellings that are closer to either the local spelling or the local pronunciation would be better.
**13. Regionalisms.** Preserving the unity of written English is essential, but this should not imply that every single regionalism needs to be tabooed. Americans will still write *gotten* and *learned* even if they look and sound ridiculous to readers in England. British writers will continue to write *got*

and *learnt* even though these look and sound every bit as ridiculous to Americans as *gotten* and *learned* seem to the British. Nothing should stop local words, local grammar, or representations of local pronunciations from being used in order to give local color, just as we use them now. Nevertheless, except when deliberately conveying local color, we should follow the same spelling conventions, wherever we live and wherever we write. Only in that way can we keep our language unified.

**14. Rare contrasts.** I argued in Point 5 above that, if a distinction in pronunciation (a phonological contrast) is found in any accent, then it should also be distinguished in a reformed spelling. *Mary*, *merry*, and *marry* are pronounced in contrasting ways in some accents of English, so they ought to be spelled differently, even though their contrasting spellings would be a problem for the millions of Americans who pronounce them all alike. This will be a burden for writers who do not have the contrast in their own speech, but this seems less serious than spelling them alike, and thereby obscuring a contrast that millions of other people observe.

Nevertheless, the number of people who make a contrast cannot be ignored. If a phonological contrast is observed by only ten people in the world, these ten can hardly expect all the other millions of English speakers to spell the words differently. What about 1000 people? 100,000 people? 10,000,000 people? It is not at all clear just where the line should be drawn or what other criteria might lead us to decide in one way rather than another, but the numbers cannot be ignored.

**15. Non-native English.** In addition to the accents of English that are spoken in the British Isles, those that were carried to North America, the Caribbean, South Africa, Australia, and New Zealand must all be taken into account when designing a better way to spell. These far-flung accents share a history of linguistic continuity with the language of the homeland. Speakers in these former colonial regions have every bit as much right to consider their language to be English as do their cousins who stayed behind. Of course, speakers of many other languages have assimilated to the English that was spread around the world from Britain, but that does not distinguish places like Australia or Canada from the home country. Britain, too, has had immigrants who brought other languages with them. The descendants of the Vikings, the Norman French, and the Huguenots long ago assimilated to the English language, even as they contributed something from their older languages to their new one. Other, more recent, immigrants have come to all the English-speaking nations from every corner of the world. They and their children continue to assimilate to whatever form of English surrounds them. Immigrant languages have enriched English everywhere, but they have not introduced serious discontinuities.

But today English is also spoken, sometimes as a first language, more often as a second, by many people in the Philippines, Malaysia, Singapore, South Asia, and the former British colonies in Africa. The English that is used in these nations has been far more heavily influenced by the native languages of the speakers than has the English that was carried around the world by migrants from Britain. We would need to know much more about these new forms of English if we wanted to take them into account in constructing a better spelling. A few eccentric localisms aside, I doubt if the added complexities would be great, and most localisms could probably be ignored for a global spelling. Nevertheless, I leave open the question of whether, and to what extent, the "new Englishes" of nations like India and Nigeria ought to be considered when devising a better way to spell. I will not take them into account in the remaining chapters.

One thing does seem certain: a simplified spelling would greatly ease the task of teaching and learning English as a second or foreign language. As the world shrinks, as a result of both rapid travel and instant electronic communication, it needs a lingua franca. For better or worse, that role has fallen to English. I mourn the decline and death of other languages under the uniformitarian onslaught of World English, and I worry that if English were to become easier to learn, it might hasten the decline of every other language. That is the best reason I know for hanging on to our traditional English spelling. It is so difficult to learn that it puts a serious impediment in the way of the smothering forward march of English. Our children, who must struggle for years to learn to spell "correctly," pay a dreadful price for keeping that impediment in place.

# 8 Consonants

... the traditional appearance of our language, its spelling, has become in
our eyes a sacred shrine and cenotaph, which we are prepared to defend to
the last drop of blue-black ink in our fountain pens.

A. Lloyd James, *The Times* (London), 20 November 1937

## Letters and the Sounds of Speech

In one way or another, the letters of every alphabetic writing system represent the sounds of the spoken language. Some writing systems, such as
Italian, Finnish, and Korean Hangŭl, represent the speech sounds in a
much more consistent way than English does, but even our English letters
do reflect, even if irregularly, the sounds of speech. In spite of some
complications and irregularities, we know what sounds *b, d, f, p, m, n,
s*, and *t* usually stand for. English *c* represents different sounds in *cent*
and *can't*, and *g* can represent the initial of either *gun* or of *gem*. We have
utterly useless consonant letters in *debt, island*, and *subtle*, and we have a
few real eccentricities such as the *gh* of *laugh, rough, dough*, and *ought*.
These irregularities give children needless pain, but by comparison with
our chaotic vowels, our consonants are models of order and regularity.
This makes the consonants the easiest place to begin.

Whether written on paper, typed onto a computer screen, or carved
into stone, letters are visible. Their visibility and their relative permanence
make us aware of them. We even give them names. The spoken sounds
that our letters stand for are more elusive. We don't talk about our audible
speech sounds as easily as we talk about our visible letters. Usually we do
not even need to give the speech sounds much explicit attention. Anyone
who is concerned with spelling, however, needs to know a great deal about
speech sounds, and about how we use letters to represent them.

The sounds of a language form a code, and we use this code to keep
the tens of thousands of words in our spoken languages distinct from one
another. To accomplish this, the individual speech sounds must be recogniz-
ably different from each other, and when they are different enough to signal
different words, linguists describe them as being "in contrast." It is these
contrastive speech sounds that we call "phonemes." The sounds that are
most often represented by *b, p, f, s, m, n*, and *h* count as different phonemes
of English because they can be used to distinguish words from one another.

*Bat*, *pat*, *fat*, *sat*, *mat*, *rat*, and *hat* can be recognized as different words because their initial phonemes are "in contrast." They are different enough to distinguish words from one another. It is these phonemes that form the code that we use to distinguish among the thousands of spoken words that every language needs.

A writing system that had one, and only one, symbol for each phoneme would be perfectly "phonemic." Each distinctive phoneme of the spoken language would always be represented by the same distinctive letter, and each letter would always represent the same phoneme. Some of our letters, such as *b*, *d*, *t*, *l*, *m*, and *n*, come reasonably close to meeting this ideal, but others do not. *Th* can represent the initial phonemes of either *thy* or *thigh*; *s* represents three different phonemes in *see*, *busy*, and *measure*. Just as some letters can represent more than one phoneme, some phonemes can be represented by more than one letter: *c* and *s* represent the same phoneme in *cell* and *sigh; f*, *ph*, and *gh* give us three ways to represent the phoneme that is found in *find*, *photo*, and *laugh*.

Different languages, and even different accents of the same language, differ in their inventory of contrasting phonemes. English consonants are much less variable than its vowels, but even consonants vary from one accent to another. Pairs such as *where/wear*, *which/witch*, and *whether/weather* are pronounced differently (they are "in contrast") by most speakers in Ireland and Scotland, and by a declining minority in the United States. Speakers who make the *wh/w* contrast have a puff of breath at the beginning of *where*, *which*, and *whether* but no puff in *wear*, *witch*, or *weather*. For most speakers in the United States and for nearly everyone in England, these pairs are pronounced as homophones. We say that *w* and *wh* have "fallen together" in some accents, while in other accents they are still "in contrast." Differences among accents, such as this one, greatly complicate the task of designing a better spelling system but, in English, the complications of accent variability become acute only with the vowels. These will be dealt with in the next chapter.

## English Consonants

Most English accents have 24 consonant phonemes, each of which is in contrast with all the other 23. This means that any two of these 24 phonemes could be used to distinguish words from one another. It also means that, ideally, we ought to have 24 different written symbols with which to represent our 24 spoken consonants. Since we need letters for vowels as well as for consonants, the 26 letters of our alphabet fail to give us enough letters to go round, so we have to augment our alphabet with digraphs: *th*, *ch*, *sh*, *ng*, and an occasional *zh*. We could make up new symbols to stand for these phonemes but, since new letters look outrageous to conservative readers, and since millions of keyboards are limited to the familiar 26 letters, digraphs would be a less disruptive choice, even for a revised spelling.

In Table 8.1, each consonant phoneme of spoken English is represented by a distinctive letter or a digraph. Anyone who reads English will find all the single letters in the table, and all of the digraphs except for *dh* and *zh*, to be thoroughly familiar. We recognize these symbols as representing English phonemes. Each of these 24 phonemes is pronounced differently enough from all the other 23 to distinguish different words from one another, so the 24 consonants are all in "contrast." *Pen/ten, tie/die, thumb/some*, and *sew/show* all have contrasting initial consonants. We call these words "minimal pairs" because they differ from each other in just one phoneme—a "minimal" difference. Minimal pairs confirm our feeling that the speech sounds that distinguish them are, indeed, contrasting phonemes. If you were to hunt hard enough you should be able to find minimal pairs for most of the pairs of phonemes found in Table 8.1: *sit/sip, son/some, wrong/long*, and so on. You won't find a minimal pair for *h* and *ng* because *h* never occurs at the end of an English word, and *ng* never occurs at the beginning. Both can occur in the middle of a word *(behind, longing)*, but I know of no pair that is identical except that one has an *h* where the other has *ng*. The speech sounds represented by *ng* and an *h* are so utterly different that we count them as separate phonemes, and we spell them with different letters.

**Table 8.1** English consonants

|  | *Front of the mouth* |  | *Back of the mouth* |  |
|---|---|---|---|---|
| Voiceless stops or affricates | p 'pot' | t 'ten' | ch 'chop' | k 'kick' |
| Voiced stops or affricates | b 'bad' | d 'day' | j 'jump' | g 'good' |
| Voiceless fricatives | f 'fat' | th 'thigh' | s 'sun' | sh 'shop' |
| Voiced fricatives | v 'vat' | dh 'thy' | z 'zoo' | zh 'azure' |
| Nasal | m 'man' | n 'nine' |  | ng 'ring' |
| Approximants | w 'wall' | l 'lip'    r 'run' | y 'yes' | h 'have' |

I will use the letters shown in Table 8.1 as convenient symbols to represent the consonant phonemes of English. These letters are familiar and reasonably unambiguous, but I do *not* mean to propose them for a reformed orthography. Spelling reformers have used most of them in their alphabets, but many decisions are needed before we can settle on a particular spelling: should the initial phoneme of *kitten* and *cake* be spelled with a *c* or a *k*, or with something else? Do we really need different letters for the contrasting initials of *thy* and *thigh*? We have no conventional spelling for the phoneme that comes in the middle of *treasure* and *azure*, so how should we represent it in a better spelling system? If we are to agree on new spelling conventions for English, these are just a few of the many questions that will need answers. The spellings that I use here are simply convenient choices for the purpose of exposition, but the spellings chosen for most reform proposals are not much different from these.

The arrangement of Table 8.1 has a clear logic. Phonemes with closure or partial closure at the lips are on the left. Phonemes that are articulated at the back of the mouth are on the right. The middle columns have the phonemes that are produced somewhere between the front and the back of the mouth. The rows distinguish the manner in which the vocal organs are articulated. For present purposes, the precise manner in which these phonemes are pronounced hardly matters. What does matter is that each phoneme is distinct from all the others. It is possible to find words that are distinguished by almost every pair of these 24 phonemes: *bit/ pit*, *bat/ sat*, *zoo/sue*, *right/bite*, *sit/sick*, *sun/some*, *Benny/Betty*, and so on. An ideal spelling system would use a different letter, or a different digraph, for each of our consonant phonemes, and each phoneme would always be represented by the same letter.

Most of the letters used in Table 8.1 will be familiar to anyone who can speak and read English, but *zh* is a rare spelling in English, and words spelled with *dh* are nearly unknown. The digraph *dh* is simply a convenient way to write the initial phoneme of *thy*, *this*, *that*, and *those*. It reflects the fact that these words have a different initial phoneme than *thigh*, *think*, *three*, and *thistle*. Our conventional spelling uses *th* for both phonemes. Compare *thy* and *thigh*, which are a "minimal pair." They show us that *dh* and *th* are, indeed, contrasting phonemes. They are different enough to distinguish different words, and we would be justified in spelling them with different letters. The digraph *zh* stands for a speech sound that is never used at the start of an English word, but it is found in the middle and, less often, at the end of perfectly ordinary words such as *measure*, *vision*, *leisure*, *usual*, *equation*, and *beige*.

Table 8.1 has a place for each of the 24 consonants of English. It does not show the consonant clusters (sometimes called "blends") that are formed when two or more consonant phonemes are grouped together, as in *blast*, *strength*, and *twelfths*. English has scores of clusters, but they are all formed from a succession of two or more of the 24 consonant phonemes.

## Alternate Spellings

Of the spellings in Table 8.1, only *zh* and *dh* depart from regular English usage, and even *zh* should be recognizable from Russian and Chinese proper names. The rest will be familiar to anyone who can read English. The spellings given in Table 8.1, however, are not the only spellings that represent these phonemes. Table 8.2 gives examples of most of the ways that most of the English consonant phonemes can be spelled. As we become skilled readers, we grow so familiar with all this variability that we hardly notice it. The wide variety of ways in which our phonemes can be spelled, however, is a serious challenge for new readers, and especially for new writers. Notice the remarkable range of spellings that can represent *sh*, for example, and notice, also, that *zh* has no spelling that can be called "regular."

In spite of all this variation, most English consonant phonemes have one spelling as the clear favorite. Spelling reformers can probably agree on *b*, *d*,

**Table 8.2** Examples of English consonant spellings

| | |
|---|---|
| **b** | boy, rob, lobby |
| **ch** | chew, teach, catch, virtue, question, cello, righteous |
| **d** | day, bad, ladder, would, called |
| **dh** | then, bathe (now always spelled *th*) |
| **f** | far, beef, telephone, cliff, enough, half |
| **g** | goat, dog, ghost, vague, buggy |
| **h** | hot, who |
| **j** | jump, gent, magic, fudge, graduate, adjust, exaggerate |
| **k** | kiss, come, school, queen, chaos, khaki, queue, pick, lilac, saccharine, liquor, lacquer |
| **l** | lip, pal, llama, bill |
| **m** | make, jam, lamb, damn, summer |
| **n** | near, man, know, gnaw, pneumonia, mnemonic, dinner, handsome, foreign |
| **ng** | long, think, zinc, finger (spelled *ng* except before the sound of *k* or *g*) |
| **p** | pie, lip, pepper, hiccough |
| **r** | red, door, wrap, rhyme, horror, myrrh, corps (In many accents, the letter *r* is not pronounced before another consonant or at the end of an utterance.) |
| **s** | say, bus, kiss, city, scene, psychic, waltz, isthmus |
| **sh** | shy, dash, chef, sugar, ancient, assure, special, nation, crescendo, patient, ambitious, precious, fuchsia, negotiate, anxious, moustache |
| **t** | ten, net, better, thyme, two, doubt, kissed, veldt, receipt |
| **th** | thick, both (always spelled *th*) |
| **v** | view, love, of, savvy |
| **w** | want, bivouac |
| **y** | yes, beyond (always spelled *y*) |
| **z** | zoo, nasal, does, dizzy |
| **zh** | vision, exposure, Asia, beige, brazier, equation, azure (no regular spelling) |

*f, g, h, j, l, m, n, ng, p, s, sh, t, v, y,* and *z.* This leaves *c/ch, c/k, f/ph, qu/kw, r, th/dh, w/wh, x,* and *zh.* For each of these, there is room for disagreement, and each will be discussed briefly at the end of the chapter.

## An Example

What would a passage of English look like if each of its 24 consonants were written consistently with the same letter or digraph? Here, as a test, are a few paragraphs selected from a story by Mark Twain called "Simplified Spelling." The story is set in Egypt at the time when the ancient hieroglyphics were still in use. Twain wrote the story using traditional spelling, but I have re-spelled it, with the consonants shown in Table 8.1. It is thus a relatively radical, although still understandable, revision. The vowels remain unchanged.

## Simplified Spelling

Dhe Simplifierz had rizen in revolt against dhe hieroglyfiks. An unkel of Kadmus ho waz out ov a job had kome to Ejypt and waz trying to introduse dhe Foenishian alfabet and get it adopted in plase of the hieroglyfiks. He was chalenjed to show kauze, and he did it to dhe best of his ability. Dhe eksibishion and diskushion took plase in the Temple of Astarte, and I was present. So also waz the Simplified Komitee, with Kroesus as foreman of the Revolt—not a large man fyzikly, but a simplified speler of aknowlejed ability. The Simplifierz were fyew; the Opozishion were multitudinous.

\* \* \* \* \*

[Kadmus konkluded:] "My argument iz before you. Wone ov the objek-shonz to the hieroglyfiks is that it takes dhe britest pupil nine yearz to get the formz and dheir meaningz by heart; it takes dhe average pupil siksteen yearz; it takes the rest of the nashon all dheir dayz to akomplish it—it is a life sentens. Dhis los of time is much too ekspensive. It coud be employed more usefuly in odher industries, and with beter rezults."

\* \* \* \* \*

Unkle Kadmus sat down, and the Opozishion roze and kombated hiz rezon-ingz in the uzhual way. Thoze people said dhat they had alwayz been uzed to dhe hieroglyfiks, that the hieroglyfiks had dear and sakred asosiashionz for dhem, dhat dhey loved to sit on a barel under an umbrela in dhe brilyant sun of Ejypt and spel out dhe owlz and eaglez and aligatorz and saw-teeth, and take an our and a haf to the Lord'z Prayer, and weep widh romantic emotion at dhe thought dhat they had, at most, but eit or ten yearz between dhemselvez and the grave for the enjoyment of dhis ekstasy, and dhat dhen possibly these Revolterz woud shove the anshient sinz and symbolz from dhe main trak and ekwip dhe people widh dhe litning-ekspres reformed alfabet that woud leave dhe hieroglyfik wheelbarrow a hundred thouzand milez behind and have not a damed asosiashion hwich koud kompel a tear, even if tearz and diamondz stood at dhe same prise in dhe market. (Twain, 1962)

Most of this passage should be understandable for anyone who can read English as it is traditionally spelled, but it needs extra time. Many plural and past-tense suffixes had to be modified, and these could slow a reader down at first, but they probably don't make the passage much more difficult. These suffixes could be kept closer to traditional spelling. Several doubled consonants have lost one member of the pair. The simplification of doubled consonants does not seem to interfere with comprehension, but in a larger sample it might cause an occasional problem. Single and double consonants often indicate different pronunciations for the preceding vowel—*ape/apple*, *diner/dinner*—so occasional ambiguities would arise if all doubled consonants were suddenly undoubled without reforming the vowels at the same time. English spelling is absurdly inconsistent on this point, however, and we could surely find a better way to indicate vowel quality than by doubling consonants.

This exercise shows that regularizing the spelling of our consonants would not be very difficult. On the other hand, even the most ardent reformer must grant that a fluent reader would be noticeably slowed by this unfamiliar spelling. Since our conventional spelling of English vowels is far more chaotic than the spelling of the consonants, the vowels call for comparatively heroic changes. These would interfere with fluent reading more severely than would a few changed consonants.

## Questions That Need Answers

Many questions need to be answered before any scheme for a reformed spelling for the English consonants could be seriously proposed. Many of these questions reflect a tension between constructing an ideal system and constructing a system that stays as close as possible to our traditional spelling. The closer we cling to our familiar spelling, the easier the transition would be, but by clinging too closely we would miss opportunities for simplification.

*A, an, the, -s, -ed.* Several English articles and suffixes change their pronunciation to fit the sounds of the word with which they are used. We are already familiar with the difference between *a* and *an*, so it would be foolish to abandon that alternation. The other articles and suffixes could be written in ways that would reflect their changing pronunciations: *a peach/ an apple*; *thee apple/thə peach*; *bats/boyz/busəz*; *calld/talkt/batəd*; *runz/ flirts/kisəz*. On the other hand, we could continue to spell them in a more traditional way by using the same spelling for consistent meaning: *bats/ boys/buss*; *calld/talkd/batd*; *runs/flirts/kiss*. If doubled consonants are used for nothing else, we might even write the plural, past, and third person singular with a single suffixed letter: *buss, chatd, kiss* for *busses, chatted, kisses*.

*c* **or** *k*. The initial consonant of *cat, call*, and *come* is pronounced just like the initial consonant of *kitten, kite*, and *keep*. Romance languages generally use *c* for this sound. Germanic languages more often use *k*. English, with its mongrel heritage, has never been able to make up its mind. In the middle and at the end of words English even allows the absurdly redundant *ck*. We don't need *ckrackers* or *ckoockiez*, but either *c* or *k* would be possible. We use *c* more often than *k* to represent this speech sound, so *c* might seem to be the better choice. On the other hand, *c* is pronounced like an *s* in words such as *city* and *central*, while *k* rarely stands for anything except this single sound so it would be less ambiguous. In this case, *c* wins on frequency, but *k* wins on its lack of ambiguity.

*c, cy*, **or** *s*. *City, cycle*, and *society* all begin with the same phoneme. *s* can now represent several different phonemes, not only the initial phoneme of *society*, but also the phonemes of *sure, busy*, and *vision*. Nevertheless, *s* is most often used for the *s* of *Suzy, some*, and *bus*, so it is the obvious choice for *sity, sycle*, and *sosiety* as well.

*ch* **or** *c*. If *kiss, kill, cat*, and *copper* all began with *k*, and if *city, certain*, and *scythe* were all spelled with an *s*, we should be able to clean up such odds and ends as *chord* by turning it into *kord*, and, if the residents desire, turning *Chicago* into *Shikago*.

That done, *c* would be found only when paired with *h*, as in *cheese, chicken*, and *each*. The *h* would become completely redundant, so we could then simplify our spelling by writing *c* without the useless *h*: *ceez, ciken, cans, kac*.

*wh* **or** *w*. Older forms of English had a clear contrast between *wh* and *w* in minimal pairs such as *where/wear, which/witch, whale/wail*, and *whether/weather*. In both England and the United States the distinction has been gradually disappearing. It hangs on better in Scotland and Ireland than in England or North America.

A bit of research is needed to find out which accents and how many people still make the distinction in speech, and to judge whether there is a clear trend for it to disappear everywhere. If no more than a small handful of wistful old folks still cherish the *h*, then it can be harmlessly dropped. On the other hand, if the difference is still retained by most Irish and Scottish speakers, it should probably be retained in spelling as well. We already have quite enough words, such as *bow*, *wind*, and *minute* that are spelled alike but pronounced differently. We don't want to present the Irish and the Scots with a word like *wich* if it could stand for either *witch* or *which*.

*zh*. This is one way to spell a consonant that does not now have a single dominant spelling. One would never guess from their spelling alone that *azure*, *pleasure*, *equation*, and *beige* all share the same consonant sound. Clearly, we need a new and consistent spelling for the middle of *pleasure* and the end of *beige*. *Zh* has never been used for ordinary English words such as *treasure* or *vision*, but it should be familiar to English readers from occasional romanizations of Russian and Chinese proper names: *Zhukov*, *Zhivago*, *Zhu*, *Zhou*. Unadorned *z* is needed for *zoo*, *zebra*, *bizy*, and *buz*, so *zh* would be a natural choice for *mezhur* and *vizhun*. The *z/zh* distinction even parallels the *s/sh* distinction. Notice that *ng* and *zh* are the only two English consonants that are never used initially in native English words. We do, occasionally, find them both in proper names: *Zhou* is Chinese and *Nguyen* is Vietnamese.

*qu*. The sound sequence that is spelled *qu*, in *quick*, *quality*, and *quirky*, could be spelled more regularly as *kw* or *cw*: *kwik*, *kwality*, *kwirky* or *cwik*, *cwality*, *cwirky*. On the other hand, *qu* is now the usual spelling for this cluster. It is unambiguous, regular, and used for nothing else. If *qu* were used consistently, it would not be much of a problem for children who must learn to read and spell. Which is more important: familiarity or consistency? *Qu* would be more familiar, but *kw* or *cw* would be more consistent with the other uses of the letters, and, perhaps, just a bit easier for new learners.

*th/dh*. The initial spoken consonant of *think*, *thought*, *thanks*, and *throw* is in clear contrast with the initial consonant of *they*, *then*, *this*, and *them*, but we are so accustomed to spelling them both with *th* that we may hardly be aware of the difference in their pronunciation. The *th* of *thigh* and the *th* of *thy* are as different phonetically as the *t* and *d* of *to* and *do*. Both pronunciations of *th* are used in some very common words. For several centuries, the readers and writers of English have used the same spelling for both phonemes without a bit of trouble. They give us no problem because English seems to have only two minimal pairs for these phonemes: *thigh* and *thy* and, for some speakers, *ether* and *either*. (Speakers who pronounce *either* with the vowel of *eye* have contrasting vowels in *either* and *ether*, so these words are not a minimal pair.) A degree of orderliness and consistency would be lost if the same letters were allowed to represent two contrasting phonemes, but it would be difficult to devise a sentence in which *thigh* and *thy* or *ether* and *either* could be confused. So far, no disaster has descended from spelling the initials of *this* and *thing* in the same way, and disaster seems unlikely to descend even if we continue to spell both these phonemes with our familiar *th*. Would it set a bad precedent to allow an ambiguous spelling here?

***ph/f.*** Most words with a *ph* have roots in ancient Greek, although they often name objects such as *telephones* and *photographs*, about which the ancient Greeks knew nothing. The Germans and Scandinavians use *f* for these words, without, it seems, any disaster. This is one place where English spelling does make etymology unusually transparent, however, and it would cause relatively little anguish to continue to spell such words as *telephone* with a *ph*. Regularity certainly calls for *f*. Etymologists would welcome *ph*. Does it matter?

***x.*** This is already a relatively rare letter in English and it could be quietly put to rest by using either *ks* or *gz* wherever *x* has been traditional: *egzample, egzibit, egzact, boks, eksklude, eksite*, or *bocs, ecsclude, ecsite*. On the other hand, retaining the familiar *x* wherever it is used now would be no more than a minor burden on the memory.

***ng.*** This digraph is used with great regularity as our traditional spelling for the final nasal consonant of such words as *clang, wrong*, and *fling*. In *finger* and *longer* the *g* does double duty, not only turning the *n* into *ng*, but also supplying the "hard" *g*. Should we write *fingger* and *longger*? That would keep their spelling safely different from *singer* and *hanger*. Only when the *ng* phoneme is followed by *k* does our present spelling now lack a *g*: *think, pink, thank, drank*. Does consistency require us to replace *think* and *thank* with *thingk* and *thangk*? No serious problem would arise if we continued to use *nk* wherever it is used in traditional spelling, but we do need to ask how many such small exceptions should be allowed.

***r.*** "Retroflex" describes the shape of the tongue when it is curled up and hunched back to form an English *r*. The sharpest divide among English accents is due to the centuries-old loss of the retroflex *-r*s, from some accents but not from others, whenever they were followed by a consonant. Preconsonantal *r*s will play a central role in the next chapter.

These are the kinds of problems that need thought, and the kinds of questions that will need answers, if the spelling of our consonants is to be reformed. Yet, by comparison with the problems of our vowels, the problems of the consonants are few and trivial.

# 9  Stressed Vowels

"A synonym is a word you use when you can't spell the other one."
Baltasar Gracián (1601–58)

## Chaos Among the Vowels

The spelling of our consonants calls for a fair bit of repair, but, when compared with our written vowels, the consonants look like models of order and regularity. Think about the many ways that we can spell a single spoken vowel: *Caesar, me, flea, leave, bee, cheese, Pete, ceiling, people, key, ski, police, amoeba, quay.* Or try: *maestro, aisle, bayou, aye, stein, eye, find, indict, diamond, die, like, sign, island, guile, buy, try, dye, type.* The only polite way to describe such incoherence is to call it "imaginative." This rampant inconsistency must certainly take part of the blame for the high rates of illiteracy in English-speaking countries. If we want the largest possible fraction of the citizenry to share the joys and privileges of literacy, then we should all be howling for change. The traditional spelling of our vowels is, quite simply, a shambles. It screams for urgent repair.

One difficulty, though a relatively minor one, is our pitifully short supply of vowel letters: *a, e, i, o, u* and, as our teachers told us, "sometimes *y* and *w*." Five letters, or even seven, are simply not enough to go round. We compensate for our shortage of letters with digraphs such as *ai, ea, ou, oo,* and an occasional trigraph such as the *eau* of *beauty.* The *-ough* of *through* and *although* counts as a quadragraph. We should be able to rid ourselves of trigraphs and quadragraphs with few regrets, but digraphs give us a decent way to augment our limited stock of vowel letters. Sadly, we have squandered the opportunity by losing control of our digraphs just as we have lost control of the single vowel letters. Think of *cheap, bread, break,* and *fear,* or *ought, you, young, should,* and *count,* spelled alike, but pronounced differently. The mess long ago passed the point where it could be fixed by a bit of patching. Patching might knock the consonants into shape, since most spoken consonants already have one clearly dominant spelling which is the natural choice for any reform. The choices are much more difficult for the vowels because so few of them have just one dominant spelling. Nothing short of a brutal revision can fix the way we write our vowels.

The problem is more difficult than simply assigning a unique spelling to each distinctive vowel phoneme. A second piece of the problem is that the accents of English vary so much. Any spelling system that is intended for use by all English speakers, whatever their accent, has to be a compromise. No sensible set of spelling conventions should privilege one English accent over another, but a spelling system cannot possibly be simultaneously perfect for speakers from all parts of the British Isles, North America, South Africa, Australia, and New Zealand, to say nothing of the millions of people throughout the world who use English as a second language. It is easy to devise a splendid spelling system for a single accent. The Appendix to this book (pages 151–64) gives a small sample of the many revised spellings that have been proposed. Each of these fits one accent very well, but a spelling system that works equally well for all English speakers, wherever in the world they learned to talk, is a more daunting challenge.

Any reform must allow people whose English accents are very different to read the same letters from the same page, and let each reader do so in his or her own accent. In some degree, we even use our own accent when we read silently. The variability of our accents needs to be emphasized, because of a strange idea that is widespread among people who are opposed to reform and who suppose that a reformed spelling would be "phonetic." This, they imagine, would require everyone to pronounce words in the same way. This is monumentally confused. Indeed, it goes absolutely counter to the goals of everyone who has any serious interest in spelling reform. We should all be able to use the same spelling but everyone should be able to continue to speak exactly as they have always spoken, using whatever familiar accents they already use. The spelling should be designed to represent the way we talk; nobody's speech should need to change in order to fit the way we spell. We can use the same spelling to represent our varied accents because all English accents are related to one another in highly systematic ways.

We must sort the words of our language into "sets," in which all the words of each set have the same spoken vowel. For example, consider what we can call the GOAT vowel. For each of us, *goat, mauve, beau, sew, go, soap, hope, doe, dough, flow, owe, oh, choke,* and *yolk* all have the same spoken vowel, but speakers who speak with different accents may pronounce their GOAT vowels in different ways. The typical British pronunciation of the GOAT vowel is different from the typical North American pronunciation, but if all the GOAT vowels were spelled with the same written symbol, each reader would simply interpret the spelling in accordance with his or her own familiar accent. This allows that same spelling to be used by people with very different accents. It is simply nonsense to imagine that a reformed spelling would require anyone to learn a new pronunciation in order to fit the spelling.

## The Distinctive Vowel Sets of English

We need to find the sets of English words in which each speaker, whatever his accent, pronounces the vowel in every word in a uniform way, even if the pronunciation of the vowel varies from one speaker to another. How do we know which words belong together in a single set? Fortunately, this question was addressed in superb detail by J. C. Wells in his book, *Accents of English* (first published in 1982). Wells surveyed the accents of the entire English-speaking world. He assigned a name (a "key word") to each set of words that an individual English speaker, wherever he grew up and whatever his home, generally pronounces with the same spoken vowel. GOAT is Wells's key word for one such set. The important generalization is this: *Speakers from different parts of the world often differ from one another in their pronunciation of the vowels of a set, but each speaker is usually consistent for all the words of each set.*

We need to deal with one major complication: different accents do not always group their words in the same way. Consider, for example, words such as *trap, have, pal, sand, hang,* and *plaid.* These all belong to Wells's TRAP set. Consider also *bath, chance, calf, last, ask, example, grasp,* and *dance* that belong to his BATH set. Most speakers in England pronounce the vowels of these two sets in very different ways, which is why they form two sets, each with its own name. Most Americans pronounce the vowels of both the TRAP and the BATH set with the same spoken vowel. It is impossible to design a spelling system that is right for both kinds of speakers. If we use different spellings for each set, most Americans will have to write different vowel letters for words that they pronounce exactly alike. If we spell the vowels of both sets in the same way, however, many speakers in England would have to use the same spelling for words that they pronounce differently. What do we do? I will argue that, on balance, it is better to require some writers (in this case the Americans) to learn different spellings for words that they pronounce with the same vowel than to confuse other readers (in this case speakers in England) by using the same spelling for words that have very different spoken vowels.

We need to start by classifying the words of English according to the pronunciation of their vowels. Whatever the accent, all the words of each set should share a vowel, but the vowels of a set can differ from one accent to another, just as the vowels of the GOAT words do. It will turn out that we need to recognize twenty-nine different sets of stressed vowels. No single accent has that many contrasting vowels, but different accents merge their vowel sets in very different ways.

For the most part, Wells based his sets on just two accents. One was the variety of British English that, at the time he wrote, was known as "RP" (Received Pronunciation). The other was a variety of American English to which he gave the name "GenAm" (General American). It may seem to be unduly restrictive to use just two accents to produce a classification that ought to be useful for all the many varieties of English, but, in fact, Wells's RP and GenAm are at the opposite poles of English variation. One or the other of these two accents has most of the features that need to be accounted for when designing a spelling system for English. They give us an excellent place to begin.

Until the latter half of the twentieth century, "RP" was the term often used for the accent that was widely accepted as the "best," or most "prestigious," accent of England. Announcers on the BBC radio and television networks were required to use RP, so it was often called "BBC English." A more varied and more interesting range of accents can now be heard on the BBC and on other British broadcasting channels, but most announcers and commentators still converge on a single accent that is widely acceptable in England. It is an accent that seems, at least to some speakers in England, to be less stuffy than the older RP, and it came about as a reaction to an RP that seemed increasingly artificial to many listeners. I have heard it suggested that nobody except an "old Colonel" would still speak traditional RP. I have even heard rumors that the Queen received elocution lessons so that she would sound less remote to her subjects. Nevertheless, an accent that is seen as less formal than RP is still recognizable as a sort of neutral accent in England. It is common in broadcasting and it shares a good deal with the older RP.

No single accent in the United States has been as consistently recognized as a "standard" as RP/BBC English once was in England, but in the 1920s, when the American radio networks were first organized, the broadcasters needed a pronunciation that would be broadly acceptable everywhere in the country. They chose one that is closer to the accents of the Midwest and western parts of the United States than to the more varied accents of the East Coast or the old South. Even now, almost a century later, few Americans except broadcasters ever make a deliberate effort to adopt this accent, but it is widely accepted. It is inoffensive, and it does not immediately reveal one's hometown.

Wells's term, "General American," never caught on among American linguists, and in England "RP" is now more likely to elicit a chuckle than respect. Neither "RP" nor "GenAm" now seems to be the right term to use, but I still need to refer to the more or less neutral and inoffensive accents that are used in the two countries. Perhaps, without too much violence to common perceptions, I can call them "Mainstream American" and "Mainstream English." I mean these terms to refer to forms of the language that are widely used and that do not immediately reveal the speaker's hometown.

Mainstream American and Mainstream English are on opposite sides of the most salient division among English accents. This is the division between rhotic accents, which have well-pronounced *r*s wherever a word is spelled with *r*, and non-rhotic accents, in which *r*s are not pronounced immediately before a consonant. Rhotic speakers say *roars* and *reared*, with similar *r* sounds both before and after the vowels. Non-rhotic speakers say something more like *rawz* and *ri²d*, without rhoticity after the vowel. (The small raised "ə" stands for the very short "uh-like" speech sound that keeps *ri²d* (*reared*) different from both *reed* and *rid.*) Most North American accents are rhotic, while the most widespread accents of England are non-rhotic, but both rhotic and non-rhotic accents can be found on both sides of the Atlantic. The accents of eastern New England, traditional New York City, and much of the American South are non-rhotic, while the accents of Ireland, Scotland, and some parts of England itself are every bit as rhotic as any accent in the New World.

Go back four centuries or so, and all English accents were rhotic, but by the eighteenth century, the accents spoken around London were losing the *r*s that were followed immediately by a consonant. This new fashion gradually spread, not only to much of England, but also to the eastern seaboard of what became the United States. Later, it spread further to Australia, New Zealand, and South Africa. The loss of so many *r*s brought a good deal of reorganization to the sound system of non-rhotic accents, and it brings headaches to would-be spelling reformers. Because rhoticity and its absence bring so many complications to the spelling system, it is easiest to deal with the vowels in two batches: first, those that have never been followed by an *r* (the "non-rhotic" vowels) and, second, those that have, or that once had, an *r* that tagged along after (the "rhotic" vowels).

## Non-rhotic Vowels: Vowels with No Following -*r* in Their History

Table 9.1 gives examples of seventeen sets of words whose vowels have never been followed by an *r*. All the words of each set share the same spoken vowel. Following Wells, I will refer to these sets as the KIT set, the DRESS set, the TRAP set, and so on. These are the "key words" and all the words of a set share the spoken vowel of the "key word." The seventeen sets of *non*-rhotic vowels are those that were recognized by Wells (1982), and I have tried to give at least one example of all the different ways in which the vowel of each set has been spelled. In every accent the words of each set are pronounced differently from those in the other sets, but in each accent a few sets have merged so that their vowels are pronounced alike. Crucially, accents differ from one another as to which sets have merged. For example, the vowels of the PALM and the BATH sets have merged in Mainstream British English, but the words of the PALM and the LOT sets have merged in Mainstream American. It is obvious that words of the DRESS and BATH sets should be spelled differently because everyone pronounces them differently, but it is not immediately clear how the PALM words should be spelled. Since every pair of vowel sets contrast with each other in some accents, any spelling system that is intended to be used by speakers of all English accents needs to have a different spelling for each of these seventeen sets.

**Table 9.1** Non-rhotic vowels. English lexical sets with no postvocalic *r*s in their history.[1]

---

KIT: pretty, bit, pin, ring, pill, minute, sieve, give, women, busy, build, gym, myth, abyss, apocalypse [e, i, ie, i-e, o, u, ui, y]

DRESS: any, many, aesthetic, said, says, bet, tend, bell, ledge, feather, bread, heifer, leopard, friend, guess, guest [a, ae, ai, ay, e, ea, ei, eo, ie, ue]

TRAP: bat, have, pal, sand, hang, plaid, meringue [a, ai, i]

BATH: shan't, chance, calf, last, ask, example, grasp, dance, demand, laugh, draught, aunt [a, au]

PALM: spa, bra, ha, bah, fa, la, mamma, bravado, salami, schwa, barrage, Sumatra, Guatemala, Bach, salaam, Shah, hurrah, palm, balm [a, aa, ah, al]

LOT: swan, waffle, quality, watch, squabble, bureaucracy, not, bomb, odd, doll, knob, rod, mop, cod, Tom, honest, profit, knowledge [a, eau, o, ow] (Americans may vacillate with the vowels of some of these words, and pronounce them with the vowel that they use for CLOTH.)

CLOTH: wash, sausage, Australia, long, wrong, soft, offer, office, Boston, cross, lost, cost, dog, gone, log, moss, loft, catalogue, cough, trough [a, au, o, ou]

THOUGHT: all, ball, talk, stalk, haul, sauce, caught, caulk, paw, dawn, awful, awe, broad, fought, ought [a, al, au, augh, aul, aw, awe, oa, ough]

FOOT: woman, wolf, good, wood, would, should, put, full, bush, butcher, pudding [o, oo, oul, u]

STRUT: come, honey, tongue, does, done, love, blood, flood, young, touch, but, rust, dull, fun, judge, rubber, cuddle, stuff, bulk, punish [o, oe, o-e, oo, ou, u]

MOUTH: bout, shout, bough, doughty, now, how, crown, cowed, fowl [ou, ough, ow]

GOAT: mauve, gauche, beau, yeoman, sew, go, no, over, most, old, sold, holy, roll, depot, soap, oath, boat, doe, rope, choke, joke, oh, yolk, brooch, soul, dough, rogue, glow, bowl, owe [au, eau, eo, ew, o, oa, oe, o-e, oh, ol, oo, ou, ough, o-ue, ow, owe]

GOOSE: beauty, sleuth, eunuch, feud, dew, knew, steward, lewd, view, do, whom, tomb, shoe, move, whose, boot, cool, you, group, through, flu, truly, sue, glue, due, flute, crude, stupid, duty, Stuart, union, music, cue, tune, cute, fruit, suit, two [eau, eu, ew, o, oe, o-e, oo, ou, ough; u, ue, u-e, ui, wo]

FLEECE: Caesar, me, equal, legal, flea, sea, bee, feel, keep, Pete, these, deceit, ceiling, people, key, ski, visa, field, diesel, police, machine, phoenix, amoeba, quay [ae, e, ea, ee, e-e, ei, eo, ey, i, ie, i-e, oe, uay]

FACE: bass (music), pale, ale, make, fame, cradle, fail, pain, campaign, straight, gauge, pay, stray, break, great, matinee, skein, veil, reign, weigh, freight, bouquet, they, obey [a, a-e, ai, au, ay, ea, ee, ei, eig, eigh, et, ey]

PRICE: maestro, aisle, bayou, aye, height, stein, eye, child, find, I, hi-fi, diamond, indict, tie, dried, bite, mile, arrive, rise, time, island, sign, high, mighty, tight, guile, buy, dry, by, dye [ae, ai, ay, aye, ei, eye, i, ia, ic, ie, i-e, is, ig, igh, ui, uy, y, ye]

CHOICE: toil, void, boy, toy [oi, oy]

---

1.    Based on J. C. Wells 1982: 127–65.

It is not likely that English speakers anywhere in the world distinguish the vowels of every one of the seventeen sets that are listed in Table 9.1. In both Mainstream American and Mainstream English, the vowels of a few sets have fallen together so that they are pronounced in exactly the same way.

Table 9.1 lists the seventeen sets and gives a number of examples of words that have the spoken vowel of each set. The letters or pairs of letters that are now used for the vowels of each set are shown in square brackets. Most readers will find that they use the same spoken vowel for all of the words that are listed together in a set, and that the spoken vowels of most sets differ from the vowel sounds of most other sets. Every speaker, however, will surely find that the vowels of a few pairs of sets will be identical to each other. The crucial fact is that the sets that are identical differ from one accent to another.

Before reading beyond the table, readers might find it interesting to look through the words of each set and discover, for themselves, which sets they pronounce with the same spoken vowel and which sets they pronounce with contrasting vowels.

Speakers of most varieties of English generally pronounce all the vowels of each set of words in the same way, but the words of each set generally have a different spoken vowel from most other sets. For example, if you are a fluent speaker of English, you will certainly pronounce the vowels of all the GOAT words in the same way. You will, however, just as certainly pronounce these GOAT vowels in a different way than many other speakers of English, and you will pronounce them differently than the vowels of most other sets.

Nobody keeps the vowels of all seventeen sets distinct from one another. For example, I speak with a rather ordinary variety of Mainstream American, and like the majority of North Americans, I use the same spoken vowel for the words of both the BATH set and the TRAP set. I use a second spoken vowel for words of both the PALM and LOT sets, and a third for words of both the CLOTH and THOUGHT sets. Because of these three mergers, most Americans distinguish only fourteen vowels that are not, and never were, followed by r. This is three fewer than the full complement of seventeen sets that Wells identifies and that have no rs in their history. This is the most common American pattern, but some Americans do distinguish the spoken vowels of one or more of the three commonly merged pairs.

This merging of Mainstream American vowels is shown in visible form in Figure 9.1, where the seventeen non-rhotic vowel sets are listed on the left. The boxes enclose sets whose words have vowels that are pronounced identically by most Americans. The boxes in the first column of Figure 9.2 enclose sets of words in which speakers of Mainstream English use the same vowel. By comparing these two figures, you can easily see some of the most important differences between the two accents.

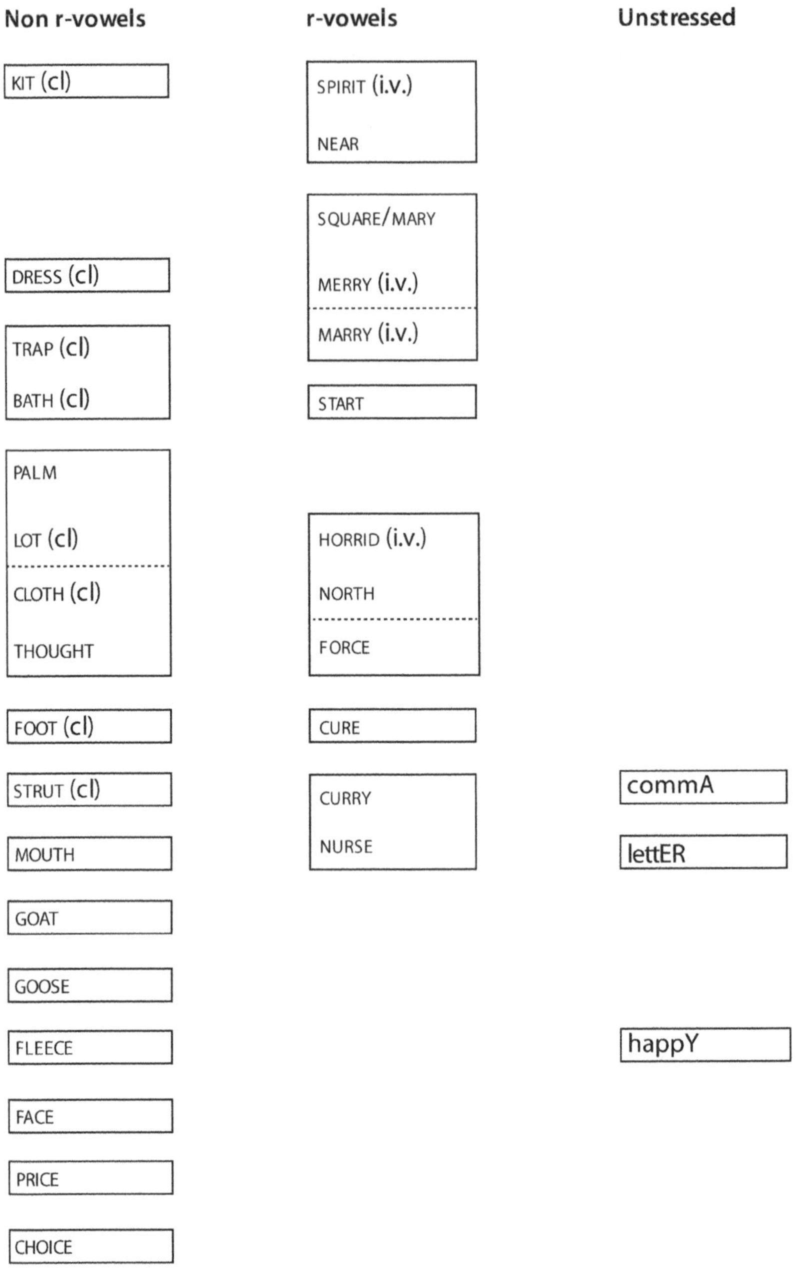

**Non r-vowels**            **r-vowels**            **Unstressed**

KIT (cl)

SPIRIT (i.v.)

NEAR

SQUARE/MARY

MERRY (i.v.)

MARRY (i.v.)

DRESS (cl)

TRAP (cl)

BATH (cl)

START

PALM

LOT (cl)

CLOTH (cl)

THOUGHT

HORRID (i.v.)

NORTH

FORCE

FOOT (cl)

CURE

STRUT (cl)

CURRY

NURSE

commA

lettER

MOUTH

GOAT

GOOSE

FLEECE

happY

FACE

PRICE

CHOICE

(cl) Closed syllables only        (i.v.) Intervocalic only

Otherwise both closed and open syllables

**Figure 9.1**  Mainstream American vowel sets

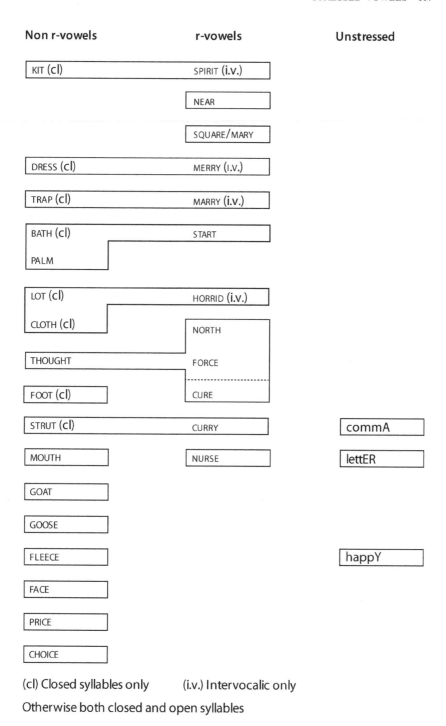

**Figure 9.2** Mainstream English vowel sets

Speakers in England are more likely to merge the BATH set with the PALM set, and to merge the LOT set with the CLOTH set. The BATH/PALM and LOT/CLOTH mergers mean that many speakers in England are left with fifteen contrasting spoken vowels for words whose vowels have never been followed by *r*. This is one more vowel than most Americans have. If a revised spelling for English were to have seventeen different ways to represent the seventeen different vowel sets, then any American who has an accent like mine would have three spoken vowels with two alternate spellings each. Many speakers in England would have just two spoken vowels that have two alternate spellings each. Neither American nor English speakers, however, would have to cope, as we all do now, with vowels that have a dozen alternative spellings. Nor would we have to cope with words such as *ought, you, young, should,* and *count,* whose vowels are pronounced differently from one another in spite of their shared spelling.

## The Rhotic Vowels

Several centuries ago, every speaker of English probably used a rhotic pronunciation for all the *r*s that were then, and that still are, found in writing. At that time, the written *r* accurately reflected the *r* that was used in the spoken language. We all continue to pronounce the *r*s that come immediately before vowels, but the single most salient difference among modern English accents is due to the loss, in some accents but not in others, of the *r*s that were once followed immediately by a consonant. When *r*s were followed by a vowel they survived everywhere in good health. When some accents, but not others, lost their *r*s before consonants, however, English accents were divided into "rhotic" and "non-rhotic" varieties. This is the difference between the rhotic Americans, who say *hard* and *start* with clear rhotic *r*s, and non-rhotic speakers in England and elsewhere, who say something more like *haad* and *staat* with no hint of rhoticity. Everyone continues to pronounce rhotic *r*s at the beginning of words (*rough, ready*), and also as the second or third member of a cluster (*crisp, try, scream*). Rhotic *r*s also remain secure between two vowels (*narrow, bury, glory, hurry*). In all these words where a rhotic *r* survives, it is followed by a vowel, and these *r*s must certainly be represented in writing. The *r*s of *hard, hoard, herd, beard, cared,* and *cured* precede a consonant, however, and they are among the thousands of words that have lost their rhotic *r*s in some accents, but that hang onto them in other accents.

The most complicated situation comes at the very end of a word, where, in non-rhotic accents, *r*s come and go depending upon whether the next word begins with a vowel or a consonant. Even non-rhotic speakers usually pronounce the *r* when a vowel follows: *Please pour a glass of wine.* When a consonant follows, the same non-rhotic speakers cheerfully omit the *r*:

*Please paw me a glass of wine.* Can rhotic and non-rhotic speakers share a common spelling? They can, but not without some care.

When *r*s disappeared from non-rhotic accents, the vowels that had preceded them were often left with a different pronunciation from the vowels that had never been followed by an *r*. Even in rhotic accents such as Mainstream American, the vowels that precede *r* are often quite different from other vowels. Indeed, in Mainstream American, the *r*s in such words as *card*, *bird*, *more*, and *poor* have almost merged with the preceding vowel to form diphthongs.

Table 9.2 sorts the rhotic vowels into twelve sets. Seven of these sets—NEAR, SQUARE, START, NORTH, FORCE, CURE, and NURSE—were recognized and named by J. C. Wells in his *Accents of English* (1982). To these seven, I have added five new sets, which I will call the SPIRIT, MERRY, MARRY, HORRID, and CURRY sets. The *r*s of these five additional sets are found only intervocalically (between two vowels), which means that even in accents that are otherwise non-rhotic, the *r*s of these sets are always pronounced because they are always followed by vowels.[2]

**Table 9.2** Rhotic vowels. English lexical sets with vowels that are, or that once were, followed by *r*.

| |
|---|
| SPIRIT: miracle, virulent, mirror, syrup, lyric, tyrannical, Syria, pyrrhic (in JCW = KIT) [ir, irr, yr, yrr] |
| NEAR: zero, serious, mysterious, query, ear, dear, weary, spear, beer, eerie, weird, here, fierce, pierce [er, ear, eer, eir, ere, ier] |
| SQUARE: Mary, vary, rarity, daring, Sarah, barbarian, area, bare, mare, spare, spared, dared, cared, laird, dairy, hairy, fairy, prairie, fair, lair, air, prayer, pear, bear, their, heir, there, where [ar, are, air, ayer, ear, eir, ere] |

*table continues*

2. This footnote is intended for the more technically inclined readers who may wonder why I have added these five sets. In Wells's original scheme, the words of the five new sets that have intervocalic *r*s were included in sets whose words were otherwise non-rhotic: SPIRIT = KIT; MARRY = TRAP; HORRID = LOT; CURRY = STRUT; MERRY = DRESS. To this American speaker, the vowels of MARRY and TRAP are simply not the same. Nor are the vowels of either HORRID and LOT sets or the CURRY and STRUT sets. Worse, MERRY, MARRY, and MARY have become homophones for me, as they have for many Americans. Wells groups MERRY, MARRY, and MARY (which I pronounce identically) with, respectively, the DRESS, TRAP, and SQUARE sets. This is appropriate for non-rhotic British English. From the perspective of Americans who pronounce *Mary*, *marry*, and *merry* identically, however, it is simply wrong to find them distributed among three different vowel sets in which all the non-*r* words have clearly contrasting vowels. My SPIRIT, MERRY, MARRY, HORRID, and CURRY sets are new. I leave the MARY words in the SQUARE set, which is where Wells put them.

**Table 9.2**–*continued*

MERRY: very, merit, cherry, ferry, terror, bury (in JCW = DRESS) [er, err, ur]

MARRY: Harold, parity, Harry, carry, arrow, narrow, harrow, carriage (in JCW = TRAP) [ar, arr]

START: car, star, farm, card, Carl, large, art, arms, sari, are, starry, jarring, aardvark, sergeant, heart, hearth [ar, are, arr, er, ear, aar]

HORRID: origin, Oregon, orange, florid, forest, foreign, lorry, horrid, Morris, porridge, quarrel, quarry, warrant (in JCW = CLOTH) [or, orr, arr]

NORTH: war, quart, or, for, horse, lord, form, assort, orbit, porpoise, normal, forty, aura, aural, Laura, Taurus [ar, or, aur]

FORCE: pork, torn, forth, export, wore, flora, oral, glory, gory, ore, adore, before, pore, hoarse, door, pour, four [or, ore, oar, oor, our]

CURE: Boer, Moor, pure, sure, furious, curious, curate, during, Ural, plural, Europe, jury, ensure, obscure, bureau [oer, oor, our, ure, ur, eur]

CURRY: worry, courage, flurry, Surrey, hurry, Murray (in JCW = STRUT) [orr, our, urr]

NURSE: term, fern, earn, serve, heard, fir, stir, bird, squirm, word, world, journey, fur, spurn, furl, curl, curve, burr, myrtle [er, ear, ir, or, our, ur, urr, yr]

## Mergers and Splits

It is unlikely that a speaker of English could be found who keeps all seventeen non-rhotic vowels and all twelve rhotic vowels distinct from one another, but the sets have merged in different ways in different accents. The boxes in Figures 9.1 and 9.2 enclose the sets that, as described by J. C. Wells, have merged in what I am calling Mainstream American and Mainstream English. Among the differences between these accents is the more extensive merging of the rhotic vowels in Mainstream American. The variety of Mainstream American that is shown in Figure 9.1 has only six rhotic vowels, while the Mainstream English shown in Figure 9.2 has ten. You will see the more extensive mergers of Mainstream American by comparing the right-hand columns of Figure 9.1 and Figure 9.2. The American mergers shown in Figure 9.1, while by no means unusual, are relatively extreme, even for American accents, so they make a particularly clear contrast to Mainstream English.

In the figures, dotted lines divide sets that have merged for some speakers, but continue to be in contrast for others. For example, some Americans distinguish vowels of the FORCE set from vowels of the NORTH set, while others merge them. These two sets are rarely, if ever, distinguished by speakers in England. Some English speakers merge vowels of the CURE set with those of the FORCE and NORTH sets, but others pronounce them differently. Perhaps, right now, in England, the CURE set is in the process of merging with the FORCE and NORTH sets. Americans rarely merge the vowel of the CURE set with anything at all.

The rather simple conclusion from all this complexity is that any reform of English orthography ought to use a distinctive spelling for each of the seventeen sets of non-rhotic vowels and for each of the twelve sets of rhotic vowels. In order to converge on a common spelling, everyone would have to learn to use different spellings for a few sets that are not distinguished in his or her own speech. That would be a burden on the memory but the burden would be almost trivial by comparison with the burden of our present spelling.

If all of this seems excessively intricate, it is well to remember that many sets remain distinct in both accents and, indeed, in all accents of English. It is the extensive similarities among the accents that allow us to understand one another when we talk, and it is also these similarities that would allow us to design a single spelling system that can be used by speakers of all English accents. It is the differences among the accents that make it such a challenging task.

## Conclusions

I have deliberately refrained from proposing specific spellings for the vowel sets. Choosing the letters is not as important as getting the sets right. Proposals for reformed spellings by Americans have an understandable, though unfortunate, tendency to spell the BATH words and the TRAP words with the same vowel letter, even though these are clearly distinguished by speakers of Mainstream English. Reciprocally, reformers who speak Mainstream English often use the same spelling for the vowels of both the BATH and PALM sets, even though most Americans pronounce them differently. If reformers could start by agreeing on the sets that need to be distinguished, all that would remain would be to assign a distinctive letter or digraph to each set, and to do so in a way that causes the least possible offense.

No accent of modern English distinguishes all 29 sets of stressed vowels from one another. If a different letter or digraph were to be assigned to each of the 29 sets, all the distinctions that are widely used in the English-speaking world would be represented in the spelling. Children would be able to learn to read and write with far less effort and delay than our present spelling system requires.

The most difficult *technical* challenge about designing a spelling system for English is to reconcile the many ways in which our spoken vowels have developed over the long course of their history so that a single spelling system of the vowels could be used by English speakers, wherever they live and whatever their accent. In the Appendix to this chapter, I consider a few of the many detailed choices that will need to be made if we are ever to have a rational spelling system. Readers who would prefer to avoid these technicalities can safely skip to the next chapter.

The really difficult challenges of spelling reform are not technical, however, but social and political. Reformers need to start by finding a way to agree among themselves on a single spelling system to promote, and then they must persuade the literate millions that something better is both possible and desirable. Every literate adult has made a very large childhood investment in learning traditional spelling. Switching would be hard for skilled readers. Enthusiasts for reform should not be blind to the genuine difficulties of a change. At the same time, even the most skilled readers and spellers ought to be able to understand how much more easily their children and grandchildren could learn to read, if only our spelling were more rational. Getting people to grasp that simple fact, and then to act on it, is the real challenge of spelling reform.

## Appendix to Chapter 9
## Some Complications and Some Choices

### A Scottish and Irish Problem with the NURSE Vowel

The classification of vowels into the sets that are displayed in Figures 9.1 and 9.2 is based on just two accents. For the most part, this classification turns out to be all that is needed for other accents of English as well, but there is one serious exception. In the accents of both rhotic Americans and non-rhotic British speakers, the vowels of large numbers of words are grouped together as the NURSE vowel. As with other vowels, this is spelled in several different ways: *fern, learn, bird, word, journey, burn, burr, myrtle*. These alternate spellings are absurd for speakers of both Mainstream American and Mainstream English, but they are less absurd for many speakers in Scotland and Ireland. Irish and Scottish accents are every bit as rhotic as Mainstream American, but they maintain many more vowel distinctions before *r* than North American accents do, and more, even, than speakers of Mainstream English do. In particular, some speakers in Scotland have one spoken vowel in *dirt* and *bird*, a second in *pert* and *heard*, and a third in *hurt* and *word* (J. C. Wells 1982: 405). These differences are hidden in the vowel classification that Wells created and that I have followed. It is Wells's classification that is reflected in Figures 9.1 and 9.2. This was appropriate for what I am calling Mainstream English and Mainstream American, but it misses contrasts that are found in some accents of Scotland and Ireland.

Our conventional spelling of words such as *dirt*, *pert*, and *hurt* is annoyingly irregular for speakers of Mainstream American or Mainstream English, who pronounce all these words with the same vowel. The spelling does reflect conservative distinctions that are still found in Scotland and, to some extent, in Ireland. Not even in Scotland and Ireland, however, does everyone distinguish three distinct vowels in *dirt*, *pert*, and *hurt*, and the distinctions have disappeared everywhere else. Should we, for the benefit of some Irish and Scottish speakers, continue to spell *dirt*, *pert*, and *hurt* with different vowel letters, even though a very large majority of English speakers use the same spoken vowel for all of them?

### Variable Mergers

Figures 9.1 and 9.2 show the mergers that have brought sharp differences between Mainstream English and Mainstream American. These mergers are of three kinds:

**1. Mergers among the rhotic vowels.** The vowels of the MERRY, MARRY, and SQUARE sets have fallen together in some, although not all, varieties of Mainstream American. In accents where they have fallen together, *Mary*, *merry*, and *marry* have become homophones. In Britain, the vowels of these three sets remain in clear contrast. In a satisfying bit of reciprocity, the vowels of the THOUGHT, NORTH, FORCE, and CURE sets have fallen together in some British accents, so that *paw*, *pour*, and *poor* have become homophones for many British speakers. *Paw*, *pour*, and *poor* remain in clear contrast for most Americans. As a result of these differing mergers, the rhotic vowels are organized in strikingly different ways in Mainstream American and Mainstream English.

**2. Mergers among the (mostly) non-rhotic vowels.** As Figures 9.1 and 9.2 show, Mainstream English and Mainstream American have merged the TRAP, BATH, START, PALM, LOT, CLOTH, and THOUGHT sets in very different ways. These differing mergers leave us with some difficult spelling problems. The exact phonetic quality of these vowels is not important for reform, but the fact that the two accents have undergone such different mergers seriously complicates the design of a unified spelling.

**3. Splits between rhotic vowels and non-rhotic vowels.** The boxes that reach across the columns of Figure 9.2 may seem to imply that several rhotic vowels have merged with non-rhotic vowels in Mainstream English, while Figure 9.1 suggests that Mainstream American has escaped such mergers. In fact, linguistic history has been quite different. It was not mergers that joined the rhotic and non-rhotic vowels of Mainstream English, but splits that divided them in Mainstream American. A few centuries ago, the *r* that followed vowels was simply an ordinary consonant that was distributed in much the same way as any other consonant. Like other consonants, *r* could occur before, after, or between any vowels at all. At that time, there would have been no reason to set off the *r* vowels as a special category. With the passage of the centuries, however, post-vocalic *r*s have become more difficult to regard as ordinary consonants that follow ordinary vowels. In Mainstream American, they can even be considered to have merged with the preceding vowels and to have formed diphthongs.[3]

---

3.   In my own speech, as in the speech of many Americans, post-vocalic *-r* can be reasonably regarded as having merged with the preceding vowels to form diphthongs. The vowels of the FLEECE, FACE, PRICE, and CHOICE sets are also diphthongs. They end with a very brief *y*-like tongue movement called a "*-y* off-glide." The vowels of the MOUTH, GOAT, and GOOSE sets have *-w* off-glides. The vowels of the NEAR, SQUARE,

The mergers and splits that now distinguish Mainstream English from Mainstream American (and, of course, the mergers and splits that distinguish other accents from one another) pose some serious challenges for the spelling reformer: how can a uniform spelling be used for accents that differ as much from one another as Mainstream English differs from Mainstream American? Mainstream English and Mainstream American have undergone very different mergers. If we can find ways to spell these vowels that are satisfactory for both accents, we will have made a good start toward a better orthography for English.

## The TRAP, BATH, and PALM sets

Before the eighteenth century, all speakers of English probably pronounced the vowels of the TRAP and BATH sets in the same way. Quite likely, they used a vowel that was not much different from the vowel that most Americans still use for the vowels of these two sets (Wells, vol. I: 232). Then, most likely in the eighteenth century, some accents in England began to shift the vowels of some of these words toward the pronunciation that all of us now use for words of the PALM set. The shifted vowel is sometimes called "long *a*," and the shift generally took place only when the vowel was followed by *f, th, s, n*, or *m*, as in *laugh, bath, class, dance*, and *example.* These are the BATH words. Mainstream English speakers now pronounce these words with the same vowel that they use for the PALM words, while Mainstream American speakers still pronounce them like the BATH words (Wells, vol. I: 135). In view of this difference between the accents, what would be the best way to spell the vowels of the TRAP, BATH, and PALM sets? No less than five different answers might be proposed.

**1.** Spell the TRAP and BATH vowels in the same way, but use a different vowel letter for the PALM set. This would suit most Americans just fine because, for most of us, the PALM set is the odd one out. It would, however, badly misrepresent the pronunciation of large numbers of speakers in England and in the southern hemisphere. Even a good many Americans from eastern New England would find this spelling disconcerting.

**2.** Use the same vowel letter for the vowels of the BATH and PALM sets but a different letter for words of the TRAP set. This should be attractive for many speakers in England, South Africa, Australia, and New Zealand. In an environment where most spelling follows pronunciation, however,

---

START, NORTH, FORCE, CURE, and NURSE sets can be regarded as diphthongs with *-r* off-glides. By considering post-vocalic *-r* to be an off-glide, we remove it from the category of consonants, and regard it, instead, as a component of the diphthongs.

Mainstream American speakers would find it absurd to spell both the BATH and PALM words with the same vowel letter.

**3.** Let American and British speakers follow different conventions, so that we could all write in a way that reflected our own speech. This would mean that all the many words of the BATH set would have one spelling in the USA and Canada but a different spelling in England, South Africa, New Zealand, and Australia. Since accents on both sides of the Atlantic vary, however, this would not really solve the problem. Some British accents follow the otherwise American pattern, while some East Coast Americans follow the pattern that is more common in England. Variable spelling for so many words might even set a dangerous precedent by encouraging increasingly different spellings for different accents. We should continue to pronounce our words in our own differing ways, but we really ought to agree on a common spelling.

None of these first three alternatives has much appeal. The next two need to be taken more seriously.

**4.** Spell all the vowels of the TRAP, BATH, and PALM sets in the same way. We now spell most of these words with "*a*", and we could continue to do so. That would make them easy to spell, of course, and it would have the advantage of familiarity. The variation in pronunciation would not be serious if we were concerned only with spelling—with going from sounds to letters. In spite of their differences in pronunciation, everyone would simply write "*a*" in all these words. Having them all spelled in the same way, however, could be difficult for new readers, for it would give them inconsistent guidance about how the words should be pronounced. A new reader, or a poor reader, might have difficulty knowing which spoken word was being represented. A foreign reader would not know how to pronounce these words when first encountering them in print. If pairs such as *Sam/psalm* and *cam/calm* were all spelled alike, the printed words could become difficult to identify. If we remove all the other distinctions among words, their written vowels really ought to reflect their differing pronunciations.

**5.** One option remains: use three different spellings for the three different sets. This would avoid homographs for words that, in some accents, are not homophones, and it would show the differences between the spoken vowels of such pairs as *bath* and *maths* that is characteristic of Mainstream English. If we were able to re-spell proper names, a great advantage of spelling the three sets differently would be to make it much easier to settle on a single pronunciation for proper names such as *Koran*, *Nevada*, and *Pakistan*.

To use three different spellings for the three different sets would conform to the guideline offered in Chapter 7, where I argued that over-differentiation is better than under-differentiation. The disadvantage, in this case, is not only that by spelling the vowels of the three sets in three different ways we would force everyone to learn some arbitrary spellings. It would also require a proliferation of distinctive letters or digraphs, one for each of the three sets. On balance, nevertheless, it is this option that seems the best.

## Orthographic *r* for Non-rhotic Speakers

Rhotic speakers would surely prefer to have every *r* that they pronounce to be shown in writing as well. That, of course, describes our present orthography. Many of these *r*s are not pronounced by non-rhotic speakers, however, so they pose an inescapable problem for reform.

In our traditional spelling, orthographic *r* can follow the vowels of three groups of sets:

1. SPIRIT, MERRY, MARRY, HORRID, CURRY. The *r*s of these five sets are always surrounded by vowels. This means that these *r*s are fully and consistently pronounced in both rhotic and non-rhotic accents. They would always need to be written, and they raise no problem at all for a reformed spelling.

2. NEAR, SQUARE, NURSE. In rhotic accents, of course, the *r*s of these three sets are always pronounced. In non-rhotic accents, they are *not* pronounced when they are followed immediately by a consonant, as they are in *neared*, *squared*, and *stirred*. (The *e*, of course, is silent.) The vowels that remain when the rhotic *r* disappears, however, are unlike any other vowels. This means that the orthographic *r*s will help to show the reader what spoken vowel the letters stand for. These *r*s, then, are just as useful for non-rhotic speakers as they are for rhotic speakers, although they represent different speech sounds for speakers of the two accents.

3. START, NORTH, FORCE, CURE. The words of these four sets pose a spelling problem for non-rhotic speakers. Mainstream English speakers have no rhoticity before consonants in words of the START set, so the spoken vowel is identical to the vowel of the PALM and BATH sets. In Mainstream English, vowels of the NORTH and FORCE sets merge, not only with each other, but also with the vowels of the THOUGHT set. Even the vowels of the CURE set may also merge with the vowels of the NORTH, FORCE, and THOUGHT sets. (All these mergers can be seen in a more visual form in Figure 9.2.) The merging of these sets inevitably presents non-rhotic speakers with a spelling problem. *Arms* and *alms* are homophones in Mainstream English, while they are in unambiguous contrast in Mainstream American. *Harm,*

*calm*, and *laugh* have the same vowel in Mainstream English, but they have three contrasting vowels in rhotic Mainstream American.

For the sake of rhotic speakers, *harm*, *scarf*, and all the other words that belong to the START set must continue to be spelled with an *r*. Pairs such as *sort/sought*, *lore/law*, *pour/paw*, *board/bawd* are generally homophones for non-rhotic speakers but, because they are in clear contrast for rhotic speakers, they must be spelled in different ways. Inevitably, this will bring a spelling problem to speakers of Mainstream English.

In what might be regarded as well-justified revenge, speakers of rhotic Mainstream American will have to spell *bath*, *calf*, and *ask* with a different vowel letter from the one they use for *bat*, *hang*, and *sand*, even though they pronounce the vowels of all of these words identically. This is the price we must pay for keeping a uniform orthography that can be used for all the accents of English. By accepting a few such spelling anomalies, speakers of varied accents will be able to converge on a common spelling. The anomalies that each speaker would have to cope with would be a very small fraction of the anomalies that every English-speaking child and every student of English as a foreign language must cope with today.

## Variable Articles and Suffixes

Our indefinite article is spelled and pronounced in one way before a consonant and in another way before a vowel: *ə pear*, *æn apple*. Because the definite article is always spelled "the," we may not notice that it also has two pronunciations. We say *thə* before a consonant but *thee* before a vowel: *thə book* and *thə hat*, but *thee apple* and *thee umbrella*. Should *the* be spelled differently before vowels and before consonants so as to match the pronunciation? Probably not. We have many pairs of related words in which a full spoken vowel alternates with a reduced schwa (e.g. *cóntrast/cəntrást*), but a writing system where schwas are constantly popping up to replace the letters for full vowels is unlikely to please anyone. *The* can keep a consistent spelling. It is such a common word that, however it is spelled, it will be quickly learned.

Our plural suffix, possessive suffix, and third person singular suffix all have three pronunciations, the choice among them depending entirely on the words to which they are attached: *cats*, *dogz*, *foxəz*; *Jack's*, *John'z*, *George'əz*; *walks*, *runz*, *kissəz*. Our past tense suffix can also be pronounced in three ways: *combd*, *washt*, *landəd*, but, except for irregular verbs, it is spelled in just one way: *combed*, *washed*, *landed*. We have some serious inconsistency here. We seem to want to represent both the meaningful units (the morphemes) and the sounds (the phonemes), but our spelling fails to do either in a consistent way. Exactly how we spell these suffixes may not matter very much. We could spell them all as they sound or we could give each of them a single consistent spelling. The real challenge is to find a way to agree on how to do it.

## Contrastive Stress

In addition to its hundreds of homophones, English has a handful of unrelated words that are kept distinct in speech by nothing except the location of stress: *ínsight* 'understanding' and *incíte* 'arouse to violence'; *trústy* 'a prisoner who is trusted' and *trustée* 'someone who is responsible for a trust'; *íncense* 'fragrant smoke' and *incénse* 'cause great anger'; *dráfty* 'having gently moving air' and *draftée* 'someone who has been drafted'. To complicate matters even more, emphatic stress can sometimes override the normal stress. *Japanése* and *Chinése* are usually stressed on their final syllables, but we can move the stress to the first syllable to emphasize a contrast: *The Jápanese drive on the left but the Chínese drive on the right.* Such examples prove, in case anyone should be in doubt, that stress is an essential and contrastive feature of the English sound system.

In spite of such examples, we should still be able to avoid any regular indication of stress in writing. English orthography, after all, has managed to survive for a good many centuries without marking stress. We have been able to live with homographs such as *bow*, *lead*, and *wind* that have sharply contrasting pronunciations for their contrastive meanings. These will no longer be homographs in any reasonable revised spelling. We should not be worried by the considerably smaller handful of words, such as *ínsight* and *incíte*, that are distinguished in speaking only by the position of stress, and that would become homographs in a revised spelling. Indeed, considerable ingenuity would be needed to construct a sentence that is ambiguous only because of a word that might be stressed in two ways. In extreme need, an accent mark would easily overcome any ambiguity.

# 10  The Unstressed Schwa

## Stress and the Schwa

The schwa is the "weak" vowel that is found in many unstressed English syllables. It is the noise of hesitation (*I, uh . . . don't know*). It is, by far, the most common of our vowels, but we do not even have a colloquial name for it. Linguists write the schwa with "ə," as in *bəlów, gáləxy, clárəfy, ənóther, díffəcult, multəpləcáshən*. Schwas are short, weak, very relaxed, and exceedingly common. They are never found in stressed syllables, but the schwas of unstressed syllables pose some serious challenges for anyone who hopes to mend the spelling of English.

The schwa is the vowel to which other English vowels are sometimes "reduced." This means that the stressed vowel of one word may be replaced by an unstressed schwa in a related word. When *prógress* is a noun, its stress is on the first syllable, and both syllables have "full" vowels. When *prəgréss* is a verb, the stress moves to the second syllable and the first vowel is reduced to a schwa. This kind of reduction is very common in English, but accents often differ in which vowels are reduced: British *frágail*, American *frágəl;* American *cápəlary*, British *cəpíləry*. Words can differ in their schwas not just from one accent to another but from one speaker to another: *mústache, məstáche*. Schwas can be extremely short, and sometimes they disappear completely: American *bátəry*, British *bátry*. The schwa is the most frequent vowel of spoken English, so we need a way to represent it in writing, but no system of spelling could possibly represent all the chaotic variability of spoken schwas. They appear in several guises:

**1. Reduced schwas.** We have many pairs of related words, one with a full vowel, the other with a schwa: *réserch/rəsérch, cónvert/cənvért, súbstənce/ səbstánshəl*. Such pairs are so common that we hardly notice their variability. I argued in Chapter 7 that many of these schwas should be spelled like the full vowel to which they are related. Writers whose spelling is shaky should be able to guess the spelling of the first vowel of the verb *prəsént* by thinking of the related noun, *présənt*. How is the second vowel of *disəbílity* spelled? If you think of *disable*, you should be able to make a good guess. What about the second and third vowels of *imməgrənt?* Think of *migrənt* and *migration* and you can find their spellings without a dictionary. If teachers let their pupils in on the secrets of vowel reduction, a reformed spelling could continue to use the same spelling for the corresponding vowels of words such as *migrant, immigrant*, and *migration*. No teacher was ever kind enough, or clever enough, to point out this simple rule to me. True, the rule does not work for every word, so I still make "mistakes" when I grope for the spelling of a reduced vowel, but my mistakes are fewer than they used to be.

**2. Free variation.** We have many sets of related words whose vowels vary, almost at random, between a full vowel and a schwa. I can reduce, in varying degrees, the vowels in words such as *division/dəvision* or *police/pəlíce*. Do I say *deecíde* or *dəcíde, pronóunce* or *prənóunce?* A vowel that varies should probably be spelled according to its fullest variant.

**3. Deletion.** The second syllable of words such as *battle, throttle, cotton, kitten*, and *Latin* may be squeezed so much that no real vowel remains. When the vowel goes, the remaining consonant forms a syllable by itself, a so-called "syllabic consonant." The spoken language gives a writer no hint about what vowel letter, if any, should be used in a syllable with a syllabic consonant. We might write these syllables with no vowel letter at all: *battl, throtl, cottn, kittn*, and *Latn*, although this would violate an expectation that every written syllable should include a written vowel. If we had a letter that could easily represent a schwa, that might be the best choice for such syllables, but we have no such letter.

**4. Invariant schwas.** Many English words have consistent and unchanging schwas. They can be found in the initial, middle or final syllable of a word, but they are never stressed: *əwáy, cəllápse, cəncérn, əbóut, fətígue, ánəmatəd, contrədíct, médəcəl, sófə, cóləmn, dístənce, cómmə, vódkə*. The existence of invariant schwas needs to be emphasized because so many other schwas alternate with something else. Most often they alternate with a full vowel but sometimes with nothing at all. This variability makes it easy to be misled into believing that *all* schwas are variable, but they are not. We need a way to spell the invariant schwa. Ideally, we should write it with a letter that is used for nothing else, something as distinctive as the linguist's "ə." Unfortunately, neither our alphabet nor our writing habits, to say nothing of our keyboards, give us any obvious candidate for the job.

**5. Accent variability.** We have many words that have a full vowel in some accents, but a schwa or nothing at all in others: *stráwbry* (British), *stráwbery* (American); *princéss* (British), *prínsəs* (American); *ləbórətry* (British), *lábrətory* (American). How do we decide, in each case, which accent to base the spelling on?

## Regional and Idiosyncratic Variation among Schwas

It is the fifth kind of variability, variability among accents, that gives us the most difficult spelling problems. Even without a change in stress, accents can differ in what gets reduced: British speakers have full vowels in *frájail*, *ájail*, *dairéction*, *vínyard*, *princéss*, and *hostéss*, while Americans have a weak syllable with a schwa: *frágəl*, *ágəl*, *dəréction*, *vínyərd*, *princəss*, and *hóstəss*. On the other hand, British speakers sometimes delete a vowel without leaving so much as a schwa behind: *sécrətry*, *diréctry*, *pátn*, *báttry*, *stráwbry*, *contémpree*, and *Snt Pául*. Americans have either a schwa or a full vowel in the unstressed syllables of these words: *sécrətary*, *dəréctəry*, *páttern*, *stráwbery*, *contémpərery*, and *Saint Pául*,

There is no fully satisfactory way to reconcile all these differences among accents, and the complexities can only grow when the accents of Ireland, Scotland, Wales, and the southern hemisphere are taken into account, as, of course, they must be. If we are to share a common spelling, we will sometimes need to choose just one alternative among several that are plausible. The least disruptive of the alternatives will often be the spelling that is appropriate for the accent with the fullest vowel. This would require everyone to learn to spell some words with full vowels rather than with the schwas (or nothing at all) of their own speech: Americans say *strawberry* but the English say *strawbree*, so give that one to the Americans with their full vowel in *-berry*. The English can say *princés* with two full vowels, while the Americans always reduce the second vowel, and say *príncəs*. That can be spelled with the full vowels of England. Use the full vowels in *laboratory*, *capillary*, and *innovative* rather than the schwas of either the American *labrətory*, *capəlary*, *inəvativ* or the British *ləborətry*, *capiləry*, *inovətive*. To use the full vowel in writing would often be the conservative choice, the spelling that is closest to tradition. Admittedly, by spelling so many words as if all the vowels are full, we will pose inescapable problems for speakers who consistently pronounce them as schwas. Unless they are familiar with English accents other than their own, they can have no way of knowing what letter should be chosen when writing them. Even these words, of course, would be no more difficult to spell than they are now. Many would be easier, because so many more of their vowel letters would conform more closely to speech than they do now.

It is tempting to let each speaker spell these variable words according to his or her own pronunciation. Our different accents rarely interfere with mutual understanding when we speak, and we should be able to understand some variation when we read. Highly literate readers, however, read much more quickly than they speak. As they take in whole words or phrases with a single saccade of their eyes, they do not want to be distracted by eccentrically variable spellings. Our orthography ought to bind us together rather than drive us apart, and if speakers with varied accents were to spell in varied ways there could be a danger that our written language would gradually lose its uniformity. We really ought to agree on a uniform spelling. Two principles should help us to make sensible choices:

**1.** When we have a choice, we should base the spelling on the fuller pronunciation rather than on the more reduced or abbreviated one. Choose the American *patern* and *strawbery* rather than the British *patn* and *strawbry*. Choose the British *intrest* and *ajayl* rather than the American *intrəst* and *ajəl*.

**2.** Other things being equal, choose the form that is most like traditional spelling. *Strawbery* and *zebra* are more like traditional spelling than British *strawbry* or American *zeebra*, so leave the *e* in *strawbery* and use just one *e* in *zebra*. *Strawbery* is justified by American pronunciation, *zebra* by British pronunciation. *Saint* has a full vowel in American, but it is often pronounced as little more than *Snt* in Britain. Give that one to the Americans. More often than not, fortunately, these two principles will point in the same direction.

One serious note of caution is still needed: all the examples in this chapter are taken from just two accents, the most widespread accents of England and the United States. None are from the accents of the other English-speaking countries. England and the USA are convenient places to begin. Not only have their accents been well described, but they are also spoken by the largest number of people, and they exhibit much of the variability that is found among English accents everywhere. Nevertheless, the limitation is a serious one that will need to be overcome. Decisions about spelling must rest on all parts of the world where English is spoken natively, not just on the most widespread accents of England and the United States. My purpose here, however, is not to advocate a particular spelling system, but only to explore the kinds of problems that will need to be dealt with if we are to escape our present tangle. Hundreds of words will require hundreds of choices. Inevitably, some of these choices will favor some accents over others. At the same time, thousands of other words can be given a single spelling that will be right for all speakers of English, wherever they live and whatever their accent. Words whose pronunciations are eccentrically varied give us a large fraction of our problems, but they are only a small fraction of the full vocabulary of English.

## Spelling Schwas

The upshot of all this discussion is actually rather simple: whenever one variant of a vowel is recognizable as its "full" pronunciation, it is that pronunciation that should be represented by the spelling. In one way or another, writers would often be able to retrieve this pronunciation without leafing through a dictionary. Often, the full pronunciation will be known from related words where the vowel is stressed. The pronunciation of the first and third vowels of *fótəgraf* shows us how the first and third vowels in *fətógrəfy* should be written. The second vowel of *fətógrəfy* returns the favor by showing how the second vowel should be spelled. Americans say *lǽbrətoree* while speakers in England say *ləbórətree*. If we spell each vowel to reflect its fullest pronunciation, we will have something like *laborutoree*—a reasonable compromise. No one would need to change pronunciation.

We will still be left with many schwas that never alternate with a full vowel, and we will need a way to write them. For example, I never use any vowel except a schwa in the first syllable of *cəmplete* or *əbove*, or in the second syllable of *blossəm*, *couplət*, or *commə*. Nor, as far as I am aware, does anybody else have anything but a schwa in these words. This leaves us with no basis in spoken English for spelling these vowels with any letter except one that represents a schwa. Here, the reformer faces a real dilemma. The invariant schwa ought to have its own symbol, but we need all our usual vowel letters for the full vowels: how should we represent invariant schwas? We can choose among several alternatives, none of them very appealing.

**1.** The best technical choice would be to use a symbol, such as *ə*, that is never used for anything else. Any such symbol would be unfamiliar to most readers, however, and it would quite likely invite rebellion. Many readers would choke on such a "funny" letter as *ə*. Even if that resistance could be overcome, the absence of *ə* from most keyboards would still be a serious problem—ultimately solvable, but hopelessly awkward during the transition.

**2.** Invent a digraph such as '*iu*' that we need for nothing else, or use a letter that has been put out of use by other reforms—perhaps *x*. The two letters of a digraph seem unreasonably bulky for the shortest vowel in the language, but to use *x* for a vowel might look sufficiently outrageous to provoke rebellion.

**3.** Represent each schwa by the letter that has been used in traditional spelling. This is the easy solution, or at least it is the easy solution for adults who already know how to spell. But it is a cop-out. It yields to tradition, and it would condemn every young learner to master a whole flotilla of totally arbitrary spellings. The most important reason for a spelling reform is to save our children from this kind of rote learning. To surrender here, for fear of a strange-looking letter, would be very sad indeed.

**4.** Finally, we might use *u* not only for the stressed vowel of *but, butter, abut,* and *destruct,* but also for unstressed schwas that do not alternate with one of the full vowels: *kumpleet, distuns, blosum.* If I had to choose among these four alternatives, I would probably opt for this one, even though it seems to violate the principle that contrasting speech sounds should always be written by different letters. In fact, however, the two pronunciations do not contrast in exactly the same contexts. The full *u* of *húgging* and *discús* is found only in stressed syllables, while a schwa appears only in *un*stressed syllables, as in *blósəm* and *bəlów.* The stressed *u* and the unstressed *ə* differ in more than just stress, but they are not so jarringly different that using the same symbol for both would be outrageous. This would be the kindest choice for children, who could confidently use *u* to stand for very weak vowels, as well as for the full vowel of words such as *of, fun, hug,* and *luv.* The worst problems might arise when a child encountered a *u* in an unknown word in writing. Even if she could guess the word's meaning from the context, she might not be able to tell whether the *u* stood for a stressed or unstressed vowel.

None of these four alternatives is entirely satisfactory. If a reformed spelling is ever to be adopted, someone will have to choose among several less than entirely satisfactory alternatives. In the long run, something like *x* or even *ə* would probably be best, but if these are sufficiently bizarre to inflame those who are dubious about any sort of reform, it would be a bad mistake to insist on one of them.

Designing a better alphabet requires so many seemingly arbitrary choices about so many hundreds of words that at some point even the most enthusiastic reformer must stop to wonder whether a reasonable spelling system is even possible. Can all the varieties of English be represented by a single set of spelling conventions and still be significantly better than our present system? Yes, they can, but much care will be needed to get the details right.

It is true that we have many hundreds of words with such idiosyncratically varied pronunciations that no spelling could be exactly right for every speaker. There is simply no way to reconcile the British *tomahto* with the American *tomeyto.* For many of our words, however, even a spelling that seems wrong to many people would still be much better for everyone than our traditional spelling. Even if we have a few hundred words like *tomato* that vary in idiosyncratic ways, we have many thousands of others with no such eccentricities. For the overwhelming majority of words, in fact, a single spelling can be right for speakers of all accents. Even where arbitrary choices need to be made, they will generally allow more reasonable spellings than those that we impose on our children now. The technical problems of devising a satisfactory spelling system for English are greater than enthusiastic reformers have sometimes imagined. They are trivial by comparison with the psychological, social, and political obstacles that have sabotaged every attempt to reform the spelling of the English language.

# 11 How Might It Look?

HOLOFERNES: . . . I abhor such fanatical phantasms, such insociable and point-device companions; such rackers of orthography, as to speak dout, fine, when he should say doubt; det, when he should pronounce debt,—d, e, b, t, not d, e, t; he clepeth a calf, cauf; half, hauf; neighbor *vocatur* nebour; neigh abbreviated ne. . . .

William Shakespeare, *Love's Labour's Lost*, V. i

## Two Trials

Scores of serious proposals have been made for revising English spelling, and I will not propose yet another. Nevertheless, we do need to experiment, so I will offer two *non*-serious proposals, one of which I regard as insufficiently radical, while the other seems too radical. Even though these are not meant to be serious proposals for reform, they should suggest the range of problems that any attempt to construct a better spelling system will have to deal with.

With my first non-serious proposal I try, not very successfully, to stay as close as possible to our traditional spelling. I will call this the "conservative trial," although it is not really conservative except by comparison with the radical trial. The radical trial shakes off tradition and reaches for a system that is maximally orderly and consistent. The radical trial is the kind of spelling system that ought to bring joy to a technically inclined linguist. Even for the radical trial, I hang on to many traditional spellings, so it is still a long way from being radical enough to satisfy the George Bernard Shaws of the world, who would tear up everything that we have now and start afresh. I would not seriously propose either my conservative or my radical spelling as a better way to write English. A more realistic reform ought to fall somewhere between the two.

Far more radical reforms than either of these would, of course, be possible, but I will assume that any reform that is worth serious consideration would use the Roman alphabet and accept a good many letters with their traditional values. Alphabets as radical as Shavian are not worth considering (see the Appendix). Even the innovative letters of the Initial Teaching Alphabet would surely be unacceptable to most readers, to say nothing of most keyboards. Within these limits, we still have a vast range of choices.

## Consonants

Assigning letters for the consonants is relatively straightforward. No one is likely to quarrel about *b, d, f, h, j, l, m, n, p, r, s, t, v,* or *z,* so they can all be used with their most common traditional English values; *sh* and *ng* are regular and easily understood, so they, too, can survive; *g* is more problematic. We now use it at the beginning of both *gym* and *get.* If we fix that foolish ambiguity by using *j* for *gym, gel, gem,* and *budge* to give us *jim, jel, jem,* and *buj,* we could then reserve the letter *g* for the "hard" *g* of *go, get,* and *bug.* That would take care of most of the consonants. A number of choices remain.

*th* is now used for both of the contrasting English phonemes that distinguish *thy* from *thigh.* The initial consonant of *thy* is "voiced" (meaning that it has vibrating vocal chords), while the contrasting initial consonant of *thigh* is unvoiced (the vocal chords do *not* vibrate during the *th*). You can feel the vibration if you hold your thumb and forefinger against your Adam's apple while you say *thy* out loud. (You will feel no vibration at all if you whisper!) The vibration will be absent from *thigh* until the vowel begins. A better orthography would spell these two phonemes in different ways. Many reformers have suggested hanging onto *th* for the unvoiced phoneme of *thigh, ether, thing, three, thistle, Kathy,* and *bath,* but using *dh* for the voiced phoneme of *thy, either, these, they, feather,* and *bathe.* We have never been much inconvenienced by using *th* for both phonemes, however, so we might stick with tradition and continue to use *th* for both. Purists would certainly prefer to have two different symbols to match the two different phonemes, so in the radical trial I use *dh* for the voiced consonant of *dhey, dhen, dhy,* and *eidher,* and keep *th* for the unvoiced consonant of *think, throw, thigh,* and *ether.* In the conservative trial I spell all these words with *th,* just as we spell them now.

*zh* can be used for the consonant that is found in the middle of *measure, azure,* and *equation,* and at the end of *beige.* This is the only English consonant that now lacks a single dominant spelling. It is never found initially in English words, but we know it from Russian and Chinese family names such as *Zhukov* and *Zhou. Zh* is the obvious spelling to use for this phoneme, and it has been the usual choice of hopeful reformers: *mezhur, azhur, eekwaizhun.*

*c, k, ck,* and *q* give us four ways to spell a single English phoneme. We manage perfectly well with just one letter each for the initials of *pie* and *tie,* and we can only blame the tangled history of our language for the absurdity of having four different ways to write the sound of *k.* Germanic languages more often use *k* for this speech sound, while *q* and *c* are more frequent in Romance. I will use *c* in the conservative trial, for words such as *cup, keep,* and *back,* but *k* in the radical trial. The ridiculously redundant *ck* deserves a peaceful burial.

If we ignore the *Kwik Kwality Kleaners*, *qu* is the only spelling that we now use for what we might otherwise write as *kw* or *cw*: *quality*, *quiet*, *bequest*. To retain *qu* would be unlikely to give anyone a spelling problem, and it would bring a comforting island of familiarity to an otherwise much-changed orthography, but it would surely offend the more dogmatic kind of reformer. The conservative choice would be *qu*, the radical one *kw*. I will use *kw* and the *Kwik Kwality Kleaners* only for the radical trial.

**ch**. We use *ch* or, occasionally, *tch* for the phoneme of *church*, *Charlie*, *pitcher*, and *rich*. Sometimes, *ch* does worm its way into words where it has no business, such as *chicanery* and *chaos*, but these can be easily repaired. If we use *k* rather than *c* to start off *kakes* and *kookys*, and if we use *s* consistently for words like *sity* and *juisy*, then the *h* of *ch* would become completely redundant. We could then be rid of the useless *h* and write a simple *c*. That would save a few key strokes and even fewer drops of ink, but not much else. For the conservative trial I will retain the *ch* of *cheez*, *choklut*, and *lunch*. For the radical trial I will use the less conventional but more parsimonious *ceez*, *coklət*, and *lunc*.

**hw/w**. The contrast between *hw* and *w*, in such pairs as *where/wear*, *which/witch*, and *whether/weather*, is disappearing from many spoken accents of English, in both England and North America. I do not know whether the *h* hangs on securely enough in the accents of Scotland and Ireland to warrant its retention in a revised spelling. I use *wh* for the conservative trial, but will drop the *h* in favor of a lonely *w* for the radical trial.

Finally, a considerable number of "silent" consonants, such as those in *calm*, *debt*, and *subtle*, ought to be quietly but firmly cast away. Minority spellings such as the *gh* of *rough* and the *ph* of *photo* could be easily regularized as *f*. There are better ways to learn about etymology than to force six-year-olds to memorize which words need *ph* and which need *gh*.

**Table 11.1** Consonants

| Conservative | Radical | |
| --- | --- | --- |
| th | th | thigh, think, ether, bath |
| th | dh | thy, these, bother, bathe |
| zh | zh | measure, beige, leisure |
| qu | kw | quick, quiet, quit, liquid |
| c | k | cup, keep, soccer, kick |
| ch | c | cheese, child, church |
| wh | w | why, when, wheel, whine |
| f | f | feel, phone, rough, off |
| s | s | cycle, messy, sit, boss |

Table 11.1 lists the consonant letters that I will use in the two trials when they differ from our present spelling conventions. Other consonants can retain their traditional values, but they ought to be regularized. In both the conservative and radical trials, for example, *busy* should lose its *s* and gain a *z*. An *s* should replace the *c* of *nice* and *mice*.

## Vowels

Bringing order to the way we write our vowels is, to put it gently, a rather more challenging task than fiddling with our consonants. In part, this is because our spoken vowels are inherently more complex than our spoken consonants, but even more, it is because English vowels are far more variable, from one accent to another, than its consonants are. This means that fixing the vowels needs more compromises than fixing the consonants. Most important, the written vowels of our present spelling give us much less to build on than our relatively orderly written consonants. Our vowels confront us with a vast confusion of choices.

The method that I follow is straightforward. I have selected a letter or digraph with which to spell each of the seventeen non-rhotic and twelve rhotic sets that I described in Chapter 9 (see Figures 9.1 and 9.2) . These sets were established by J. C. Wells in his *Accents of English* (1982), except that I added five new sets to his list. It requires no special imagination to assign the letter *i* to words of the KIT set. *Bit, pin, pill, simple*, and hundreds of other words can keep their familiar *i*. *Women, busy, myth*, and *sieve* would need to be re-spelled. They might turn out to look something like *wimen, bizy, mith*, and *siv*. *Sign, mine*, and many other words would need to have their *i* replaced by something else. To a skilled reader of English, these new spellings are likely to seem childish, or even illiterate, but the consistent spelling of this and other speech sounds would hugely ease the burden on the several million English-speaking children who start school each year. They would learn to read their language much more easily than they do now, and they would not be even slightly put off by the childish nature of the spelling.

In assigning letters or digraphs to the lexical sets, we might try, conservatively, to hang on to as much of our traditional spelling as possible. Or we might try, radically, to achieve the most orderly and coherent spelling that we can devise. Conservative continuity would be the less disruptive, but too much conservatism would undermine the whole point of reform. If we were starting from scratch to design an alphabet for a language that had never before been written, we would certainly choose something very different from our familiar English orthography. Any realistic reform would fall somewhere between the extremes of changing nothing at all and starting totally fresh.

Table 11.2 lists the vowel letters that I use for the two trials. For the conservative trial I try to minimize the difference from our traditional spelling, but no serious reform of the English vowels could avoid some major changes from our present spelling. For the radical trial, I try, instead, to minimize the irregularities of the spelling, but still cling to tradition wherever it seems natural to do so. With just one exception, I have limited the spelling in both trials to our familiar twenty-six letters. The exception is the linguist's schwa (ə), and even that I use only in the radical trial. If we had a letter that could naturally and easily represent a schwa, we could more easily distinguish it from the full vowels, but we have no such letter. I would not really recommend alarming conservative readers by using such an unfamiliar letter as a schwa. Nevertheless, for the radical trial only, I will use ə to represent the common unstressed vowel of such words as *əbuv*, *kəlaps*, and *pokət*.

**Table 11.2** Vowels

| Non-*r* vowels | | | *r* vowels | | |
|---|---|---|---|---|---|
| | Conservative trial | Radical trial | | Conservative trial | Radical trial |
| KIT | i | i | SPIRIT (iv) | ir | ir |
| | | | NEAR | ear | iər |
| | | | SQUARE/MARY | air | eər |
| DRESS | e | e | MERRY (iv) | err | err |
| TRAP | a | ae | MARRY (iv) | arr | arr |
| BATH | aa | a | START | ar | ar |
| PALM | ah | aa | | | |
| LOT | o | o | HORRID (iv) | orr | orr |
| CLOTH | au | ou | NORTH | or | or |
| THOUGHT | aw | au | FORCE | oar | oər |
| FOOT | ou | oo | CURE | oor | uər |
| STRUT | u | u | CURRY (iv) | urr | urr |
| MOUTH | ow | aw | NURSE | ur | ur |
| GOAT | oa | ow | | | |
| GOOSE | oo | uw | Unstressed vowels | | |
| FLEECE | ee | iy | lettER | er | er |
| FACE | ai | ey | commA | u | ə |
| PRICE | ie | ay | happY | y | iy |
| CHOICE | oi | oy | | | |
| | | | (iv intervocalic only) | | |

Wells recognizes two other unstressed vowels in addition to the ordinary schwa. These are the vowels in the unstressed second syllables of *letter* and *happy*; *er* is a satisfactory spelling for the unstressed final syllable of *letter*, and *y* or *iy* should do for the unstressed vowel in *happy*. In the conservative trial I use *u* for the ordinary schwa of *commu* and *buleev*. Many other choices would, of course, be possible. Note that in sets marked with "iv" (intervocalic), *r*s that have vowels both before and after are always pronounced.

## Conservative Trial

My conservative and radical re-spellings are illustrated here by the first few paragraphs of Jane Austen's *Pride and Prejudice*. Even readers who are most skeptical about spelling reform must grant that the re-spelled passages are not terribly difficult to read. No doubt, they look peculiar, and perhaps they look childish, but they are understandable. They would not force any reader of English to go back to school in order to learn to read again. No one would have to lug around a dictionary in order to figure out what the clumps of letters mean. At the same time, even the most passionate enthusiast for spelling reform must grant that the re-spellings slow reading down. It drags. Fluent readers of traditional spelling will need to pause repeatedly to sound out words. With time and practice, reading would gradually speed up again, but we would all need to start by relying on the context, and on relatively laborious sounding-out, in order to understand some of the words. With enough experience, the unfamiliar letter combinations would seem less strange until, finally, the sentences would be understood as quickly and easily as our sentences are understood now. Still, regaining the ability to take in entire words or phrases with a single saccade would need time and plenty of patience.

"*The*" gives us an awkward problem. It is usually pronounced as *thə*, but before a vowel it becomes *thee*. "*The*" is such a common word that, whatever its spelling, it would be quickly learned, so it is not really necessary to change its spelling before vowels. I use a conservative *the* in the conservative trial, but I alternate between *dhə* and *dhiy* in the radical trial.

The first trial is conservative only by comparison with the even less conservative re-spelling of the radical trial. Many other re-spellings would, of course, be possible and the two spellings offered here are meant to be no more than suggestive. They are not serious proposals for a reformed English spelling. Using the choices for the conservative trial, Jane Austen's *Pride and Prejudice* would begin as shown on page 144.

## Radical Trial

The second, and more radical, trial shares a good many spellings with the conservative trial but it deviates somewhat further from our traditional spelling. Two changes are particularly noticeable. First, many diphthongs have been spelled as if they consisted of two parts. The first part is much like an ordinary vowel, while the second part represents a very short movement of the tongue or lips that linguists call an "off-glide." In Mainstream American, though less clearly in Mainstream English, the FLEECE, FACE, PRICE, and CHOICE vowels end in a slight *y*-like off-glide, so they are all spelled here with a final *y: fliys, feys, prays, coys* (choice). Similarly, the MOUTH, GOAT, and GOOSE vowels end with a *w*-like off-glide, so they are written as *mawth, gowt, guws*. In Mainstream American, the *-r* that follows a vowel can be regarded as a third off-glide: *spirit, start, north, nurse,* and so on.

The second change from the conservative trial is that I use a schwa, *ə*, for the unstressed neutral vowel. The difficulties of using a schwa were discussed in Chapter 9. Apart from the resistance that could be expected from conservative readers, the worst, and probably fatal, problem with *ə* is its absence from most keyboards.

## The (Almost) Last Word

Designing a better spelling system for English is a pleasant game. Anyone can play. Many spellings have been proposed that would be far better than our present one. Those that are included in the Appendix at the end of the book show that, although reformers have come at different times and from different places, their proposals have much in common. Many of the changes that have been proposed would immediately make reading much easier to learn. Even a quick scan of the examples given in the Appendix will show that reformers, over the course of many years and speaking very different accents, have proposed spelling systems that have much in common.

Far more difficult than designing a better spelling system is, first, reaching wide agreement on one particular set of reforms and, second, persuading everyone who can already read to accept the changes. These have always been the stumbling blocks. Most adults (though not those of us who have always been incompetent spellers) seem to have forgotten their own struggles when first learning to read and write. Having no way of knowing how much more easily literacy can be gained in a language with a rational spelling, English speakers generally imagine that it is normal for children to take several years to gain full competence in

# Conservative Trial

## Chapter Wun

It iz u trooth yoonivursuly acnolijd that u singgul man in puzeshun uv u goud forchoon must bee in waunt uv u wief.

However litul noan the feelingz or vyooz uv such u man mai bee aun hiz furst enturing u naiburhoud, this trooth iz soa wel ficst in the miendz uv the surownding famleez that hee iz cunsidurd az the rietfoul property uv sum wun or uther uv thair dawterz.

"Mie dear Mr. Benut," sed hiz laidy too him wun dai, "hav yoo hurd that Netherfeeld Parc iz let at last?"

Mr. Benut reeplied that hee had not. "But it iz," reeturnd shee; "for Mrs. Laung haz just been hear, and shee toald mee awl ubowt it."

Mr. Benut maid noa ansur.

"Doo not yoo waunt too noa hoo haz taicun it?" cried hiz wief impaishuntly.

"Yoo waunt too tel mee, and ai hav noa ubjecshun too hearing it."

That wuz invitaishun unuf.

"Wie mie dear, yoo must noa, Mrs. Laung sez that Netherfeeld iz taicun bie u yung man uv larj forchoon frum the north of Inglund; that hee caim down on Munday in u shaiz and foar too see the plais, and wuz soa much deelaitud with it that hee ugreed with Mr. Moris imeedeeutly; that hee iz too taic puzeshun bufor Miculmus, and sum uv hiz survunts ar too bee in the hows bie the end uv necst weec."

"Whut iz hiz naim?"

"Binglee."

"Iz hee marreed or singgul?"

"Oa! singgul mai dear, too bee shoor. U singgul man uv larj forchoon; for or fiev thowzund u year. Whut a fien thing for ow gurlz."

"How soa? How can it ufect them?"

"Mai dear Mr. Benut," reeplied hiz wief, "how can yoo bee soa taiersum! Yoo must noa that ie am thingking uv hiz marrying wun uv them."

"Iz that hiz deezien in setuling hear?"

"Deezien! Nonsens, how can yoo tawk soa! But it iz verry liecly that hee mai fawl in luv with wun uv them, and thairfor yoo must vizit him az soon az hee cumz."

"Ie see noa ucaizhun for that. Yoo and the gurlz mai goa, or yoo mai send them bai themselvz, which perhaps wil bee stil beter, for az yoo ar az hansum az eny uv them, Mr. Binglee miet liek yoo the best uv the party."

"Mie dear, yoo flater mee. Ie surtunly *hav* had mie shair of byooty, but ie doo not preetend too bee enything ecstrordinery now. When u woumun haz fiev groan-up dawterz, shee awt too giv oaver thingking uv her oan byooty."

# Radical Trial

## Capter Wun

It iz ə truwth yuwniversəliy aeknolijd dhaet ə singgəl maen in pəzeshən əv ə good forcuwn must biy in wount əv ə wayf.

Hawever litəl nown dhə fiylingz or vyuwz uv suc ə maen mey biy oun hiz furst entering ə neyberhood, dhis truwth iz sow wel fikst in dhə mayndz uv dhə serawnding famliyz dhaet hiy iz kənsiderd az dhə raytfool propertiy uv sum wun or udher uv theər dauterz.

"May diər Mr. Benət," sed hiz leydiy tuw him wun dey, "haev yuw hurd dhaet Nedherfiyld Park iz let aet laest?"

Mr. Benət riyplayd thaet hiy haed not. "But it iz," riyturnd shiy; "for Mrs. Loung haz just biyn hiər aend shiy towld miy aul əbawt it."

Mr. Benət meyd now aenser.

"Duw not yuw wount tuw now huw haez teykən it?" krayd hiz wayf impeyshəntliy.

"Yuw wont too tel miy aend ay haev now əbjekshən tuw hiəring it."

Dhaet wuz inviteyshən ənuf.

"Way may diər, yuw must now, Mrs. Loung sez that Nedherfiyld iz teykən bay u yung man uv larj forcuwn frəm dhə north uv Inglənd; dhat hiy keym dawn on Mundiy in u sheyz and foar tuw siy dhə pleys, and wuz sow muc diylaytəd widh it dhat hiy agriyd widt Mr. Morris imiydiyətliy; thaet hiy iz tuw teyk pəzeshən bəfoar Mikəlməs, and sum uv hiz servunts ar tuw biy in dhə haws bay dhee end uv nekst wiyk."

"Wut iz hiz neym?"

"Bingliy."

"Iz hiy marriyd or singgəl?"

"Ow! singgəl, may diər, tuw biy shuər! ə singgul maen uv larj forchuwn; foar or fayv thawzənd ə yiər. Wut a fayn thing for awər gurlz."

"Haw sow? Haw kan it əfekt dhem?"

"May diər Mr. Benət," riplayd hiz wayf, "haw kaen yuw biy sow tayersum! Yuw must now dhaet ay am thingking uv hiz marriying wun uv them."

"Iz that hiz diyzayn in setəling hiər?"

"Diyzayn! Nonsens, haw kaen yuw tauk sow! But it iz verry laykliy dhat hiy mey faul in luv widh wun uv dhem, aend dheərfor yuw must vizit him az suwn az hiy kumz."

"Ay siy now əkeyzhun for dhat. Yuw aend dhə gurlz mey gow, or yuw mey send dhem bay dhemselvz, wic perhaps wil biy stil beter, for az yuw ar az hansum az eny uv dhem, Mr. Bingliy mayt layk yuw dhə best uv dhe partiy."

"May diər, yuw flaeter miy. Ay surtunliy *haev* haed may sheər uv byuwtiy, but ay duw not priytend tuw biy eniything ekstrordəneriy naw. Wen ə woomən haez fayv grown-up dauterz, shiy aut tuw giv owver thing-king uv hur own byuwtiy."

reading. It is not normal at all, but rather it is the result of our complex and illogical spelling. The vested interest that good readers have in our traditional spelling, along with their ignorance about the ease with which literacy can be acquired when orthography is closer to speech, encourages skilled adult readers to dig in their heels in firm resistance to any change. Worst of all, our class-segregated society leaves many educated speakers ignorant of the many who fail. Vested interest and sheer ignorance have conspired to limit support for reform to an eccentric fringe of enthusiasts. It is very easy to forget, or simply to ignore, how many of our fellow citizens never manage to gain much skill with reading and writing. Illiterate adults are segregated by their poverty and they are badly over-represented in our prisons.

A more rational spelling would not be a magic solution to all our problems of illiteracy, but fixing our spelling ought to be one important part of any solution. Even the best spellers would, in the end, profit. Remember the Korean women who, through many generations, were able to pass down the ability to read Hangul, even without help from formal schooling. Would a better system of spelling English make it as easy for us to teach our children to read?

# 12 English Spelling: Optimal or Absurd?

English orthography, despite its often cited inconsistencies, comes remarkably close to being an optimal orthographic system for English.
Noam Chomsky and Morris Halle, *The Sound Pattern of English* (1968)

Here we have Noam Chomsky, certainly the most eminent linguist of the last half century, along with his only slightly less eminent collaborator Morris Halle, singing the virtues of English spelling. Their message seems unambiguous, and it grabs our attention because it flies so defiantly in the face of common sense. Must we take them seriously simply because we know them to be brilliant linguists? Or should we, instead, just laugh at the absurdity of their claim?

If we want to extract some sense from their assertion, we need to start by asking just what they could really have meant by calling our spelling "close to … optimal." Perhaps they simply wanted to remind us that many of our letters—such as *b*, *d*, *m*, *n*, and *p*—have entirely regular pronunciations. Perhaps they wanted to point out that pairs of letters such as *ch*, *sh*, and *ng* perform admirably to overcome the limitations of our meager supply of twenty-six single letters. Perhaps they would assert that a skilled reader can often make a very good guess about the pronunciation of an unknown word without ever needing to leaf through a dictionary for help. Try *ozocerite*, *tacamahac*, or *Chatelperonian*, or consider nonsense words such as *mipe*, *pring*, *trut*, or *pleet*. Who can have much doubt about how to pronounce these words and syllables? This hardly looks like chaos. We must give Chomsky and Halle their due: English spelling is by no means totally irrational.

When I first encountered the claim that our spelling is "near optimal," however, I shrugged it off as deliberately provocative. It looked like an effective way to dispose of the opposite fallacy—the notion that English spelling follows no rules at all—but I hardly imagined that anyone would take this new fallacy seriously. Nevertheless, the oracular statements of Noam Chomsky are difficult to shrug off. People who should know better really seem to have imagined that our spelling system is rather good.

Of course, it must be understood that Chomsky and Halle were looking for "underlying rules," rules that lie behind the superficial irregularities of casual speech, and they did, indeed, find many regularities. Still, in the face of seventeen ways to spell a single spoken vowel—*aisle*, *aye*, *height*, *stein*, *eye*, *child*, *diamond*, *indict*, *tie*, *bite*, *island*, *sign*, *high*, *guile*, *buy*, *dry*, and *dye*—it seems a bit rich to claim that our spelling is "remarkably close to being an optimal orthographic system for English." "Optimal" is not the word that comes most easily to mind. Admittedly, the vowel of *aisle* and *high* is an extreme example of orthographic chaos, but every one of our vowels can be spelled in more ways than one, and a half-dozen can be spelled in ten or more different ways.

Perhaps Chomsky and Halle were not thinking about the writer's problem of finding the right spelling for a known word, but of the reader's problem of finding the right word in a string of letters. But think of *busy, put, but, flu*. Here, the poor letter *u* can have any of four different pronunciations. Not a single one of our five vowel letters is limited to representing just one spoken vowel: *any, bat, palm, all; pretty, pet; bit, ski, price; women, do, mop, some*. So what were Chomsky and Halle trying to tell us? Were they being deliberately outrageous, hoping to catch the attention of their readers? If so, they were certainly successful. Some readers, who should have known better, meekly accepted their assertion that our orthography is "close to being optimal."

I hold a very different view of our spelling, of course. It is a view that was wonderfully expressed in a long poem called "The Chaos" that was written many years ago by a Netherlander named Gerald Nolst Trenité. An early version of the poem, with just 146 lines, was published in 1920, but between then and his death in 1946 Trenité kept adding to it. The final version reached 274 lines, and it is well worth a visit to the web to read it.[1] Here are its first five stanzas.

> Dearest *creature* in *creation*
> Studying English *pronunciation,*
>   I will teach you in my verse
>   Sounds like *corpse, corps, horse* and *worse.*

> I will keep you, *Susy, busy,*
> Make your *head* with *heat* grow dizzy.
>   *Tear* in eye, your dress you'll *tear*;
>   *Queer*, fair *seer, hear* my *prayer.*

> *Pray*, console your loving *poet,*
> Make my coat look *new*, dear, *sew* it!
>   Just compare *heart, hear* and *heard,*
>   *Dies* and *diet, lord* and *word.*

---

1.  "Chris Upward introduces The Classic Concordance of Cacographic Chaos," *Journal of the Simplified Spelling Society*, 1994/2: 27–30. (http://ncf.idallen.com/ english.html). Upward provides a useful and interesting commentary on the poem. To view various other versions, Google its first line: "Dearest creature in creation."

*Sword* and *sward, retain* and *Britain*
(Mind the latter how it's *written*).
   *Made* has not the sound of *bade*,
   *Say-said, pay-paid, laid* but *plaid*.

Now I surely will not *plague* you
With such words as *vague* and *ague*,
   But be careful how you *speak*.
   Say: *gush, bush, steak, streak, break, bleak*.

Sixty-three more stanzas follow in the same vein. The poem gives us hundreds of examples of vowels that have parallel spellings but differing pronunciations: *demon/lemon, heathen/heather, rounded/wounded, hood/hoot, valise/revise, friend/fiend, tomb/bomb/comb, bloat/broad, stranger/anger, daughter/laughter* and many more. The poem even gives a sample of word pairs that are (absurdly) spelled identically, even though they have both different meanings and different pronunciations: *minute, desert, buffet, gill, putting, invalid, Polish,tear*.

Trenité's poem is the perfect antidote to the strange idea that English spelling "comes remarkably close to being an optimal orthographic system for English."

English spelling is, in fact, a very long way from optimal. I have no doubt that people differ greatly in their native ability to learn to spell, but I still find it puzzling that so many of my friends, starting with those with whom I shared third grade, and continuing with those with whom I share retirement, have found spelling so easy. I must have been just as puzzling to my teachers and my friends as they have been to me. A few children, at the opposite end from my spot on the bell curve, probably learned to spell each word the first time they saw it, but the bulk of English-speaking children must be in the middle of the range. These are the children who never spelled so badly that they dreaded a spelling bee, and who have forgotten the years when mistakes were inevitable. Some kind of amnesia must set in so they don't remember the struggle. Even children in the middle of the curve, those who were neither brilliant at spelling nor hopeless, must have used a great deal of time and energy in learning to spell—time and energy that could have been much better used for something more important.

The poor marks that I always received in English were surely due, at least in part, to my spelling. The marks persuaded me that my verbal aptitude was on the frail side, and I thought I had better stick to technical subjects where, I presumed, verbal aptitude was less crucial. Fortunately, I managed to hang in long enough to reach the stage where I could find people who would not only type my papers but correct my spelling. Suddenly I overcame my fear of writing, and suddenly my marks improved.

Thousands of children in English-speaking countries are less fortunate than I was. Many have parents who are themselves poorly educated and who cannot help their children when the schools fail them. Shockingly high numbers of children never learn to read or write well enough to participate fully in our literate society. Of course spelling is not the only reason for our high rates of illiteracy, but it is an important piece of the problem and it could be changed if only we had the will. Tragically, all the people with the power to bring change also have a vested interest in the absurd spelling that they worked so hard to learn. They will gain nothing from spelling reform.

A century ago, even as late as the experiments with ITA in the 1960s, spelling reform was a respectable topic that respectable people could support. Since then, it has been little more than a game for a few eccentrics. The last few years, however, have seen the publication of three fine books on the nature and history of English spelling: David Wolman's *Righting the Mother Tongue* (2008), Simon Horobin's *Does Spelling Matter?* (2013), and David Crystal's *Spell It Out* (2012). Wolman, a confessed bad speller, does not take a decisive stand on reform, but Horobin and Crystal both come down firmly against it. We have, they argue, far too much invested in our present orthography for a reform to be feasible. Their conservatism saddens me. Vested interest is difficult to overcome, and it can be difficult to recognize, even in oneself. At least, however, these authors are bringing spelling back into public view.

This book is an argument for the other side.

# Appendix
# The Table of Vowels

## Introduction

The table of vowels on pages 160–4 gives a selection of the many ways by which the spoken vowels of English have been represented on paper. Each column shows the symbols that have been used by a linguist, or by a dictionary, or proposed by a hopeful spelling reformer. Each row shows the symbols that have been used to represent one of the distinctive spoken vowels of the English language.

The rows are organized, primarily, according to the classification of vowels that J. C. Wells used in his book *Accents of English* (1982). I describe this classification in some detail in Chapter 9. As I explained there, I have found it useful to add five new sets to the twenty-four sets of stressed vowels that Wells recognized. These five sets all have intervocalic *r*s, and each of them is given a row in the table, along with rows for the twenty-four sets of stressed vowels that Wells both recognized and named.

In addition to the twenty-nine sets of stressed vowels, the table also has rows for three sets of unstressed vowels. Wells named these sets "lettER," "happY," and "commA." I have added one final row for what I will call the FEUD set, which I will explain below.

It is important to emphasize the fact that the vowels of most accents of English can, without much difficulty, be fitted into this classification. The most important exception is that some accents in Scotland and Ireland make finer distinctions among the vowels of the NURSE set than are found in most other accents of English (see the Appendix to Chapter 9). Every accent makes most of the phonological distinctions that this classification allows for, but no single accent makes them all. The fact that it is possible to group our vowels in this way suggests an encouraging conclusion: whatever their diversity, all the accents of English really do have a great deal in common. We are right to consider them all to be varieties of a single language, and we are on firm ground in wanting to construct a writing system that can be used by speakers of all our many accents. No other language, not French, German or Russian, to say nothing of Chinese or Zulu, has vowels that could be forced into this classification. Speakers who justify their own resistance to reform by arguing that English accents are too diverse to allow an orthography that is both uniform and phonologically reasonable is, quite simply, wrong.

## Rows

Twenty-four of the thirty-three rows of vowel sets that are shown in the table correspond to the sets of stressed vowels that J. C. Wells recognized in his *Accents of English* (1982). I have labeled these twenty-four rows with the key words that Wells assigned to them: KIT, DRESS, TRAP, and so on. To Wells's twenty-four sets, I have added five other sets whose *r*s are always intervocalic. These sets were described in Chapter 9 (pages 111–22), where I called them the SPIRIT, MERRY, MARRY, HORRID, and CURRY sets. Because the *r*s of these five new sets are always followed by another vowel, they are always fully pronounced, even by speakers of non-rhotic accents such as Mainstream English. These intervocalic *r*s are never lost in the way final and preconsonantal *r*s are lost in non-rhotic accents (as in *far away*, but *fa from town*). The five vowel sets that I have added to Wells's inventory, and that always have an "intervocalic" *r*, are marked in the table as "iv."

In addition to these sets of stressed vowels, Wells also recognized three sets of unstressed vowels that he called lettER, happY, and commA. These sets will be found near the bottom of the table.

I have added one final vowel set to the inventory of rows, but only because a number of proposals for reformed spellings treat its vowel as distinctive. This is the vowel of words such as *few*, *cute*, and *beauty*, which is sometimes referred to as "long *u*." These words have a vowel that is similar to the GOOSE vowel, but it is preceded by *y*: *fyoo*, *cyoot*, *byooty*. If the *y* in these words is considered to be a part of the vowel, then the table needs a row for words that have this "long *u*." Implicitly, however, Wells treats this *y* not as a part of the vowel but, rather, as a consonant that precedes the vowel. Often, as in *few*, *beauty*, and *cute*, it can be regarded as part of a consonant cluster: *fy*, *by*, *cy*. Wells does not give a special place for "long u" in his classification of vowels, and I follow Wells by treating the *y* as a consonant, either part of a cluster, as in *fyoo* and *pyootrid*, or alone as in *yoo* and *yoosful*. In order to accommodate proposals for reformed spellings that give a special place to the vowel of *feud*, *putrid*, and *cute*, I have added a row for it at the bottom of the table, and I have named it the FEUD vowel.

In British accents this "long *u*" is found in some words that begin with *t*, *d*, or *n*, as in *tyune*, *nyew*, and *dyew*. The *y* after these consonants has been lost from most North American accents. This is why the English sometimes think Americans sound *stoopid* when they say *stoopid* rather that *styoopid*. If the *y* of such words as *few*, *beauty*, *new*, and *stupid* is treated as forming a cluster with the preceding consonant (*fyew*, *byeauty*, *nyew*, *styupid*), no separate FEUD vowel needs to be recognized. Spelling proposals that treat the *y*, implicitly, as a part of an initial cluster, rather than as a component of the vowel, lack an entry for the FEUD vowel.

In Chapter 9, all the sets of stressed vowels are treated as different from one another because, in one accent or another, every set contrasts with every other set. In no single accent, however, does every set contrast with every other set. Every accent has a few merged sets, but the mergers differ from one accent to another. The most difficult problems that the spelling reformer must cope with arise from the varied ways in which the vowel sets have merged in different accents. Figures 9.1 and 9.2 (pages 116 and 117) should help readers to visualize the differing mergings of the Mainstream American and Mainstream English accents.

The most important way in which this vowel classification differs from that of Wells is my sharp separation of the sets that have post-vocalic *r*s in rhotic accents from the sets that do not have them. I feel that this separation is called for because, in the history of the English accents, vowels that are, or that once were, followed by *r* have developed in very different ways from vowels that have no history of a following *r*. English spelling reform is made considerably more challenging because of the divergent ways in which *r*, and the vowels that now precede *r* or that did precede *r* in the past, have developed over the course of the last few centuries.

## Columns

Each column of the table shows a transcription that has been used, or at least proposed, as a way to represent the English vowels. These transcriptions are of three types. Columns 1 to 7 give transcriptions that have been used by linguists to represent the vowels of several English accents. The symbols in most of these columns are those that were used by J. C. Wells, but other linguists have used very similar sets of symbols. Column 3 shows an alternative transcription for one form of what I have called "Mainstream American". This represents the author's speech, which is a rather ordinary form of American English. I find this one more revealing than the transcription used by Wells, but this is an esthetic preference and it implies no significant difference in our understanding of the General American accent.

Columns 8 to 15 give the symbols used by several dictionaries to show the pronunciation of British, American, or Australian English.

The columns from 16 onward all show transcriptions that have been proposed as reformed spellings for English. Some were proposed for special purposes, many were proposed in the rather touching hope that they would replace our traditional spelling.

More detailed information for each column follows.

## Linguistic Transcriptions

**1.** "RP" or "Received Pronunciation" was the term that Wells (henceforth referred to as JCW) used for the most prominent British pronunciation of his day. I prefer to use "Mainstream English" for the respectable accent that is now widely used in England, but for the purpose of this column there is little difference. Most of the symbols in the RP/Mainstream English column are those used by Wells, in his *Accents of English*, but I have added "(r)" for the sets whose vowels can be (but are not always) followed immediately by a pronounced *r*. The parentheses suggest the variability of this *r* in RP/ Mainstream English and in other non-rhotic accents. The *r* is pronounced when a vowel follows, but not when a consonant follows: *nea the house* but *near a house; the sofa by the door*, but *the sofar in the hall.*

Wells groups the words of the lexical sets to which I give the names SPIRIT, MERRY, MARRY, HORRID, and CURRY with, respectively, the KIT, DRESS, TRAP, CLOTH, and STRUT sets, all of which are otherwise non-rhotic. The *r*s of my five added sets are *always* followed by a vowel, so these *r*s are *always* pronounced, even in non-rhotic accents. For that reason, the *r*s of these sets are shown, in column 1, without parentheses.

JCW's transcription shows the following mergers: BATH = PALM = START; LOT = CLOTH = HORRID; THOUGHT = NORTH = FORCE; STRUT = CURRY; lettER = commA. Some Mainstream English speakers, though not all, also merge the CURE vowels with the THOUGHT, NORTH, and FORCE vowels.

**2.** Mainstream American/GenAm. "GenAm" was Wells's term for the most widespread North American accent. I use "Mainstream American." The symbols in the second column are those used by JCW, except that I have added *r*, or used *ɚ* for those sets that speakers of Mainstream English always pronounce with a rhotic *r*.

**3.** Mainstream American 2. The third column offers an alternative transcription for one variety of North American English, that of the present author. The differences between JCW's transcription and mine are minor, but mine could be regarded as somewhat more "phonological," while JCW's stays closer to the phonetics. The FORCE and NORTH vowels remain distinct in some American accents but they have merged in mine. My symbols imply that my accent has just seven stressed monophthongal vowels: *i, e, æ, a, o, ʋ,* and *ʌ*. All other stressed vowels can be assigned to one of three sets of diphthongs which are distinguished from one another by three contrasting off-glides: *w, y,* or *r*. My accent is characterized by the following mergers: TRAP = BATH; PALM = LOT; CLOTH = THOUGHT; SPIRIT = NEAR; SQUARE = MERRY = MARRY; HORRID = NORTH = FORCE; CURRY = NURSE. These mergers are all widespread in North American accents of English, although, even among Americans, they are by no means universal.

**4 to 7** (London, Wales, Scotland, Ireland). These four columns give JCW's symbols for several regional accents of the British Isles. Where two alternatives are shown in a single cell, it means that there is variability within the accent. I have no certain knowledge of the pronunciation of the vowels of the SPIRIT, MERRY, MARRY, HORRID, or CURRY sets in these non-Mainstream English/NonRP accents, but JCW groups the words of these five sets with, respectively, his KIT, DRESS, TRAP, CLOTH, and STRUT sets, so I presume that, except for the added *r*, the vowel of SPIRIT is pronounced like the vowel of KIT, and so on. In Ireland and Scotland the *r*s of these five sets are always pronounced (which is to say that these accents are rhotic), so I show them in the table with a following *r*. The accents of London and Wales are non-rhotic, so an *r* is heard only when a vowel follows. I write these variable *r*s as "(r)." JCW gives additional examples for some sets, a few of which I have included in the appropriate cells of the table. The blanks for the HORRID set in the Irish and Scottish columns are an admission of my own ignorance.

Some Scottish and Irish accents of English have a serious complication: for some Scottish and Irish speakers, the words that are shown with the NURSE vowel are divided among two or even three sets, each with contrasting vowels. These preserve old distinctions that have disappeared in all other accents of modern English. In some Scottish accents, *dirt* and *bird* have ɪr; *pert* and *heard* have ɛr; *hurt* and *word* have ʌr (Wells 1982: 409). These distinctions are not reflected in JCW's vowel sets, or in mine, and the distinctions are not universal, even in Scotland or Ireland. I discuss this aspect of the Irish and Scottish accents in the Appendix to Chapter 9, but I leave open the question of whether these vowel contrasts are sufficiently widespread to justify contrastive spellings in a reformed orthography.

Of course, there is much variability within each of these accents, but I follow JCW's transcriptions, which represent accents that are typical and widespread.

## Dictionary Keys

The symbols in columns 8 to 15 have been used as guides to pronunciation in several British, Australian and American dictionaries. The *Longman Pronunciation Dictionary* gives both British and American pronunciations, but the others confine themselves to the pronunciation of a single accent. It is immediately clear that the *OED* and the *Cambridge English Pronouncing Dictionary* are British, because vowels of the LOT and CLOTH sets are spelled in the same way, as are the vowels of the BATH and PALM sets. American dictionaries generally indicate, instead, the identity of the TRAP and BATH sets, and also of the CLOTH and THOUGHT sets. British dictionaries use more symbols derived from linguistic phonetics. American dictionaries more often attach diacritical marks ("accents") to the letters in order to distinguish the different speech sounds.

The alternative spellings that are used by several of the American dictionaries are simply a recognition that accents in the United States can vary.

**8.** *The Oxford English Dictionary*, 2nd. edition. Oxford: Oxford University Press, 1989. The use of ɒ for both the LOT and CLOTH vowels, and the use of ɑ: for both the BATH and PALM vowels clearly shows that the transcription represents a British accent rather than an American one. The parenthesized *r*s are pronounced only when a vowel follows. This is the defining characteristic of a non-rhotic accent. Intervocalic *r*s are always pronounced, so sets whose *r*s are always intervocalic are written without parentheses.

**9.** *Cambridge English Pronouncing Dictionary*. Cambridge and New York: Cambridge University Press, 2006. The symbols used in this dictionary differ only in very minor ways from those used in the 1989 *OED*.

**10.** *Australian Oxford Dictionary*. Oxford and Melbourne: Oxford University Press, 2004. A few of the symbols used in the *AOD* differ from those in the *OED*. Presumably, these represent different phonetic realizations of the vowels. The vowel *system* shown in the *AOD* (the way in which words are grouped as having the same or different vowels) is virtually identical to the Mainstream English system shown by the *OED*, however.

**11 and 12.** *Longman Pronunciation Dictionary*, 3rd. edition (2008). This pronouncing dictionary gives pronunciations for both RP/Mainstream English and GenAm/Mainstream American. The GenAm transcription used in the Longman dictionary avoids the accent marks that are used by most American publishers. This is, by far, the best of any of the dictionaries that are included here in showing the types and range of variations that characterize the pronunciation of many words.

**13.** *Webster's New International Dictionary of the English Language*. Springfield, MA: G. & C. Merriam Company (1944). This is the largest American dictionary and the closest the United States comes to a rival of the *OED*. The phonetic symbols (diacritics) that are used for three of the vowel sets are unavailable to me, so I have been forced to make substitutions: 1. Instead of ŏŏ, a single, but longer, breve mark should stretch over both vowel letters. 2. Instead of ōō, a single long mark should stretch over both letters. 3. ę, which represents the vowel of the NEAR set, should have a macron above it, in addition to the small hook below.

**14.** *Funk & Wagnalls Standard Dictionary of the English Language.* New York and London: Funk & Wagnalls, 1973. This and *The American College Dictionary* use symbols that are very similar to Webster's. They both share the stretched breve mark and the stretched macron with *Webster's New International.*

**15.** *The American College Dictionary.* Clarence L. Barnhart (ed.). New York: Harper & Brothers Publishers, 1950.

## Reform Proposals

Columns 16 through 26 show the symbols that have been used in a number of proposals for revised English spellings. In addition to the symbols used for each vowel, several of these columns have examples of words for which the symbol is intended.

**16.** A. J. Ellis. The symbols in this column are those proposed in a remarkable book called *A Plea for Phonetic Spelling*, written by a man named Alexander John Ellis, and published in 1848. Unlike more recent spelling reformers, Ellis does not seem to have given his system a new name, but simply called it the "Phonetic Alphabet." The symbols that Ellis used are often different from any that would be proposed today, but his *system*, as far as it goes, is very close to more modern proposals. Ellis was English, so he probably would have taken it for granted that his British readers would use the same vowel for both the BATH and PALM words, but a different vowel for both the CLOTH and LOT words, although his examples do not make that definite. Ellis really does give "ope," whatever that may have meant to him, as his example for vowels like that of "GOAT." Typographic limitations mean that a few of the symbols shown in the table are slightly different from those found in Ellis's book. Most seriously, I have not been able to reproduce anything close to the symbol he used for the GOOSE vowel. It was similar to "ɯ," but the central ascending spike was much shorter than the left and right spikes. Ellis made no special provision for vowels that were followed by *r*.

**17.** Nue Speling/New Spelling. This spelling system was once supported by the Simplified Spelling Society of Great Britain. It is described by P. A. D. MacCarthy (1969). His article does not give spellings for the vowels of the BATH, CLOTH, SPIRIT, or MERRY sets. Words of both the NORTH and FORCE sets seem to be spelled with *or*. Nue Speling uses *uer* for words of the CURE set in which the spoken vowel begins with a *y*. It has *uur* for *poor* and other words that have the CURE vowel but that lack a preceding *y* sound. Thus Nue Speling would have *kuer* "cure," but *tuur* "tour." http://www.spellingsociety. org/journals/pamflets/p12ns90.php

**18.** Regspel/Traditional Spelling Regularized. Regspel is the work of Stephen Linstead of the English Spelling Society. He has proposed several versions, this one being the latest that I am aware of: http://spellingsociety. org/uploaded_views/pv15linstead-personal-view1419715177.pdf

**19.** World English Spelling. WES was a reform proposal by the US-based Simplified Spelling Society, and is described by Godfrey Dewey in *English Spelling* (1971). In addition to *er*, which is used in unstressed syllables (*further, coller, moter)*, WES offers *ur* for stressed syllables (*hur, urly, furst, wurk, murmur)*.

**20.** Truespel. The American roots of Truespel are shown clearly by the sets that it groups together: PALM = LOT; CLOTH = THOUGHT; SQUARE = MERRY = MARRY. Like the vowels of *goose* and *food*, the vowels of *new* and *due* are spelled *ue*, with no indication of the preceding *y* that is found in the Mainstream English pronunciation of these words. *Few* and *beauty*, however, are spelled *fyu* and *byutee*. All these spellings reflect American pronunciation rather than British. Truespel has an automated re-speller that is easy to use: type in a text using traditional spelling, hit a key, and get a translation into Truespel: http://truespel.com

**21.** NuEnglish. This is a second American proposal for which there is a computerized re-speller and, as with Truespel, it is unambiguously American. Its preferred spelling for the "long" vowels (pronounced like their names) uses a macron: $\bar{a}, \bar{e}, \bar{\imath}, \bar{o}, \bar{u}$, but digraphs with *e* are offered as alternatives: *ae, ee, ie, oe, ue*. The re-speller will translate a text into NuEnglish. After reaching the link, click on the "re-speller" button at the top: http:// nuenglish.org

**22.** SoundSpel. This spelling apparently dates back to the early part of the twentieth century. It was, at one time, endorsed by something called "The American Literary Council." It has a more nuanced spelling of the *r* vowels than many proposed reforms: http://en.wikipedia.org/wiki/SoundSpel

**23.** Rifaurmd Lojikl Inglish. This is still another American product, for which an electronic translator, different from the one used for Truespel, is available. Rifaurmd Lojikl Inglish reveals its American origins in the usual way: the vowels of the TRAP and BATH sets are spelled alike, as are the vowels of the CLOTH and THOUGHT sets. Translators for Rifaurmd Lojikl Inglish, and for several other re-spellings, can be found at http://www. wyrdplay.org/spelling-converter.html

**24.** ITA. The Initial Teaching Alphabet was promoted by Sir James Pitman, and it was tried out extensively during the 1960s in both British and American schools. It was intended as an easy alphabet for children, one that could get them started quickly with reading. It was hoped that after a year or two with ITA the transition to traditional spelling would be reasonably easy. ITA is described at some length in Chapter 5.

**25.** Shavian. These symbols were designed by Kingsley Read, the winner of a contest funded by the will of George Bernard Shaw. The contestants were required to design a new alphabet for English. Read's symbols are cursive, designed to be written rapidly, but they do not resemble any familiar alphabet. They have never been taken seriously as a possible alphabet for practical use. It is not clear how words of the BATH and CLOTH lexical sets should be written. http://www.omniglot.com/writing/shavian. htm

**26.** Deseret. This alphabet was invented by Mormons in the mid-nineteenth century and promoted, for a time, by the Mormon Church. Parts of the Book of Mormon and four other books were printed in Deseret but, even among Mormons, the alphabet did not finally catch on as an alternative to our traditional alphabet. The descriptions of the vowels ("Short I," "Long O," etc.) are those given in the Omniglot source, but I have had to use some guesswork in my identification of the Deseret letters with the vowel sets used in the table. These guesses should not be relied on. http://www.omniglot.com/writing/deseret.htm

| | Key word (augmented from JCW) | 1 Mainstream English (JCW) | 2 Mainstream American (JCW) | 3 Mainstream American (RB) | 4 London (JCW) | 5 Wales (JCW) | 6 Scotland (JCW) | 7 Ireland (JCW) |
|---|---|---|---|---|---|---|---|---|
| **Non r-vowels** | KIT | ɪ | ɪ | i | ɪ | ɪ | ɪ | ɪ |
| | DRESS | e | ɛ | e | e | ɛ | ɛ | ɛ |
| | TRAP | æ | æ | æ | æ | a | a | æ |
| | BATH | ɑː | æ | æ | ɑː | a, aː | a | æ, aː |
| | PALM | ɑː(r) | ɑ | a | ɑː(r) | aː(r) | a | aː |
| | LOT | ɒ | ɑ | a | ɒ | ɒ | ɔ, ɑ | ɑ |
| | CLOTH | ɒ | ɔ | o | ɒ | ɒ, ɔː | ɔ, ɑ | ɒ, ɔː |
| | THOUGHT | ɔː(r) | ɔ | o | oː, ɔə(r) | ɔː(r) | ɔ | ɔː |
| | FOOT | ʊ | ʊ | ʊ | ʊ | ʊ | u | ʊ |
| | STRUT | ʌ | ʌ | ʌ | ʌ | ə | ʌ | ʌ |
| | MOUTH | aʊ | aʊ | aw | æʊ | əu | ʌu | aʊ |
| | GOAT | əʊ | o | ow | ʌʊ | ou | o | oː |
| | GOOSE | uː | u | uw | uː | uː | u | uː |
| | FLEECE | iː | i | iy | ii | iː | i | iː |
| | FACE | eɪ | eɪ | ey | ʌɪ | ei | e | eː |
| | PRICE | aɪ | aɪ | ay | ɑɪ | əi | ae, ʌi | aɪ |
| | CHOICE | ɔɪ | ɔɪ | oy | ɔɪ | ɔɪ | ɒɪ | ɔɪ |
| **r-vowels** | SPIRIT (iv) | ɪr | ɪr | ir | ɪr | ɪr | ɪr spirit (myrrh) | ɪ spirit, myrrh |
| | NEAR | ɪə(r) | ɪr | ir | iə(r) | jɜː(r), iːə(r) | ɪr beer, fierce, weary | iː beer, fierce |
| | SQUARE | ɛə(r) | ɛr | er | eə(r) | ɛː(r) | er fairy, air, scarce | eː air, fairy |
| | MERRY (iv) | er | ɛr | er | er | ɛr | ɛr ferry | ɛː ferry |
| | MARRY (iv) | ær | ɛr | er | ær | ar | ar marry | æ marry, Marion |
| | START | ɑː(r) | ɑr | ar | ɑː(r) | aː(r) | ar bar, start | aː bar, barn |
| | HORRID (iv) | ɒr | ɔr | or | ɒr | ɒr, ɔːr | | |
| | NORTH | ɔː(r) | ɔr | or | oː, ɔə(r) | ɔː(r) | ɔr sorry, war | ɒr, ɔːr for, war, horse |
| | FORCE | ɔː(r) | or | or | oː, ɔə(r) | ɔː(r) | or story, hoarse, wore | oːr wore, hoarse |
| | CURE | ʊə(r) | ʊr | ur | uə(r) | uːə(r) | ur jury, poor, gourd | uːr poor, jury |
| | CURRY (iv) | ʌr | ɜr | ɝ | ʌr | ər | ʌr hurry | ʌr, ʊr hurry |
| | NURSE | ɜː(r) | ɜr | ɝ | ɜː(r) | ɜː(r) | ɜr, ʌr, ɪr pert, hurt, dirt, purr, gourd | ʌr, ɛr purr, nurse |
| | lettER | ə(r) | ər/ɚ | ɝ | ə(r) | ə(r) | ər | ər |
| | happY | ɪ | ɪ | iy | ii | [i] = /iː/ | e, ɪ, i | iː |
| | commA | ə(r) | ə | ə | ə(r) | ə(r) | ʌ | ə |
| | FEUD | | | | | | | |

| | DICTIONARY KEYS | | | | | | | |
| | 8 | 9 | 10 | 11 | 12 | 13 | 14 | 15 |
| Key word (augmented from JCW) | *OED* | *CUP* | *AOD* | Longman ME | Longman MA | *Webster's* | *F &W* | *ACD* |
| **Non r-vowels** | | | | | | | | |
| KIT | ɪ | ɪ | ɪ | ɪ | ɪ | ĭ | i | ĭ |
| DRESS | ɛ | e | e | e | e | ĕ | e | ĕ |
| TRAP | æ | æ | æ | æ | æ | ă | a | ă |
| BATH | ɑː | ɑː | aː | aː | æ | à | a~ă | ă~ä |
| PALM | ɑː | ɑː | aː | aː | ɑː | ä | ä | ä |
| LOT | ɒ | ɒ | ɒ | ɒ | ɑː | ŏ | o | ŏ |
| CLOTH | ɒ | ɒ | ɒ | ɒ | ɔː | ǒ | ô | ô~ŏ |
| THOUGHT | ɔː | ɔː | ɔː | ɔː | ɔː | ô | ô | ô |
| FOOT | ʊ | ʊ | ʊ | ɷ | ʊ | ŏŏ | ŏŏ | ŏŏ |
| STRUT | ʌ | ʌ | ʌ | ʌ | ʌ | ŭ | u | ŭ |
| MOUTH | aʊ | aʊ | aʊ | aʊ | aʊ | ou | ou | ou |
| GOAT | əʊ | əʊ | oʊ | əʊ | oʊ | ō | ō | ō |
| GOOSE | uː | uː | uː | uː | uː | ōō | ōō | ōō |
| FLEECE | iː | iː | iː | iː | iː | ē | ē | ē |
| FACE | eɪ | eɪ | eɪ | eɪ | eɪ | ā | ā | ā |
| PRICE | aɪ | aɪ | aɪ | aɪ | aɪ | ī | ī | ī |
| CHOICE | ɔɪ | ɔɪ | ɔɪ | ɔɪ | ɔɪ | oi | oi | oi |
| **r-vowels** | | | | | | | | |
| SPIRIT (iv) | ɪr | ɪr | ɪr | ɪr | ɪr | ir | ir | ĭr |
| NEAR (ə) | ɪə(r) | ɪə(r) | ɪə(r) | ɪə(r) | ɪᵊr | ę | ir | ĭ |
| SQUARE (ə) | ɛə(r) | eə(r) | eə(r) | eə(r) | eᵊr | âr | âr | âr |
| MERRY (iv) | ɛr | er | er | er | ɪᵊr | ĕr | er | ĕr |
| MARRY (iv) | ær | ær | ær | ær | er | ăr | ar | ăr |
| START (mono) | ɑː(r) | ɑː(r) | aː(r) | ɑː(r) | ɑːr | är | är | är |
| HORRID (iv) | ɒr | ɒr | ɒr | ɒr | ɔːr | ŏr | ôr~or | ôr |
| NORTH (ə) | ɔː(r) | ɔː(r) | ɔː(r) | ɔː(r) | ɔːr | ôr | ôr | ôr |
| FORCE (ə) | ɔə(r) | ɔːr | ɔː(r) | ɔː(r) | ɔːr~oʊ | ōr | ôr~ ōr | ōr |
| CURE (ə) | ʊə(r) | ʊə(r) | uːə(r) | ʊə(r), ɔː(r) | ʊᵊr | ūr | ŏŏr | ŏŏr |
| CURRY (iv) | ʌr | ʌr | ʌr | ʌr | ɚ | ûr | ŭr | ûr |
| NURSE (mono) | ɜː(r) | ɜː(r) | əː(r) | ɜː(r) | ɝ | ûr | ûr | ûr |
| LetteR | ə(r) | ə(r) | ə(r) | ə(r) | ᵊr | ĕr | ər | ər |
| happY | ɪ | i | iː | i | i | ĭ | ē | ĭ |
| commA | ə | ə | ə | ə | ə | à | ə | ə |
| FEUD | | | | | | | | |

Key: *OED: The Oxford English Dictionary*, 2nd. edition. Oxford: Oxford University Press (1989); *CUP: Cambridge English Pronouncing Dictionary.* Cambridge and New York: Cambridge University Press (2006); *AOD: Australian Oxford Dictionary.* Oxford and Melbourne: Oxford University Press (2004); Longman ME and Longman MA: *Longman Pronunciation Dictionary*, 3rd. edition (2008); *Webster's: Webster's New International Dictionary of the English Language.* Springfield MA: G. & C. Merriam Company (1944); *F & W: Funk & Wagnalls Standard Dictionary of the English Language.* New York and London: Funk & Wagnalls (1973); *ACD: The American College Dictionary,* Clarence L. Barnhart (ed.). New York: Harper & Brothers Publishers (1950).

| | | REFORM PROPOSALS | | | |
|---|---|---|---|---|---|
| | | 16 | 17 | 18 | 19 |
| | Key word (JCW) | A. J. Ellis | Nue Speling | Regspel | World English Spelling |
| Non r-vowels | KIT | i ill | i hit | i pit | i it, him, pretty, give |
| | DRESS | e ell | e pet | e pet | e edge, men, said |
| | TRAP | ɑ am | a hat | a pat | a at, man, ask |
| | BATH | | | | |
| | PALM | ą alms | aa calm | | aa alms, father, bath |
| | LOT | o olive | o hot | o pot | o on, bother, not, was |
| | CLOTH | | | | |
| | THOUGHT | ɵ all | au call | aw awl | au author, law, water |
| | FOOT | ɯ foot | oo foot | ou could | uu full, (sure), good |
| | STRUT | u up | u hut | u pun | u up, other, but, some |
| | MOUTH | γ owl | ou count | ow fowl | ou out, pound, now |
| | GOAT | ω ope | oe goat | oe flow | oe old, note, goes, so |
| | GOOSE | food (see text) | uu goose | oo food | oo fool, move, too |
| | FLEECE | ε eel | ee feet | ee feed | ee each, here, see, be |
| | FACE | a ale | ae fate | ae made | ae age, main, say |
| | PRICE | į isle | ie fight | ie lie | ie ice, tie, kind, by |
| | CHOICE | σ oil | oi coin | oy boy | oi oil, point, boy |
| r-vowels | SPIRIT (iv) | | | | |
| | NEAR (ə) | | eer fear | eer near | eer here |
| | SQUARE (ə) | | aer fair | ear bear | aer air, care, their |
| | MERRY (iv) | | | | |
| | MARRY (iv) | | arr carry | | |
| | START (mono) | | ar starry | ar hard | ar army, market, far |
| | HORRID (iv) | | orr sorry | | |
| | NORTH (ə) | | | or order | or order, north, for, story |
| | FORCE (ə) | | or story | | |
| | CURE (ə) | | uur/uer poor/pure | | uur sure, your |
| | CURRY (iv) | | urr furry | | |
| | NURSE (mono) | | ur turn | er herd | ur her, early, first, work |
| | LetteR | | er sister | | er collar, motor, murmur |
| | happY | | i happy | y simply | |
| | commA | | | u campus | |
| | FEUD | ų mule | ue feud | ew yew | ue use, music, due, few |

| | | REFORM PROPOSALS | | | |
|---|---|---|---|---|---|
| | | 20 | 21 | 22 | 23 |
| | Key word (JCW) | Truespel | NuEnglish | SoundSpel | Rifaurmd Lojikl Inglish |
| Non r-vowels | KIT | i  kit, give | i | i  in, tip, gives | i |
| | DRESS | e dress, said | e | e  ebb, end, set, bed | e |
| | TRAP | a rag, have | a | a  act, at, bag | a |
| | BATH | a bath, laugh | a | | a |
| | PALM | aa palm, father | a | aa alms, calm, father | aa |
| | LOT | aa  top, rob | o | o  ox, odd, hot | o |
| | CLOTH | au long, cough | au | au/aw auto, saw, fraud | au |
| | THOUGHT | au broad, law | au | | au |
| | FOOT | oo put, would | oo | uu bush, put,  good | uu |
| | STRUT | u blood, love | u | u  up, but, fun, love | u |
| | MOUTH | ou bough, now | ou | ou/ow  mouth, how, power | ou |
| | GOAT | oe  choke, sew | ō, oe | oe  old, toe, only, boat | oe |
| | GOOSE | ue  food, do, new | ū, ue | oo  ooze, moon, flu | oo |
| | FLEECE | ee  me, leave | ē, ee | ee  eel, eat, feet | ee |
| | FACE | ae pale, say | ā, ae | ae  aim, aid, same | ae |
| | PRICE | ie eye, high | ī, ie | ie  ice, tie, ride | ie |
| | CHOICE | oi boy | oi | oi  oil, noise, loyal | oi |
| r-vowels | SPIRIT (iv) | eer syrup, miracle | ir | | ir |
| | NEAR (ə) | ee spear, beer | ir | eer near, hear, serious | eer |
| | SQUARE (ə) | air  fairy, bear | ar | air  air, hair, where | air |
| | MERRY (iv) | air very, bear | er | err  berry | er |
| | MARRY (iv) | air carry, arrow | ar | arr  carry | ar |
| | START (mono) | aar car, heart | or | ar  card, far, are, dollar | aar |
| | HORRID (iv) | or  borrow, origin | oer, ōr | orr  sorry | aur, or |
| | NORTH (ə) | or for, orbit | oer, ōr | or  for, north, war | aur |
| | FORCE (ə) | or oral, pork | oer, ōr | or  four, force (oer | aur |
| | CURE (ə) | uer  sure, poor | ur, oor | uer/oor cure, poor | uer, oor |
| | CURRY (iv) | er  worry, courage | ur | ur  courage | ur |
| | NURSE (mono) | er  earn, term | ur | er  her, early, mercy | eur |
| | LetteR | er better, quicker | ur | | r |
| | happY | ee  dirty, heavy | ē, ee, | y  city | y |
| | commA | u, i comma, focus | u, i | | |
| | FEUD | yue  beauty, few | ue | | ue |

| | | REFORM PROPOSALS | | |
|---|---|---|---|---|
| | | 24 | 25 | 26 |
| | Key word (JCW) | ITA | Shavian | Deseret |
| Non r-vowels | KIT | i in | ) if | ᛏ ᛏ Short I /ɪ/ |
| | DRESS | e egg | ᒪ egg | ᗡ ᗡ Short E /ɛ/ |
| | TRAP | a at | ⅃ ash | ⅃ ⅃ Short A /æ/ |
| | BATH | | | |
| | PALM | ɑ father | ꜱ ah | ϑ ə Long A /ɑː/ |
| | LOT | o odd | ⌐ on | ⅃ ⅃ Short Ah/ɒ/ |
| | CLOTH | | | |
| | THOUGHT | au all | ꝛ awe | θ ө Long Ah /ɔː/ |
| | FOOT | ω book | V wool | ꝗ ꝗ Short Oo /ʊ/ |
| | STRUT | u up | 7 up | ⊦ ⊦ Short O /ʌ/ |
| | MOUTH | ou owl | ⟨ out | θ ə Ow /aʊ/ |
| | GOAT | œ oak | 0 oak | O o Long O /oʊ/ |
| | GOOSE | ω goose | ʌ ooze | Ɵ ɵ Long Oo /uː/ |
| | FLEECE | ɛɛ, eat; y > happy | ꜰ eat | ∂ ə Long I /iː/ |
| | FACE | æ ape | ꜱ age | Ɛ ɛ Long E /eɪ/ |
| | PRICE | ie ice | 7 ice | ⅃ ⅃ Ay /aɪ/ |
| | CHOICE | ɔi oil | ⟩ oil | |
| r-vowels | SPIRIT (iv) | | | |
| | NEAR (ə) | | ʋɔ ear | |
| | SQUARE (ə) | | ꓵ air | |
| | MERRY (iv) | | | |
| | MARRY (iv) | | | |
| | START (mono) | | Ω are | |
| | HORRID (iv) | | | |
| | NORTH (ə) | | ʊ or | |
| | FORCE (ə) | | | |
| | CURE (ə) | | | |
| | CURRY (iv) | | | |
| | NURSE (mono) | iR, eR, uR | ꙍ urge | |
| | LetteR | | ꓵ array | |
| | happY | | | |
| | commA | | ⌐ ado | |
| | FEUD | U beautiful | ꙍ yew | |

# Bibliography

Adams, Marilyn Jager. 1994. *Beginning to Read: Thinking and Learning About Print.* Cambridge, MA: MIT Press.

Barnhart, Clarence L. (ed.). 1950. *The American College Dictionary.* New York and London: Harper & Brothers Publishers.

Bell, Masha. 2009. *Rules and Exceptions of English Spelling.* Cambridge: Pegasus Educational.

Bullock, Alan. 1975. A Language for Life: Report of the Committee of Inquiry Appointed by the Secretary of State for Education and Science under the Chairmanship of Sir Alan Bullock. London: H.M.S.O.

Chall, Jeanne S. 1996. *Learning to Read: The Great Debate: An Inquiry into the Science, Art, and Ideology of Old and New Methods of Teaching Children to Read.* 1910–1965. Third edition, Fort Worth: Harcourt Brace College Publishers.(First published 1966).

Chomsky, Noam, and Morris Halle. 1968. *The Sound Pattern of English.* New York: Harper & Row.

Clackler, Bob C. 1933. *Let's End Our Literary Crisis: The Desperately Needed Idea Whose Time Has Come.* Literacy Research Associates.

Crystal, David. 2008. *Txtng: The gr8 db8.* Oxford: Oxford University Press.

Crystal, David. 2012. *Spell It Out: The Singular Story of English Spelling.* London: Profile Books.

Dewey, Godfrey. 1971. *English Spelling: Roadblock to Reading.* New York: Teachers College Press.

Dobson, E. J. 1968. *English Pronunciation 1500–1700.* Oxford: Clarendon Press.

Downing, John A. 1979. *Reading and Reasoning.* New York: Springer-Verlag. http://dx.doi.org/10.1007/978-1-4757-1707-5.

Ellis, Alexander John. 1848. *A Plea for Phonetic Spelling, Or, the Necessity of Orthographic Reform.* London: F. Pitman.

Flesch, Rudolf. 1955. *Why Johnny Can't Read—And What You Can Do About It.* New York: Harper.

Flesch, Rudolf. 1981. *Why Johnny Still Can't Read: A New Look at the Scandal of Our Schools.* New York: Harper & Row.

Franklin, Benjamin, and Benjamin Vaughan. 1779. *Political, Miscellaneous, and Philosophical Pieces.* London: J. Johnson.

*Funk & Wagnalls Standard Dictionary of the English Language.* 1973. New York: Funk & Wagnalls.

Goodman, Kenneth S. 1986. *What's Whole in Whole Language.* Portsmouth, NH: Heinemann.

Goodman, Kenneth S. 1993. *Ken Goodman's Phonics Phacts.* Portsmouth, NH: Heinemann.

Goodman, Kenneth S. 1996. *On Reading.* Portsmouth, NH: Heinemann.

Goodman, Kenneth S., Olive S. Niles and National Council of Teachers of English. 1970. Reading Process and Program [Champaign, IL]: Commission on the English Curriculum, National Council of Teachers of English.

Gove, Philip Babcock (ed.). 1986. *Webster's Third New International Dictionary.* Springfield, MA: Merriam-Webster.

Greenberg, Robert D. 2004. *Language and Identity in the Balkans: Serbo-Croat and Its Disintegration.* Oxford: Oxford University Press.

Hall, Robert A. 1961. *Sound and Spelling in English.* Philadelphia: Chilton Co. Book Division.

Hart, John. 1969 [1569]. *An Orthographie, 1569* (facsimile edition). Menston, West Yorkshire: The Scolar Press Limited.

Haugen, Einar. 1966. *Language Conflict and Language Planning; The Case of Modern Norwegian.* Cambridge, MA: Harvard University Press. http://dx.doi.org/10.4159/harvard.978067 4498709.

Horobin, Simon. 2013. *Does Spelling Matter?* Oxford: Oxford University Press.

Ives, Kenneth H. 1979. *Written Dialects N Spelling Reforms: History N Alternatives.* Progresiv Publishr.

Johnson, Samuel. 1755. *Dictionary of the English Language.* London: Noble.

Johnson, Sally A. 2005. *Spelling Trouble? Language, Ideology and the Reform of German Orthography.* Bristol: Multilingual Matters.

Jones, Daniel, Peter Roach, James Hartman, and Jane Setter. 2003. *English Pronouncing Dictionary.* Cambridge and New York: Cambridge University Press.

Kim, Chŏng-Su and Ross King. 2005. *The History and Future of Hangeul: Korea's Indigenous Script.* Kent: Global Oriental.

Kozol, Jonathan. 1985. *Illiterate America.* Garden City, NY: Anchor Press/Doubleday.

Landerl, Karin, Heinz Wimmer, and Uta Frith. 1997. "The impact of orthographic consistency on dyslexia: A German-English comparison." *Cognition* 63(3): 315–34. http://dx.doi.org/ 10.1016/S0010-0277(97)00005-X.

Laubach, Frank Charles. 1959. *English Spelling Made Easy for the World.* New York: privately published.

MacCarthy, P. A. D. 1969. "New Spelling with Old Letters. Alphabets for English". In W. Haas (ed.), *Alphabets for English.* Manchester: Manchester University Press.

McCuen, Gary E. 1988. *Illiteracy in America.* Hudson, WI: G. E. McCuen Publications.

Moore, Bruce. 2004. *Australian Oxford Dictionary.* Melbourne and Victoria: Oxford University Press.

Mulcaster, Richard. 1582. *The first part of the elementarie which entreateth chefelie of the right writing of our English tung, set furth by Richard Mulcaster.* Imprinted at London: By Thomas Vautroullier dwelling in the blak-friers by Lud-gate.

Oney, Banu, and Susan R. Goldman. 1984. "Decoding and comprehension skills in Turkish and English: Effects of the regularity of grapheme-phoneme correspondence." *Journal of Educational Psychology* 76(4): 557–68. http://dx.doi.org/10.1037/0022-0663.76.4.557.

Osselton, N. E. 1963. "Formal and informal spelling in the eighteenth century." *English Studies* 44: 267–75.

Pitman, James, and John Richard St John. 1969. *Alphabets and Reading; The Initial Teaching Alphabet.* New York: Pitman.

Pressley, Michael. 2006. *Reading Instruction That Works: The Case for Balanced Teaching.* New York: Guilford Press.

Raven, Isobel. 2005. *The Future of Phonics.* Victoria, BC: Trafford.

Rayner, Keith, and Alexander Pollatsek. 1989. *The Psychology of Reading.* Englewood Cliffs, NJ: Prentice Hall.

Riemer, George. 1964. *How They Murdered the Second "R".* New York: W. W. Norton.

Roach, Peter, James Hartman, Jane Setter, and Daniel Jones. 2006. *Cambridge English Pronouncing Dictionary.* Cambridge and New York: Cambridge University Press.

Robertson, Stuart. 1954. *The Development of Modern English.* New York: Prentice Hall.

Sampson, Geoffrey. 1985. *Writing Systems: A Linguistic Introduction.* Stanford: Stanford University Press.

Scragg, D. G. 1974. *A History of English Spelling.* Manchester and New York: Manchester University Press and Barnes & Noble Books.

Seymour, Philip H. K., Mikko Aro, and Jane M. Erskine. 2003. "Foundation literacy acquisition in European orthographies." *British Journal of Psychology* 94(2): 143–7. http://dx.doi.org/10.1348/000712603321661859.

Silverman, Sanford S. 2003. *Spelling for the 21st Century.* Cleveland.

Simplified Spelling Board. 1920. *Handbook of Simplified Spelling.*

Simpson, John, and Edmund Weiner (eds). 1989. *The Oxford English Dictionary.* Oxford and New York: Clarendon Press and Oxford University Press.

Soanes, Catherine, and Angus Stevenson (eds). 2005. *Oxford Dictionary of English.* Oxford and New York: Oxford University Press.

Stanovich, Keith E. 2000. *Progress in Understanding Reading: Scientific Foundations and New Frontiers.* New York: Guilford Press.

Taylor, Insup. 1980. *The Korean Writing System: An Alphabet? A Syllabary? A Logography? Processing of Visible Language,* ed. by M. E. W. Paul, A. Kohlers, and Herman Bouma, pp. 67–82. New York: Plenum Press.

Thorsdad, G[wenllian]. 1991. "The effect of orthography on the acquisition of literacy skills." *British Journal of Psychology* 82(4): 527–37. http://dx.doi.org/10.1111/j.2044-8295.1991.tb02418.x.

Twain, Mark. 1962. *Letters from the Earth,* edited by Bernard DeVoto. New York: Harper & Row.

Vallins, George Henry. 1954. *Spelling.* London: Andre Deutsch.

Venezky, Richard L. 1999. *The American Way of Spelling: The Structure and Origins of American English Orthography.* New York: Guilford Press.

Waldman, Niall McLeod. 2004. *Spelling Dearest: The Down and Dirty Nitty-Gritty History of English Spelling.* What The Dickens Press.

*Webster's New International Dictionary of the English Language.* 1944. Springfield, MA: G. & C. Merriam.

Webster, Noah. 1884. *An American Dictionary of the English Language.* Springfield, MA: G. & C. Merriam.

Webster, Noah, and Benjamin Franklin. 1789. *Dissertations on the English language: with notes historical and critical: to which is added, by way of appendix, an essay on a reformed mode of spelling with Dr. Franklin's arguments on that subject.* [Boston]: Printed at Boston, for the author, by Isaiah Thomas and Company.

Wells, J. C. 1982. *Accents of English.* Cambridge and New York: Cambridge University Press.

Wells, J. C. 2008. *Longman Pronunciation Dictionary.* Harlow, Essex: Pearson Education Limited.

Wells, Ronald A. 1973. *Dictionaries and the Authoritarian Tradition. A Study in English Usage and Lexicography.* The Hague: Mouton. http://dx.doi.org/10.1515/9783110805949.

Wijk, Axel. 1959. *Regularized English: An Investigation into the English Spelling Reform Problem with a New, Detailed Plan for a Possible Solution.* Stockholm: Almqvist & Wiksell.

Wikipedia. History of Dutch orthography. http://en.wikipedia.org/wiki/History_of_Dutch_orthography.

Wolman, David. 2008. *Righting the Mother Tongue: From Olde English to Email, the Tangled Story of English Spelling.* New York: Smithsonian Books/Collins.

Zachrisson, R. E. 1931–32. "Four hundred years of English spelling reform." *Studia Neophilologica* 4(1): 1–69. http://dx.doi.org/10.1080/00393273108586757

# Index

# Spellbound

## Untangling English Spelling

Robbins Burling

*Spellbound* considers the history of English spelling and provides suggestions for modern-day reform of its irregularities.

The first half of the book reviews the history of English spelling and the reasons for the many irregularities of our modern language. The author argues that the irregular spelling of English contributes seriously to the high rate of illiteracy in the English-speaking world. He then reviews some of the many attempts to reform the spelling of other languages, some of which were successful and others not. During the first half of the twentieth century there was a flurry of interest in reforms for English but since then reform has been little more than the object of humor. *Spellbound* considers the reasons for this opposition to reform.

The book then turns to current proposals for the reform of English spelling. It describes the criteria that should govern the choice among alternative reforms and considers in detail the relatively easily reformed consonants and the much more difficult vowels. Special attention is given to ways of designing a spelling that is equally suitable for the many and diverse dialects of spoken English. While the author recognizes that a unified spelling could not be perfect for any single dialect, he argues that it could be very much better than our present spelling for all dialects. *Spellbound* concludes by looking at possible ways by which reforms might be brought about today.

**Robbins Burling** is Professor Emeritus at the University of Michigan, where he taught linguistics and anthropology from 1963 until his retirement in 1995. He is the author of a number of books including *The Talking Ape: How Language Evolved* (Oxford University Press, 2007). Since the early grades, he has been a hopelessly poor speller.

Cover design: Gus Hunnybun

www.equinoxpub.com

Printed in Great Britain

ISBN 978-1-78179-131-8

9 781781 791318